34.95

D1590826

Improving Memory and Study Skills:
Advances in Theory and Practice

Douglas Herrmann
Indiana State University, Terre Haute, IN

Douglas Raybeck
Hamilton College, Clinton, NY

Michael Gruneberg
University of Wales, Swansea, Wales

Improving Memory and Study Skills: Advances in Theory and Practice

Hogrefe & Huber Publishers
Seattle · Toronto · Bern · Göttingen

Library of Congress Cataloging-in-Publication Data

is available via the Library of Congress Marc Database under the
LC Control Number 2001099463.

National Library of Canada Cataloguing-in-Publication Data

Main entry under title:

Herrmann, Douglas J.
Improving memory and study skills: advances in theory and practice

Includes bibliographical references and index.
ISBN 0-88937-235-7

1. Study skills. 2. Memory. 3. Mnemonics. I. Raybeck, Douglas.
II. Gruneberg, Michael M. III. Title

BF385.H468 2002   371.3'028'1   C2002-900023-8

Hogrefe & Huber Publishers

USA: P.O. Box 2487, Kirkland, WA 98083-2487
                  Phone (425) 820-1500, Fax (425) 823-8324

CANADA: 12 Bruce Park Avenue, Toronto, Ontario M4P 2S3
                  Phone (416) 482-6339

SWITZERLAND: Länggass-Strasse 76, CH-3000 Bern 9
                  Phone (031) 300-4500, Fax (031) 300-4590

GERMANY: Rohnsweg 25, D-37085 Göttingen
                  Phone (0551) 496090, Fax (0551) 4960988

Printed and bound in Germany
ISBN 0-88937-235-7

Table of Contents

Preface for Students

This book presents the latest and most advanced approach to the improvement of memory and study skills. It is based in part on a revision and extension of a prior book, *Improving Student Memory*, written by D. Herrmann, D. Raybeck, and Dan Gutman and published by Hogrefe and Huber in 1993.

Improving Memory and Study Skills: Advances in Theory and Practice presents a new "multimodal" framework to improving cognitive functioning. Some aspects of this framework were introduced in *Improving Student Memory*. However, a number of investigations were conducted in the 1990's that both supported the multimodal approach and, at the same time, increased understanding of the many factors that affect memory and academic performance.

The multimodal framework rests on three assumptions. First, the improvement of memory and study skills requires consideration of a person's powers for learning, remembering, and reasoning. In addition, memory and skill improvement is influenced by all modes of psychological functioning, such as a person's physiological state, emotive state, and states elicited by the physical environment and social context. Second, memory and skill improvement requires practice with the use of procedures that particularly address the content covered in an educational course. Third, students benefit the most from learning new procedures if they understand the reasons why these procedures are effective.

This book presents both the methods and the rationale that has led to the new approach. Students who make a serious effort to learn the theory and techniques covered in this book will be prepared to improve their memory and study skills for those courses that previously challenged them most.

Preface for Teachers

Improving Memory and Study Skills was written to serve as a primary text for a course on study skills. It may also be useful for courses designed to orient students to college life and its expectations.

This book offers many recommendations to improve academic performance (Rego & Sousa, 1999). It also explains the scientific reasons for the procedures it recommends. It describes the manner in which memory performance depends on a person's total psychological functioning, including how a person manages their lifestyle. We have endeavored to ground each explanation in concrete examples, and we have supplied evidence why particular procedures are effective. The authors hope that this book will assist teachers in applying its recommendations to the classroom.

Many students today are stretched in trying to meet all their goals. If the students are not extremely active in campus affairs, they are busy holding a second job or assisting in family responsibilities. Improvements in memory and study skills help them get more out of the limited time they can invest in studying. For those students who hold ambitions that require high grades, memory and skill improvements make the attainment of those goals much more likely.

Students today need education in improving their memory and study skills more than ever before. The students in this generation are predicted to encounter jobs that are more technical than any previous generation. Because technology is continually spiraling upward, today's student is expected to experience several job shifts throughout his or her career. Thus, students not only need better memory and study skills to cope with the current demands of college life, they also need to acquire as many memory and study skills as possible so that they will be able to learn the information pertinent to the many jobs they will hold throughout their careers. In addition to preparing for a challenging professional life, they will need mental skills for their personal lives more than any previous generation. In the past three decades there has been considerable growth of laws and court decisions that affect everyday life. Like it or not, as a person's life progresses they will need to learn about many of these changes in the law. For example, laws have been changing as they pertain to: marriage - divorce - annulment - having children - adopting children - buying and owning property - paying taxes - inheriting money - buying insurance - making a will - being sued - and suing someone. To keep abreast of these aspects of modern life, and to avoid being misled, students will want to have excellent learning and remembering skills.

Fortunately, numerous researchers in several different fields have investigated aspects of memory, learning, studying, and remembering that simply were not subjected to scientific scrutiny in the past. As a result, we now have a much better sense of the advantages of certain study practices, and we have greater appreciation of the interrelationships between physical/emotional health and mental powers. Learning and remembering is now seen as being affected by a person's entire psychology. Consequently, because the brain is a biological entity, it is important to understand that the execution of cognitive processing depends on both physiological and psychological factors.

We are much better able today to supply students with recommendations that may actually improve their academic performance. If students come to appreciate the interrelationship between academic performance and physical/emotional well being, they will adopt habits that promote academic success.

Finally, you may be interested in having your students obtain and study the CD-Rom, *The Nature of Memory*, which can be ordered with *Improving Memory and Study Skills*. This CD-Rom, made by the Practical Memory Institute, presents compelling graphics and information that are pertinent to the content of this book. It familiarizes students with the multimodal theory of memory, the philosophy of memory, how to monitor one's memory performance, the history of scholarship on memory, and external aids to memory. If your students study this CD-Rom, it will make your job and their jobs easier.

TO
DONNA, KAREN, and RHONA

Acknowledgment

We are grateful to everyone who has encouraged us in writing this book. We thank our families for their support during the project. In addition, we thank the numerous students who studied *Improving Student Memory* and for their comments about that book. Finally, thanks are due to Steve Andrzejewski, Robert Beck, Rob Dimbleby, Jared Jobe, Cathy McEvoy, Paul Mullin, Rick Parente, David Payne, Dana Plude, Alan Searleman, Judy Swez and Carol Yoder for a variety of kinds of help.

Section I.

Fundamentals

1. Scientific Theory of Studying and Academic Success

Attending college provides the opportunity to prepare for the rest of one's life, both professionally and personally. This book describes the most important thing, other than a major, that can be gained from a college education – an increased mental ability to study, learn, and remember.

Why You Are Reading this Book?

You will develop an increased mental ability to learn and remember by learning what is presented in this book. This chapter will orient you to the mental skills you will be learning about in the following chapters.

Enhancing your college experience. An increased mental ability to learn and remember will obviously increase your performance academically. It will also prepare you to learn and remember in your career. Improving your ability to learn will improve your study skills, and by improving your ability to remember, you will develop your test-taking skills. Furthermore, improving your study skills not only means you will learn more when you study, but also that you will study more efficiently. Efficient studying will give you extra time which you can either devote to bettering your grades or to having more fun while maintaining your grade average (Hattie, Biggs, & Purdie, 1996).

The most important thing you can get from college – an increased ability to learn and remember. The most important reason for improving your memory and study skills is not to get good grades. Nor is it to increase your status on campus, to make the financial aid office support you, or to make your parents or sweetheart be nice to you. The primary reason for trying to improve your memory and study skills is to give you the mental skills that you will need for your career and personal life.

The challenge to your generation. More than any previous generation, you and your classmates will need to have a variety of mental skills for your future *careers*. Today's jobs have become more complex in the past two decades than in the prior century. You and others of your generation will need to learn new job responsibilities and technologies throughout your career.

It has been estimated that job knowledge will be completely revised every three to seven years of a person's career. Most members of this generation will need to continually update professional knowledge and skills. Across your entire career (which will be somewhere between 30 to 45 years), most people will switch jobs at least three times, such as from sales to management to advertising. Some of your classmates will have to switch jobs a dozen times.

Each time a person takes a new job, a great deal of learning is required, as they must learn the responsibilities of that job. In some cases the job may require you to carry out tasks that you have never done before. In addition, you have to learn the names and capabilities of your bosses and co-workers. You will also need to learn more mundane things, such as the spatial layout of an office, where to get supplies, and what forms of assistance are available.

It is important to recognize that your careers are expected to involve more challenging mental tasks than those of your parents or grandparents. The parents of your generation will have switched jobs less often than you will have. The grandparents of your generation may have stayed in a particular job throughout their lives.

More than any previous generation, you will also need mental skills to learn about common tasks encountered in your *personal life*. You will have to learn and remember more than was required of previous generations because of the growth of laws and court decisions that affect everyday life.

Consider some of the knowledge you will need for your personal life, knowledge that was much simpler for your parents and grandparents. For example, if you plan to marry, you may want to know a little bit about the recent laws affecting marriage, such as the laws governing prenuptial agreements. If you marry, you may well have children. Having and raising children is much more technical than before. If you have children, you will need to learn what is involved in raising children and what rights your children have to be given educational support. If you decide to adopt children, it is necessary to understand adoption law. Perhaps, unfortunately, you may also want to know about the procedures for annulment and about divorce law. With the current divorce rate being at more than 50%, understanding divorce processes will be important for many members of your generation.

Whether you remain single or not, there are still other cognitive tasks that you cannot avoid having to learn about. Eventually you will probably be interested in buying and owning a house. Mortgage options are more detailed than previously, and these change continuously. Of course, you could decide to rent; however, rental agreements are also more complex than in the past. You will have to pay income taxes, and as your income increases, paying taxes becomes more annoying and demanding. You will likely want to buy life insurance. Reading life insurance policies is tremendously challenging. If you are half as successful as your teachers want you to be, you will want to have a will to direct the disposition of your possessions after you leave this world. And, if you are lucky, you may inherit money and/or property, which can be especially complicated if you have a relative who contests your share of an estate. A further possible problem in life is if you decide to sue someone; you will want to learn a lot about how the law regulates this process. Alternatively, someone may decide to sue you and again you will need to understand how this process is regulated. Personal tasks can sometimes require as much learning and remembering as the demands of a job.

The increased difficulty of higher education. Getting an education requires a lot of hard work. Every generation has to learn more than the previous generation. Each coming generation is provided with more years of education than in the past. Thus, today's generation needs to be more capable of learning and remembering than previous generations.

Fortunately, science has increased our understanding of how we learn and remember, as well as how to reason, solve problems, and make decisions. The old approach to improving studying and academic performance (test taking, writing term papers, oral reports) focused just on the ideas. Without a doubt, ideas are at the core of education. However, it is no longer sufficient for students to acquire only skills that deal with ideas. Science has shown that the best approach to studying and academic performance is multifaceted (Druckman & Swets, 1988; Herrmann & Searleman, 1990, 1992; Herrmann, Plude, Yoder, & Mullin, 1999; McEvoy, 1992; Poon, 1980).

Acquiring memory and study skills. To study more effectively and perform well academically, you also need to learn how to keep your mind sharp by getting into the best physical and mental condition. You need to adopt a more positive and realistic attitude about your academic courses.

Through making better use of the environment, such as taking good notes, learning is facilitated. Acquiring better habits when taking tests will improve your academic performance, such as planning the use of time when taking an exam.

And, of course, the more you learn about ways that make your mind function optimally, the better your academic performance will be. As you learn and practice your memory and study skills in different courses, you can develop your overall understanding of how to learn and remember.

Acquiring athletic skills. The approach recommended in science is very much like the approaches that are successful for developing other kinds of skills. For example, suppose you wanted to improve your performance at a sport, like tennis, golf, or football. If you were truly serious about improving, you would work on as many different methods as possible that would lead to a better performance.

You would seek out the appropriate information for getting into the best physical and mental condition to win. You would work on adopting a more positive and realistic attitude about your abilities. By taking care to learn the customs of play and the tactics that suit specific arenas or opponents, you would be prepared to execute play appropriate to the situations that arise. You would acquire a greater appreciation of how environmental factors, such as the condition of the court or playing field, affect the game. Naturally, the more you practice, the better your performance will be. Good players of all sports have an encyclopedic knowledge of the things to do that lead to a fit condition for the game, a proper attitude toward playing and players, a detailed knowledge of how to use the environment, an ability to deal with specific situations, and effective ways of practicing. The same is true for people who master learning and study skills.

The importance of memory to study skills. This book teaches both memory and study skills to facilitate academic performance. Why does this book emphasize memory so much in its treatment of study skills?

Memory is crucial to the effective use of study skills. Firstly, study skills involve learning which, of course, entails creating memories for knowledge. Additionally, test taking is largely an exercise in remembering. To a degree, tests – as well as term papers – may also call for reasoning, problem solving, and decision making. However, people cannot reason, solve problems, and make decisions on exams and term papers if they have not first learned the basic knowledge pertinent to these. Thus, the most important kind of skills that you can acquire for studying and academic performance are those that enhance your memory (Herrmann, 1990a; Herrmann & Searleman, 1990, 1992; Hertzog, 1992).

General and task specific skills. Some skills are fairly general in that they affect a wide variety of academic tasks in the same way. For example, a general skill that all students use is rehearsal. Rehearsal is a general skill because it can be used when studying for most courses. Other skills are very specific; in fact most study skills are specific. The skills needed for learning vocabulary have little to do with the skills required for studying diagrams or equations. Learning a poem requires different skills to those for learning about a document or a story. Because study skills are usually specific, various psychologists have sought to develop new methods of memory improvement that are most effective when applied to certain tasks. Later in the book we will offer suggestions for the development of skills for a variety of specific tasks, such as studying poems, documents, stories, and other kinds of material.

The Job Description of a Student

To ensure that this book covers everything that it should, the content of the book has been designed to meet the demands of the job of a student. Every job has a description. In the military, industry, and medicine, each person who performs a certain job is expected to know his or her job description. This is the same for students, and it is helpful for students to appreciate the requirements for the job of a student.

Students everywhere have the same job description. If they are to be successful in college, they need to perform the tasks called for by this. Here is a summary of the tasks that make up a student's job description:

- Identify what a course requires
- Read books and articles in-depth
- Extract meaning from what is read and heard in class
- Prepare for exams
- Take exams
- Write term papers
- Stay in shape: physically and emotionally
- Be socially appropriate
- Take note of the environment
- Continually educate themselves about new ideas concerning the above tasks

The Job Description in More Detail

Identify what a course requires. A student can expect to be successful only to the extent that they understand the professor's objectives. The biggest clue to what a professor requires from students is the course syllabus. It provides a road map of where the professor wishes to take the students. A good sense of the direction the course is taking will enable you to better determine which parts of the course are important. It is important not to become so immersed in detail that the general direction of the course is missed. The sooner an overall picture of the course is gained, the sooner students do well on exams and term papers.

In-depth reading procedures. Simply turning the pages and reading the words on the pages is seldom sufficient for truly understanding the course material. Reading is best viewed as an active process. Rather than simply passively receiving wisdom, the essential points of the text have to be looked for. In the next section, we will supply you with some specific techniques to promote your understanding, retention, and ability to deal critically with the material you read.

Techniques for extracting meaning. A student has to do a large number of assignments from widely differing courses. It is impossible to memorize everything that a course presents, and indeed this is not necessary. Instead, the most important information should be extracted, which relates both to each specific assignment and to the more general objectives of the course. There are a variety of techniques discussed below that can be employed to extract the meaning from books, lectures, and other material, such as videos or sites on the Web. These techniques require actively sifting through the relevant information to find what must be known and understood.

The most valuable ability for meaning extraction is note taking. Most instructors will try to make just a few major points in a single class. Everything else serves to illustrate the key concepts (Van Locke, 1999). Therefore, developing the ability to recognize the major points of a lecture is important, and also the need for sufficient detail, so that the lecture notes can be later reconstructed.

Exam preparation. Most students dread examinations. Having taken an exam, many students are surprised to discover that they did not do as well as they had expected. After learning about the skills for exam taking described below, students will have less trouble preparing for exams.

Examinations are usually designed to test the understanding as well as the recall of course material. Many instructors assume that students remember the material to which they were exposed, and they want to see what the students can do with it. Can they construct answers to questions that they may not have encountered before? Preparing for an examination benefits from both an active approach and a continuing attempt to maintain an overview of the instructor's objectives.

Exam strategies. Many students, who spend a considerable amount of time and energy preparing for an examination, dive into an exam and forge ahead without a plan. You will discover that you will do better on exams if you decide at the beginning how much time you will spend on each part of the exam.

Exams come in different forms, such as multiple choice exams and essay exams. The approach for dealing with multiple choice questions is quite different from that needed for essay questions. Later sections of this book offer specific advice for answering different types of exams. We encourage you to stay in control of your answers rather than letting the questions push you around.

Taking care of yourself. A student must be in good physical shape in order to do well when performing academic tasks. Variables that affect a person's physical state include exercise, sleep, food, time of day, etc. It is important to keep track of your chemical consumption, such as caffeine, nicotine, and alcohol, which can interfere with learning and remembering (Kolakowsky, 1997; Snel & Lorist, 1998).

Similarly, you should be aware of the over-the-counter and prescription medicines that you take. Many medications dull your senses and make it hard to concentrate. If you get sick, you are likely to become slower mentally and make more mistakes.

Your emotional, attitudinal, and motivational states affect your willingness to study and take tests. It is important to maintain good self esteem and be in a positive emotional state when you are in class and when you study (Ginter & Dwinell, 1994). Keep your eye on the positive consequences of good grades when you prepare for and take exams.

Be socially appropriate. Social interactions are important to success in college. Remember that people differ in how they study. Others can give you good advice about how to do your best in various courses. However, remember that a person will get the best advice from other students regarding how to study from other students like themselves.

Your relationships with other students can affect how well you do and how much help you get from others. Stay away from students who attempt to be buddy-buddy with the professor or teaching assistant. People who are friends with the "apple polisher" will also be seen the same way. If other students were to perceive you this way, it will be the end of help from them.

When you answer questions in class or take oral exams, present yourself in a credible way. Even when a person has successfully recalled something in a social context, he or she may still have a problem convincing others that what has been recalled is correct. There are five ways you can increase the likelihood that others will believe in what you recall. Express your recall with an appropriate degree of confidence. Strive to make the contents of your recall include the most essential details. Claim an honest level of confidence in the accuracy of what you say you know. Express your certitude or doubt prudently. Avoid overstatement or understatement in your confidence in what your have recalled. Alternatively, do not be shy; sit up and speak confidently if you are sure of what you know.

Screen your recall to be sure that you don't "blurt out" something that you actually know to be wrong. Give extra scrutiny to answers that come quickly and seem very familiar. If you cannot recall something while studying, try the Yoga method of recall. Lay down in a quiet spot where you won't be disturbed. Relax the muscles in your body. When you are really relaxed, put questions to yourself about the information you would like to recall.

Make use of the physical environment. Use the physical environment to focus on what you need to learn. Color code your notes using different colors to show what is the most important, the next most important, and so on.

Use tape recorders to record a summary of points needed for a test. Then you can listen to the tape when you have to do other chores, such as house cleaning or while driving to school or work. Time your study sessions carefully and set alarms for when you need to move on to another topic.

Continuing education. You ability to study, learn, and remember will increase across your college years, indeed across your life. The sooner you acquire effective study skills, the better off you will be. Even when your skills are good, continue to increase your understanding of how to improve your mental functioning.

Each year there are new books, magazine articles, and cassettes on how to improve study skills, and occasional TV shows on specific scientific developments in research on memory and study skills. Participating in courses or training programs on study skill improvement can challenge and inform you even more fully. Every college and university offers courses on how to improve study techniques. It is easy to forget some of these skills, so refresher courses are periodically a good thing. Continued study of memory will deepen your theoretical understanding, enabling you to make better use of your mind in college and subsequently in your career.

This Book's Plan for Improving Your Academic Performance

The approach to the improvement of memory and study skills presented in this book is very new (Neisser, 1978). It has been practiced mainly in a small number of universities and colleges, where it has been developed. This book provides you with the latest detailed account of the new scientific method in a form available to the general public (Herrmann, Raybeck, & Gutman, 1993). You will be presented with information and practical guidance for memory improvement based on the latest scientific knowledge in the field. Because of investigations by research psychologists and educational psychologists, many more ways to improve memory ability and study skills are available today than existed just a few years ago.

The approach of this book is comprehensive. You will learn about the memory skills appropriate for certain academic tasks, while also learning techniques for facilitating your attitude, physical condition, emotive state, conversational skills, and for using physical memory aids, all of which have been found to reduce memory failures (Herrmann & Searleman, 1990, 1992; Herrmann et al., 1999; Herrmann, Weingartner, Searleman, & McEvoy, 1992; Poon, 1980; Yesavage, Sheikh, & Lapp, 1989). More than any previous book, this book prepares you not only for the kinds of tasks encountered in college, but also for the learning and remembering tasks you will encounter in your careers.

This book will assist you in improving your ability to study by thoroughly acquainting you with the different ways to manipulate your memory. The book is made up of twelve chapters divided into five sections. The first section consists of three chapters that review the fundamental ideas for understanding how one improves one's memory and study skills. Chapter 1, this chapter, provides an overview of the book. Chapter 2 presents the latest theory on how people can make the best use of their memory and study skills. Chapter 3 gives you an opportunity to assess the current state of your memory and study skills within the framework of this theory, and explores other important ways of looking at memory and study skills.

The second section addresses the importance of how you feel when you attempt to study or take a test. Chapters 4 and 5 examine ways to deal with your emotional state and physical state when learning and remembering are called for.

The third section addresses how information is stored in memory during learning and retrieved from memory during remembering. Chapter 6 provides a thorough grounding in the fundamentals of manipulations of memory and study skills. The following chapter, Chapter 7, explains further how technical manipulations, known generally as mnemonics, can enhance mental processing ever further. Chapter 8 reviews the manipulations of memory for many different everyday memory tasks that confront students and most other people. The recommendations in this chapter illustrate the claim that most memory tasks require a specific approach. Chapter 9 extends this theme to learning and test taking tasks encountered in college, offering specific advice on how to deal with particular tasks.

The fourth section addresses a topic not commonly recognized in textbooks on study skills; how the world around a person affects their performance. Chapter 10 shows how the physical environment, including devices sold at high tech and trendy stores, can speed up learning and assist you on term papers and open book exams. Similarly, Chapter 11 demonstrates how social situations can give you clues (without cheating) to perform better than you might expect.

Finally, the fifth section integrates the knowledge examined in the previous sections (concerning the fundamentals, how you feel, and storing and remembering information). Chapter 12 teaches you how to tackle studying in a forceful manner by creating or using repertoires of skills drawn from the previous chapters that are especially useful for certain academic tasks. Chapter 12 takes another look at theory in order to give you a clear overview of the study process. Finally, there is a brief epilogue, which is best appreciated by simply reading it after you have finished the other chapters.

Summary

More than any previous generation, your generation will need to have many mental skills for your professional lives. The approach recommended by science to improve memory and study skills is very much like the approaches that work best for developing other kinds of skills.

To study more effectively and perform better academically, you need to acquire better methods to learn and remember. You also need to learn how to keep your mind sharp by getting into the best physical and mental condition to learn and remember. By adopting a more positive and realistic attitude about your academic courses, you can overcome psychological obstacles to studying and remembering. Take care to learn the tactics that suit specific courses or professors. Your academic performance can also be enhanced if you mentally rehearse your plan for how to take an exam; knowing the "mental game" of strategies of test taking can give you an advantage on the actual exam.

Thus, this book is designed to give you information and practical guidance for memory improvement based on the latest scientific knowledge in the field. As mentioned above, research has made great strides in understanding how to improve memory ability. Although further investigation is needed to refine and balance the methods of the new approach presented here, most scientists agree with the variety of memory improvement skills that we recommend.

2. The Memory System

Where is Your Memory?

Before you can choose the best way to improve your memory and study skills, you have to know how your memory works. The memory system is located in the brain and the brain stem (at the top of the spinal cord). As with other parts of the brain, the memory system receives information from the senses and sends signals that enable us to respond with speech or gestures (Squire, 1987; Squire & Butters, 1984).

Different portions of the brain seem to perform different memory functions (see Figure 1). A part of the brain stem is involved in registering information into long-term memory. The temporal lobes (the parts of the brain that lie alongside your ears) are also involved in registering memories. Additionally, different types of memories are located in different parts of the brain. People who have suffered brain damage in a certain area (as

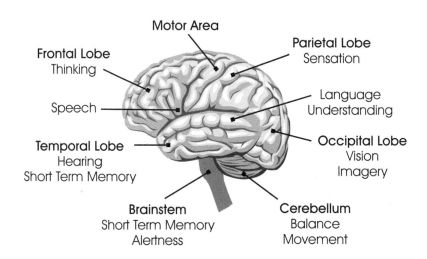

Figure 1. Location of the Memory Processing Centers in the Brain

might result from an auto accident) may have great difficulty learning abstract concepts and yet be able to acquire motor skills.

Because the memory system is made of brain tissue, your memory performance is affected by the state of the brain. Poor health, fatigue, malnourishment, and substance abuse can all lead to poor memory performance. Thus, one of the most obvious – but often neglected – ways to increase the efficiency of the memory system is to improve your physical condition.

Memory Processing

Although many memory functions have been located in the brain, many more functions have yet to be located. Nevertheless, even when it is unclear where certain processes occur in the brain, there is still a good understanding of how memory processes may malfunction. When memory fails us, it does so in one of three ways. It can fail to register something initially in memory; it can fail to retain over time that which was successfully registered; or it can fail to remember something, despite successful registration and retention (Talland, 1968). The theory many psychologists advance assumes that memory performance is due to a system of several components, each with its own specific job to do (e.g., Atkinson & Shiffrin, 1968; Baddeley, 1986, 1990; Craik & Lockhart, 1972; Fodor, 1983; Herrmann et al., 2001; Loftus, 1980; Wilson, 1987). Much like a stereo or hi-fi system, each component of the memory system contributes to the overall functioning of the system.

Figure 2 presents a simplified sketch of the functional components of the memory system and their connections. The system consists of four components: the senses, a working memory, a long-term memory, and a central processor. Working memory can contain any perceptions that are picked up by the senses (Biederman, 1987; Broadbent, 1958; Gibson, 1979; Yantis, 2001) or long-term memories that have just been remembered. The contents of working memory fade in about one minute, unless they are attended to. The central processor controls the amount of attention given to the contents of working memory (Anderson, 1983; Shiffrin & Schneider, 1977).

A memory trace is registered according to a basic sequence. Information in the world around us is picked up by the senses and then transferred to working memory. From working memory, the information and the situation in which it is encountered is absorbed into long-term memory (Brent

& Myers, 2000; Greeno, Smith, & Moore, 1993; Lave, 1988; Scribner, 1984). That which is learned, while pertaining to the situation of learning, is distributed over parts of the learning environment including graphics and what others in class say (Bell & Winn, 2000). The remembering of a trace also occurs according to a basic sequence. Attention is paid to a sight, sound, smell, taste, or touch and it is perceived. The new perception elicits thoughts in memory. Those thoughts related to the trace information stimulate the trace in long-term memory. When the trace has been sufficiently stimulated, it emerges from long-term memory.

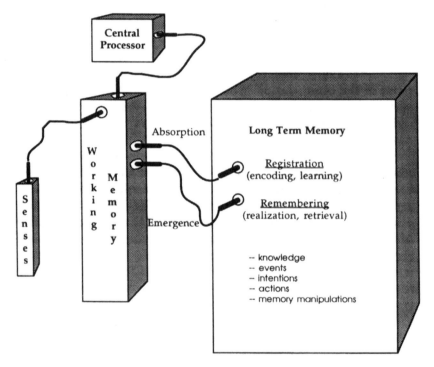

Figure 2. A Schematic Model of the Human Memory System

The Role of Psychological Modes other than Memory in Learning and Remembering

The memory system presented in Figure 2 explains many facts about learning and studying, and about remembering and test taking. For example, the model shows that information in memory is initially very unstable. Unless a person devotes effort to thinking about what is in working memory, a durable memory will not be formed. Traditionally, memory and other cognitive functions, such as those involved with thinking, have been explained by this model in terms of thought processes and what is being thought about.

However, the processing components of the memory system are not the whole story of academic performance. In addition to study and test taking processes, it is recognized that academic performance depends also on psychological *modes* of processing other than the learning and remembering (Barnard & Teasdale, 1991; Bendiksen & Bendiksen, 1992, 1996; Brunning, Schraw, & Ronning, 1999; Druckman & Bjork, 1994; Herrmann & Parente, 1994; Herrmann & Plude, 1996; Herrmann & Searleman, 1990; Herrmann et al., 1999; Mullin, Herrmann, & Searleman, 1993; McEvoy, 1992; Poon, 1980; Searleman & Herrmann, 1994; Sternberg, 1986; West, 1985; Zachs & Hasher, 1992).

Specifically, it has been found that memory and academic performance in general depends on four general categories of modes at the time that memory processing occurs. These four mode categories include cognitive processes in general, physiological states, emotive states, and cognitive characteristics unique to the individual. The multimodal account of memory and study skills is explained next.

Mode Categories

The four mode categories are defined as follows. The first category, called *informational*, includes modes that determine the content of what is learned and later remembered. This category includes the traditional view of academic performance but, as will be seen below, it also includes modes not normally considered in accounts of such performance. The second mode category, called *physiological*, includes modes that affect a person's physiological state at the time of memory processing. The third category, called *emotive*, includes three modes that affect a person's tendency or inclination at the time of memory processing. The fourth category, called *individual*, consists of modes that influence the way that a person performs memory and study tasks differently to others.

These four categories vary in the ways that they are used by people. The first category typically involves *active*, conscious processes. People know when they are studying and taking a test, and they know what they are doing to try to perform these tasks. It is sometimes said that a person consciously exerts executive control over their learning and remembering processes (Baddeley, 1986; also see Pollens, McBratnie, & Burton, 1988).

When people study or take tests, they rely on knowledge gained over a lifetime. This kind of knowledge is special in that if the knowledge is accurate and comprehensive, it will guide a person to academic success. Such knowledge is referred to as metamemory or metacognitive knowledge, where the 'meta' indicates that it is about the processes that control or regulate memory and cognition (Brown, 1978; Miller, Galanter, & Pribram, 1960; Sternberg, 1985).

Alternatively, when people study and take tests, they pay less or no attention to their physiological state, emotive state, and individual ways of doing things. They continue to experience their physiological state and emotive states, and their unique ways, but their concern for the academic task at hand leads people to be passive with regards to these three mode categories. A person can choose to actively do things to improve their physiological state, emotive state, and individual approach, but usually it is too late to try to alter these mode categories. If a person wants to optimize the normally passive categories, it requires planning and forethought (Parente & Herrmann, 1996).

Specific Modes

Current theory holds that there are three modes in each of the four mode categories. In the future, it is likely that research will suggest other modes for some of these categories. Given that there are three modes per category and that there are four categories, the current theory holds that there are 12 modes overall that influence academic performance.

Figure 3 illustrates how the modes influence learning and remembering. The boxes in the center of the figure represent the cognitive system, which includes sensory processes, cognitive processes, storage of memory, and responding (such as remembering the solution for an answer on a test). The circle at the top of the figure represents the passive processes and how they influence the components of the cognitive system. The circle at the bottom of the figure represents the active processes.

Each cognitive, physiological, and emotive mode is represented in the figure by a letter. The individual modes are not labeled in the figure because these modes pertain to the unique features of an individual that may originate in any of the components or the other modes.

The figure illustrates as well that the different modes may affect each other. For example, a person's health status influences both learning and remembering but it may also influence his/her motivation, perceived com-

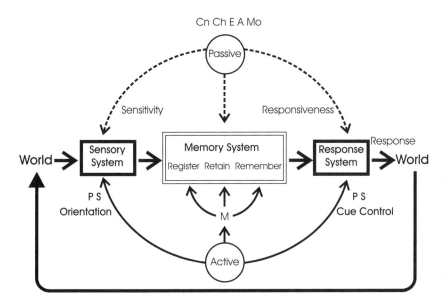

Figure 3. A Multimodal Model of Memory: M – memory, P – physical environment, S – social environment, Cn – physical condition, Ch – chemical state, E – emotional state, A – attitudes, Mo – motivation.

petence, and willingness to engage in challenging memory strategies. Similarly, a person's impression of their ability to learn or be tested in a certain academic course may have an impact on their academic tasks, performance, motivation, and, at least indirectly, on their overall stamina or energy level in confronting challenging memory tasks.

Description of Specific Modes

Information Modes

These modes include mental manipulations, manipulations of the physical environment, and manipulations of the social environment. These modes involve mental activity and behavior, usually to influence the information needed to learn or to be used to seek a cue to facilitate remembering. In general, these modes involve attentional monitoring during the memory task, and thus require active control on the part of the individual who is practicing these manipulations.

A *mental manipulation* is when a person thinks of a word, image, or some information and then alters the way the word, image, or information is thought about. For example, rehearsal is a mental manipulation because it requires a person to think about something over and over again, such as by repeating this thing to oneself again and again. Mental manipulations consist of the mental processes that have always been the mainstay of memory and study skills training.

Physical environment manipulations use physical records or other stimuli for storing information or for cueing retrieval. For example, notes can be taken, books may be underlined or highlighted, or alarms can be set in order to help an individual remember.

Social manipulations consist of behaviors and conversational ploys that increase the opportunities for (or appearance of) successful memory performance. For example, a student who is not listening may claim not to have heard what a professor said and ask the professor to repeat what was just said. A person can also avoid answering a question in class by repeating the question back with some additional commentary about the importance of the topic.

Physiological Modes

A person's learning and remembering take place in their body, so it is obvious that these may be affected by a person's physiological state (McGaugh, 1989; Wheeler & Magaletta, 1997). These modes pertain to a person's well being. They include physical state, exposure to chemicals via substance use, and health status.

Physical condition. The physical state mode includes the overall condition of the individual, which depends on such factors as the degree of exercise and amount of sleep experienced.

Chemical state. The chemical state of an individual (such as the use of alcohol, stimulants, or illegal substances) may impair memory and performance on academic tasks. Examples of substances that can interfere with one's chemical state include: caffeine, alcohol, nicotine, over-the-counter drugs, prescription medicines, and illicit substances such as marijuana.

Health. Ill health can impair a person's learning and remembering (Mathews, Davies, Westerman, & Stammers, 2000). Even minor conditions, such as the common cold, affect memory function.

The physiological modes affect the ability of the individual to engage in and control active memory processing. These modes also interfere with executive functioning, that is, the capability to control memory and study processes (Baddeley, 1986; also see Pollens et al., 1988). Students who are in a good state to perform a memory task are free of substances and medications that negatively affect mental processing. They are also well rested, in good physical condition, and healthy.

Emotive Modes

A person's learning and remembering obviously can be affected by their emotional state. Emotive states include a person's emotionality, attitudes, and motivation (Yoder & Elias, 1989). Students who are in a good position to study and take tests have moderate emotions, typical attitudes, and positive motivation.

Emotionality, especially if it is extreme, renders a person unable to learn or think.

Attitudes will interfere with cognitive performance if the attitudes are negative or unrealistic.

Motivational states can be critical as to whether or not someone attempts a task and how hard they work on the task.

Thus, emotive modes first affect a person's "strength" when attempting a study task. These modes also affect the "willingness" of the individual to study particular tasks.

Individual Differences

People differ from each other in the way that they perform memory and study tasks. These differences originate from an individual's expertise at studying and test taking, their style of approach to studying and test taking, and their confidence in themselves when attempting to study or take tests (Gruneberg & Sykes, 1993; Read, Lindsay, & Nicholls, 1998). Individual differences in cognitive expertise explain why people with apparently the same abilities differ in their performance on certain tasks.

Memory expertise. Many people develop special memory *expertise* due to repeated experience with a certain memory task, such as an accountant who can easily remember numbers.

Style. Such differences in the style with which people approach studying and test taking explain the contrast in the details and length of answers that students with the same understanding of material can generate. Differences in personal cognitive style, for example, whether one is error prone or conservative, also influence whether or not difficult memory tasks are undertaken and, once attempted, whether and to what extent the attempt is successful.

Confidence. Finally, people differ widely in confidence. A person's performance on a task depends on how much confidence they have in their ability to do that task. If a person lacks confidence in their memory and study skills, he or she may be unwilling even to attempt memory tasks.

Thus, the multimodal model of memory, as applied to academic performance, is complex, involving at least a dozen modes. Table 1 below lists several examples of changes in the different modes that can produce a reduction in a student's memory performance.

Table 2-1. Mode Changes that may Influence Memory

INFORMATION MODES	
Mental Manipulations	Reduced familiarity with mental strategies because of being educated in a poorer school district.
Physical Environment	Failure to perceive or take notice of cues in the environment that might foster encoding or the cueing of retrieval, because of a lack of experience in using cues to aid memory.
Social Environment	Failure to perceive or take notice of social cues to learn or recall because of a lack of awareness of the cues provided by other members of one's cohort.
PHYSIOLOGICAL MODES	
Physical State	Sleep patterns. Students often sleep irregularly. Sometimes, such as before a test, they sleep less. Decreased and disrupted sleep leads to a poorer memory. Also one's ability to study, take tests, and write term papers varies with the time of day. What and how much one eats affects brain function. Students often eat less and less adequately, especially if a person lives far from the dining hall.
Substance Use	Many substances interfere with abilities to learn and think. Students who are not middle aged take few medications. Nevertheless, when they do so, they are likely to take medicines that interfere with cognition, for example: analgesics (pain relievers), antibiotics, antihistamines for allergies or a cold, antidepressants, and others.
Health	Students often act as if they will live forever. Even when they are sick or injured, they soon bounce back and carry on with life as usual. However, any illness, even something minor, is likely to make a person feel less comfortable, be distracted by their symptoms, and possibly fatigued. These states impair the ability to learn and remember.

EMOTIVE MODES

Emotional State	Everyone has their good and bad days. Student life, due to its nature of constantly testing people, is a more volatile time than when people are older. Intense emotions and negative emotions work against good academic performance.
Attitudinal State	As people age, their attitudes may solidify, disposing them to acquire certain kinds of information more easily than others.
Motivational State	Rewards and punishments probably affect everyone in predictable ways. In many cases, students do poorly because the rewards are few. People who can reward themselves often do well in college.

INDIVIDUAL DIFFERENCES

Expertise	People who have been given a good high school education, or who enjoy studying and test taking, are likely to acquire the skills needed for college, and, because of continual career changes, for future jobs.
Personal Style	Regardless of age, people adopt cognitive styles for studying and test taking. People who are field dependent may be better at verbatim recall than people who are field independent. Type A ambitious people remember deadlines for papers better than Type B laid-back people, who may forget a deadline altogether.
Memory Confidence	Because people differ in what memory tasks they are good at, they also differ in how much confidence they have in attempting particular tasks.

Findings about the Effects of Different Modes on Memory

Investigations Designed to Test the Multimodal Model

Links between memory and one or more modes prior to the multimodal model. Many researchers have previously argued that it is an oversimplification to assume that memory originates only in the information mode. These researchers have demonstrated the effects of one or more psychological systems on memory. Much of this research has focused just on memory (Bendiksen & Bendiksen, 1992, 1996; Bracy, 1986; Cavanaugh & Baskind, 1996; Cavanaugh, Kramer, Sinnott, Camp, & Markley, 1985; Davies & Thomson, 1988; Goethals & Solomon, 1989; Herrmann et al., 1992; Herrmann & Palmisano, 1992; Herrmann & Plude, 1996; Herrmann & Searleman, 1990; McEvoy & Moon, 1988; Parente & Herrmann, 1996; Poon, 1980; Poon, Rubin, & Wilson, 1988; Schacter, 1984; Stigsdotter-

Neely & Backman, 1993; Wolkowitz & Weingartner, 1988; Wyer & Srull, 1986; Yoder & Elias, 1991; Zacks & Hasher, 1992).

Memory performance has been found to be affected by modes other than information, such as those concerning emotions, the environment, and social situations (Beatty, Herrmann, Puskar, & Kerwin, 1998; Bendiksen & Bendiksen, 1992, 1996; Best, 1992; Herrmann & Parente, 1994; Mullin et al., 1993; Herrmann, 1994; Reason, 1990). It has been recognized that physiological and emotive states are useful to explain memory functioning in children (Lewis & Sullivan, 1994; Sameroff & Feise, 1990), and older people (Elias, Elias, & Elias, 1990; Rubert, Eisdorfer, & Loewenstein, 1996). A number of case studies have shown that different individuals achieved improvements in memory by employing the multimodal approach.

Memory performance of college students. What should interest most of the readers of this book is that two studies demonstrated that memory performance of students may be explained by the multimodal model. The model assumes that people who possess superior cognitive, physiological, and emotive states will have good memory performance, whereas those who possess inferior cognitive, physiological, and emotive states will have poor memory performance. The first and second investigations addressed the relationship between the modes and memory performance of college students at two different universities, one in the Midwest and one in the East (Herrmann et al., 1999).

The first investigation addressed whether ratings of memory performance were related to ratings of the quality of functioning of nine modes. Students were free to relate their memory performance to school situations or to everyday life. Twenty-nine adult students (ages 18 to 67), who were enrolled in a course about improving memory and thinking, participated in this investigation. Each participant recorded their observations about their memory effectiveness and about the status of eight modes: physical condition, chemical state, attitudes, emotions, motivation, mental manipulations, physical manipulations, and social environment. The results demonstrated that the ratings of memory performance were predicted by the ratings of the different modes. The results indicated that the emotive systems predicted memory functioning better than the physiological or cognitive systems.

The second investigation also addressed whether ratings of memory performance of students would be related to ratings of the quality of functioning of nine modes. Thirty college undergraduates followed a procedure similar to that used in the first investigation. The same modes assessed in the first investigation were also assessed in the second investigation, except that the participants also rated their health. Memory was assessed by a single rating, as was done in the first investigation. The results again demonstrated that the student ratings of memory performance were predicted by the ratings of the different modes. The results indicated that the emotive systems predicted memory functioning better than the physiological or cognitive systems. An overall analysis of memory and all modes showed that use of chemical substances, motivation, use of social manipulations, and the absence of physical manipulations accounted for 56% of the variation in reported memory performance.

How changes in modes relate to changes in memory ratings. Another way of demonstrating the credibility of the multimodal model is to consider whether memory performance will change with corresponding changes in the modes. One investigation assessed whether changes in memory varied with changes in the modes produced by treatment in a substance abuse program. Eighteen veterans, who were victims of mixed substance abuse, voluntarily participated in a treatment program. Their memory performance and the status of the nine modes were assessed by a psychiatric technician in the first and last week of a six-week program. From the first to the sixth week, the patients were given psychogenic and chemical therapy for their addiction. Because the patients stopped using the adverse substance, the memory ratings improved from pretest to posttest, as did the mode ratings. Moreover, the mode ratings were more strongly related after treatment than before. Ratings increased across the treatment period more for the emotive modes than was the case for the cognitive and physiological modes. It should be noted that this investigation also asked the patients to rate the quality of their thinking. These ratings also improved across the treatment period. Thinking was related to both the emotive and cognitive modes.

Effects of treatments designed to alter modes and memory performance. Yet another way to test the multimodal model is to examine the effects of treatments designed to alter the different mode categories. In the preceding study, mode changes were investigated as a function of treatments for drug addiction; no training in cognitive processes was given to influence memory performance. The following investigation examined the effects of treatments on the different modes, including training in memory processing on memory performance.

This investigation sought to remedy memory losses that workers in a paint factor experienced when they were exposed to toxic levels of paint solvent fumes. The investigation provided the victims with a treatment program over nine weeks that was specifically designed to improve all of the modes of the victims. Specifically, the participants were educated in the rationale of the multimodal approach. They also attended a series of 18 training sessions that sought to teach procedures to improve memory functioning. These sessions also devoted time for participants to address emotional and social difficulties. Memory performance improved from pre- to post-intervention, although the magnitude of change was small and not highly consistent. The participants' perception of adjustment also improved significantly after the intervention. Although at the six month follow-up there had been some regression towards pre-intervention functioning, the frequency and intensity of symptoms were much less than prior to the treatment. Complaints about memory problems in everyday life decreased substantially across the training period. Complaints of an emotional nature also decreased over time. Thus, the results clearly showed that the memory capabilities of patients improved because of the treatment (Bendiksen & Bendiksen, 1992, 1996). The researchers concluded that successful treatment of cognitively impaired persons requires a multimodal approach. It should be noted that people with other kinds of neurological impairments have benefited from this approach (Parente & Herrmann, 1996).

Other multimodal models. The multimodal model presented here is not the only model presented. Other researchers have proposed models with multimodal assumptions to address the effects of certain modes other than memory (see Barnard & Teasdale, 1991; Cavanaugh et al., 1985; Humphreys & Revelle, 1984; McEvoy, 1992; McEvoy & Moon, 1988). The major difference between these models and the present model is that the present model was designed to provide a comprehensive account of the influence of modes in general. Nevertheless, the existence of these other models demonstrates that other researchers have also thought that it was important to try to provide a theoretical account of mode effects.

General Discussion of the Multimodal Approach

The investigations examined in this chapter clearly support approaching memory from a multi-system perspective that includes modes from the different categories. Firstly, many previously cited studies have linked the quality of particular modes with improved memory performance. Secondly, the research showed that the memory of college students was dependent on the status of different modes, as was expected. Thirdly, a study was discussed that showed interventions of a physiological and emotive nature in a drug abuse treatment program produced a change in memory performance, despite no memory training being provided. Fourthly, a study, that provided memory training and treatments to improve the cognitive and emotive modes of people who were neurologically-impaired because of exposure to toxic fumes at a paint factory, reported improvements in the participant's memory capabilities.

Across the different investigations, it is clear that different conditions influence the size of the effects observed. Nevertheless, it is also clear that the different modes affect learning and remembering. It is obvious that rehearsal and remembering strategies are not enough for a student to perform at his or her best. Students who attempt to improve the quality of as many modes as possible will find rewards in improved grades. If a student is not really interested in improving grades, he or she can learn and remember what is necessary with less study time by ensuring the modes are in good shape. The following chapters explain what one needs to know to improve one's modes in order to improve academic performance.

The Multimodal Theory of Study Skill Improvement

The multicomponent theory and the multimodal theory of memory suggest a path to study skill improvement much broader than traditional methods. Since memory and academic performance depend on so many modes, a person cannot expect that a few study skills will prepare them for any task or all tasks. The best formula for a substantial improvement holds that you should take care of all of your modes when studying and test taking. Doing so will improve your memory performance by optimizing the amount of attention given to memory tasks (Norman, 1982; Poon, 1980; Wilson, 1987; Wilson & Moffat, 1984; Yesavage et al., 1989).

This book offers more skills than any one person would want to learn. The choice of skills to learn will be those that are especially suited to the tasks an individual needs to perform better in (Flippo & Caverly, 1991; Shepherd, 1987; Weinstein, Goetz, & Alexander, 1989). Current evidence indicates that manipulations that have been designed to be task specific improve memory more effectively than general manipulations. You are best off acquiring skills that appeal to you and acquiring more than one skill for an academic task. If you have a repertoire of skills, you can choose which one applies best to the task at hand.

Forming repertoires of manipulations. There are many reasons why tasks challenge us. We may have difficulty with an academic task because our informational skills are insufficient. Our physical state and emotive state may be suboptimal at that particular time. Also, our individual study skills may not be appropriate to a task. One can attempt to rely on one skill to cope with a task, but when a task is especially annoying to us, it pays to develop a repertoire made up of a number of skills.

When you find a task troublesome, select a few skills that you can apply when the task arises. A task repertoire of manipulations will prepare you to respond quickly and accurately. Research shows that two or three skills lead to better memory performance than one. When a task is already annoying, the extra effort in preparation will be worth it to you.

The Need for a Complete Approach to Improving Memory and Study Skills

The theory of memory and study skill improvement advanced here prescribes a comprehensive and specific approach to memory problems encountered while studying and facilitating memory processing (Herrmann & Parente, 1994; Herrmann & Plude, 1996; Herrmann & Searleman, 1990; McEvoy, 1992; Poon, 1980; Yesavage et al., 1989). This approach is very similar to the approaches that work best for developing other kinds of skills.

The next chapter will provide you with an opportunity to make an assessment of the memory problems on which you would most like to improve. Subsequent chapters explain how you can improve at each of the different kinds of manipulations that affect memory performance. Finally, later chapters will describe how you combine the different kinds of manipulations into repertoires that will enable you to better deal with the memory tasks you find troublesome.

Summary

Memory and academic performance in general depends on psychological modes that belong to four categories: cognitive process in general, physiological states, emotive states, and cognitive characteristics unique to the individual. Study skill improvement depends on changing several aspects of the way a person approaches their academic responsibilities and life in general.

The different modes improve memory performance partly because they prepare a person to pay attention better. The intensity and the distribution of your attention can be improved through intentional and incidental "manipulations" of the memory situation.

No one study skill will work for all courses or for all tasks within courses. Modern memory research shows that developing a repertoire of mental manipulations – made up of the right combinations of manipulations to fit specific memory tasks – gives the best results in improving academic performance.

3. Self Assessment of Memory and Study Skills

Check Your Memory Abilities

How good is your memory? Really? Most people think they know the answer to this question, but research has shown that none of us have a very clear idea of how well our memory works. For example, people are often completely wrong when they claim they are good at a certain memory task or bad at another. Although people feel that they remember accurately, much of what they remember is actually just beliefs (Cavanaugh, Feldman, & Hertzog, 1998; Hertzog, Park, Morrell, & Martin, 2000).

There are various reasons why we perceive our abilities incorrectly. One is that our culture teaches – incorrectly – that memory ability is like a muscle – it's either strong or weak. Because we conceive of memory in this single-minded manner, we often fail to notice that people are good at some memory tasks and poor at others. It is a fact that no one's memory is uniformly good or uniformly bad across all situations. Some people come to be known as having a "good memory," but this happens because they are good at valuable memory tasks, such as remembering names or important information. People come to be known as having a "bad memory" because they fail at conspicuous tasks, such as remembering birthdays, anniversaries, and obligations in general.

Another reason why we do not have a clear impression of our memory abilities is because we do not keep a systematic record of how often we succeed or fail at memory tasks. Our lives are often filled with events that at the time seem more important than how we fare at certain memory tasks. Because we pay little attention to how well our memory performs, we do not remember what our memory abilities are like (Herrmann, 1990a;

Klatzky, 1984; Lachman, Steinberg, & Trotter, 1987; Morris, 1984; Perlmutter, 1988). The same can be said for study skills in general: we do not take the time or effort to find out whether our skills are really effective.

Obviously, a realistic appraisal of your memory abilities and study skills is essential to setting worthwhile goals for academic improvement. Additionally, a remedy for a deficient ability can only be found if this ability is precisely identified in the first place. Thus, this chapter has the purpose of helping you identify which abilities need improving. Once you have acquired a realistic evaluation of your memory abilities, you will be in the right position to direct your efforts to improve your memory. Identification of those abilities which are strong will give you confidence to attempt tasks to which these abilities apply. Furthermore, knowing which of your abilities are already strong will save you from wasting effort to improve abilities that need no improvement. Identification of memory abilities that are weak will allow you to develop ways to either avoid the tasks pertinent to these abilities or to improve these abilities. Thus, knowing your memory strengths and weaknesses enables you to hold reasonable expectations for yourself and to set goals for efforts to improve your memory.

Memory and study skills differ among people in other ways as well. One way is that people vary in how much they need to engage in intellectual tasks (Cacioppo & Petty, 1982). Another factor is personality. Some people are very ambitious and others are laid back (Searleman & Gaydusek, 1996). Intelligence affects the amount learned and the style in which the learning occurs (Gardner, 1993). Some people are more error prone than other people (Broadbent, Cooper, Fitzgerald & Parkes, 1982; Norman, 1981); i.e., the tendency to make errors in studying, test taking, and other aspects of academic performance. Later in the book we will discuss further how we differ from each other.

This chapter is intended to aid you in deciding how good your memory really is, especially as it is applied to studying and surviving in college. The chapter will begin by explaining how memory abilities are evaluated by professionals in psychology and by other books on memory improvement (Flippo & Caverly, 1991; Forrest-Pressley, MacKinnon, & Waller, 1985; Weinstein et al., 1989). The chapter will then provide you with two procedures that you can use to make a partial evaluation of your memory. One procedure consists of extensive questionnaires, which you may use to make a thorough inventory of impressions of your memory performance. A second procedure consists of carrying out a diary study of your memory performance over an interval of a few weeks. Finally, you will examine your responses to the questionnaires and the diary, identify your memory strengths and weaknesses, and set goals for your memory-improvement efforts.

Standard Methods for Evaluating Study Skills

The evaluative methods recommended in this chapter do not measure memory performance as reliably as a memory-performance examination administered by a professional would (Grafman, 1984; Poon et al., 1986; Sternberg, 1985; Wechsler, 1945; Wilding & Valentine, 1988). Nonetheless, they are substantially better than self-administered memory tasks or tests administered to you by nonprofessionals, which have been recommended by previous memory-improvement books.

The method used here couples a memory questionnaire concerning study practices with the keeping of a memory diary (Herrmann, 1990a; see also Dixon, Hertzog, & Hultsch, 1986). The use of a memory diary provides a means of corroborating or challenging the observations recorded on the questionnaire. Memory diaries are generally regarded by professionals as yielding more accurate information about you than the questionnaire, because the diary record is made shortly after a memory task, whereas a questionnaire is usually taken considerably later (Reason & Mycielska, 1983).

Memory Questionnaires

There are numerous memory and study tasks in our lives. The questionnaires below address many of these tasks. Four questionnaires are presented here to allow you to judge your performance in four categories of memory tasks: knowledge, events, intentions, and actions. Thus, when you have completed these questionnaires, you will be able to assess your overall performance in each of these memory-task categories as well as for each of the many specific tasks within each category.

Knowledge. Primary, secondary, and higher education require us to acquire a great deal of information. Depending on our interests, we have learned more about some subjects and less about others. We may have avoided or lacked a chance to study some subjects at all. Similarly, our jobs and hobbies have led us to acquire quite a lot of knowledge. Our knowledge for information learned in and out of school is a separate matter from what we know about the events of our lives, the obligations we have to others, or our physical skills.

The Study Practices Inventory

Improved academic performance requires improvements in study practices. In this inventory you are asked to check off the study practices that you engage in. Also, there are questions about the effects of certain study practices. The point of this inventory is to make you more sensitive to what study practices you should employ that you are not employing now.

As you answer the questions, please realize that the goal is not to get a high score. The goal is to give you the opportunity to collect information about your study practices. An increased awareness of how you study will enable you to get more out of this book.

Attitudes

Please check off which behaviors apply to you.

1. When you are alone, do you find yourself thinking about course material simply because you are interested in this material? _____
2. Do you talk about your reading assignments with others in your class? _____
3. Do you talk about your written assignments with others in your class? _____
4. Do you ask your professors to clarify what they just said during a lecture? _____
5. Do you find mistakes in your textbooks? _____
6. Do you review your notes within a couple days of class? _____
7. Do you daydream in class? _____
8. Do you work on assignments for another course while in a class? _____
9. When you write a paper for a course, do you ask someone else to read over the paper and revise it before finally submitting it? _____
10. Do you almost always arrive to class early or on time? _____

Attitude total score = _____

Note.   Questions 1-7: score 1 point for every question you check off (doing the right thing)
Questions 8-10: score 1 point for every question you say no to (avoiding doing the wrong things)
Total Score = sum of points

Mental Processing Challenges

Please check off which behaviors apply to you.

I find it difficult

1. to get oriented to a course in the beginning   _____
2. to remember information on a quiz   _____
3. to make inferences   _____
4. organizing the information I get in class   _____
5. to take an essay test   _____
6. to find the right words I want to say   _____
7. to keep up with the pace of my teachers   _____
8. to say what the message is of something I have read   _____
9. to think fast   _____
10. to read critically   _____

Mental processing challenges total score = _____

Note. Total score: 10 — No. of items checked out of 10

Innovative Study Procedures

Please check off which behaviors apply to you.

I am creative in my school work by

1. distinguishing between facts and opinion   _____
2. seeking understanding of new concepts through recalling the meanings of other concepts   _____
3. thinking of the applications of abstract ideas   _____
4. thinking of similar ideas   _____
5. identifying ideas that are the opposite of new terms   _____
6. anticipating how I might later remember the information I am studying   _____
7. paraphrasing ideas to be learned   _____
8. visualizing situations that are relevant to ideas being studied   _____

9. generating questions I expect to be answered when reading a textbook   _____
10. figuring out ways I might remember information on a test   _____

Innovative Study Procedures Total = _____

Note. Total score: No. of items checked out of 10

Remembering Ability

Please check off which behaviors apply to you.

I remember accurately when asked questions

1. about definitions   _____
2. about factual information   _____
3. about names of people mentioned in class or assignments _____
4. about statistics   _____
5. in a multiple choice format   _____
6. in a fill in the blank format   _____
7. about dates   _____
8. about graphs   _____
9. about tables   _____
10. about legal information   _____

Remembering Ability Total = _____

Note. Total score: No. of items checked out of 10

Study Habits

Please check off which behaviors apply to you.

I generally

1. do not cram for exams   _____
2. study in the same place   _____
3. study alone or with one or two serious students   _____

4. make outlines, graphs, charts, and diagrams to help me learn ____

5. take notes on notes, and notes on notes on notes when preparing for an exam ____

6. plan how much time I will spend reviewing each topic when I start to study for an exam ____

7. try to formulate questions that will be on an exam when I start to study for it ____

8. rehearse out loud when I study for an exam ____

9. try to restate or paraphrase material when I study for an exam ____

10. make acronyms of terms that have to be learned (IBM is an acronym for International Business Machines) when I study for an exam ____

Study Habits Total = _____

Note. Total score: No. of items checked out of 10

Class Preparation

Please check off which behaviors apply to you.

I generally

1. read headings in a textbook before reading an assignment ____
2. read the chapter summary before reading an assignment ____
3. examine figures and tables before reading an assignment ____
4. read questions at the end of the chapter before reading an assignment ____
5. develop an outline when I study ____
6. review my notes after class ____
7. get down to my studies easily ____
8. keep a schedule of my day and my studying ____
9. complete all assignments ____
10. check two or more sources to understand a difficult concept ____

Class Preparation Total = _____

Note. Total score: No. of items checked out of 10

Use of Study Procedures

Please check off which behaviors apply to you.

When you study for an exam, which of the methods below do you use?

1. rehearse, repeat over and over   _____
2. study my class notes   _____
3. study notes I have made of my class notes   _____
4. organize the information that helps me remember   _____
5. make an acronym of key terms (making another word from the first letter of the terms to be learned)   _____
6. organize words into a sentence   _____
7. make diagrams, sketches, and maps of ideas to learn   _____
8. associate material to be learned with knowledge I already have   _____
9. form images of terms to be learned, objects referred to by the terms, and situations   _____
10. flash cards   _____

Use of Study Procedures Total = _____

Note. Total score: No. of items checked out of 10

Study Skill Knowledge

Coding key:
Circle + if the action on the left enhances learning and/or remembering
Circle 0 if the action on the left has no effect on learning and/or remembering
Circle − if the action on the left impairs learning and/or remembering

---

Action   *Effect on*
                                                   Learning/Remembering

Taking down notes on most or all of what a professor says	+	0	−
Underlining most or all of what you read in textbooks	+	0	−
Studying mostly on the night before an exam	+	0	−
Taking an exam mid morning	+	0	−
Studying with classical music when one usually studies with rock'n roll	+	0	−
Studying in a slightly uncomfortable chair	+	0	−
Staying up very late when you study for exams	+	0	−
Some noise in the background while studying	+	0	−
Studying with a group of people	+	0	−
Studying in a slightly cool room	+	0	−

***Study Skill Knowledge Total* =**

Note. Total score: Count the number of correct answers.
Answer key: − − − + − +− + − + in the order of the questions.
Note that the correct answers pertain to the effect of the action on most people.

Knowledge of the Effects of Self Care on Academic Performance

Coding key:
Circle + if the action on the left enhances learning and/or remembering

Circle 0 if the action on the left has no effect on learning and/or remembering

Circle − if the action on the left impairs learning and/or remembering

Action   *Effect on*
                                                              Learning/Remembering

Action			
Drinking three cups of coffee prior to an exam	+	0	−
Having a minor cold when you take an exam	+	0	−
Regularly smoking cigarettes and/or cigars	+	0	−
Drinking lemonade after studying	+	0	−
Eating chocolate bars while studying	+	0	−
Taking an antibiotic prior to studying	+	0	−
Depression	+	0	−
Being physically fit	+	0	−
Knowing that someone else in class dislikes you	+	0	−
Being in a rut because of a very predictable life style	+	0	−

Knowledge of Self Care Effects =

Note. Total score: Count the number of correct answers.
Answer key: − − − + − + − + − + in the order of the questions.
Note that the correct answers pertain to the effect of the action on most people.

Scoring Scheme for the Study Skills Inventory (see also notes under each Section)

Copy the total scores from above and insert these scores in the table below.

Attitudes total score =
(No. of items checked out of 10)   _____

Mental Processing Challenges total =
(No. of items checked out of 10)   _____

Innovative Study Procedures total =
(No. of items checked out of 10)   _____

Remembering Ability total =
(No. of items checked out of 10)   _____

Study Habits total =
(No. of items checked out of 10)   _____

Class Preparation total =
(No. of items checked out of 10)   _____

Use of Study Procedures total =
(No. of items checked out of 10)   _____

Study Skill Knowledge total =
(No. of items checked out of 10)   _____

Knowledge of the Effects Self Care total=
(No. of items checked out of 10)   _____

Total (No. of items checked out of 90 + 10)   _____

Interpretation. As noted above, the purpose of this inventory is to increase your awareness of your study practices and to assist you in deciding which study practices you feel are most effective for you and which practices could stand improvement. Generally, the higher the score the better a person's study habits are. However, because each person is different, the optimum number of practices is a matter for each person.

Memory/Study Skills Diary

Questionnaires provide a good means for taking stock of our memory abilities and study skills. However, many of our successes and failures at remembering occur without us noticing them, making some of our questionnaire answers less accurate than we would like. Another way to learn about how your mind performs in everyday life is by keeping a diary of your memory performance and use of study skills. A diary provides a good way to gain a more direct account of how you actually perform on academic tasks (Herrmann, 1990a; Reason & Mycielska, 1983). If you forget an answer to a question in class, record it in your diary. If you are trying to study but your mind keeps on straying off to nonacademic subjects, record this in your diary. By keeping a diary for one or more weeks, you can discover that some aspects of your performance are better and some are worse than you suspected.

Keeping a memory/study skills diary is relatively simple. You decide to pay attention to your failures at a selected set of tasks, such as taking notes in class or completion of a reading assignment. During the diary period, you make a note of each failure. In order to get an accurate impression of your typical performance, keep the diary for at least one week, but preferably you should keep it for a month. After keeping a diary for some interval, total up how often you forgot for each task. The totals will indicate what aspects of studying and exam taking are most challenging for you. The chances are that you will find that you failed at some tasks much less often than you expected. Table 3-1 below lists a set of tasks that might be recommended for a first diary. These tasks are recommended because they are important to many people, and because they are fairly easy to observe. You may add other tasks to this set, and, of course, you could keep additional diaries in the future that deal with other memory and study tasks.

You can keep a memory/study skills diary in whatever form suits you best, whether on 3-by-5 cards or in a notebook. People usually find that a checklist facilitates keeping track of failures. Table 3-2 below presents a list that you can use or modify to your liking. Photocopy this page and carry a copy with you for one to four weeks.

Each time you detect that you have failed in one of the ways listed, put a check mark alongside the relevant task. Also enter a few words that describe the failure so that you can later reflect on the event and on how you might better cope with similar situations in the future. Sometimes your memory failure will occur while you are with other people. If you feel shy or awkward about making your record at that time, wait until you are alone to enter a check on the diary checklist. However, the longer you wait to make a check, the greater the chances are that you will forget your failure – making your diary record less accurate than it could be. Table 3-3 gives an example of a completed diary record sheet.

You can choose to monitor any one of many aspects of your study practices. For starters, we suggest that you keep a diary on three practices: reading practices, note-taking practices, and practices for taking note of and retaining recent information.

Table 3-1. Recommended Tasks for a Memory/Study Diary

Reading	Effective reading of assignments is obviously important to learning and studying in college. Nevertheless, there are some mistakes that many students make in reading.
What Is This About?	Most students want to get their reading done and then relax. Conscquently, they jump right in.
False Start	It usually pays to skim over a reading assignment before starting to read in earnest. Failing to skim and making a fast start at reading makes it hard for anyone to get into the material.
Taking Notes	It is important for students to take notes in college because much of the material covered in a course is presented in class. The textbook will present some of the information, but not all of it. Therefore, students have to be good at taking notes. However, note taking does not mean becoming a human tape recorder. Instead, a good note taker is a good observer, recording the essence of what has been presented. Taking good notes is an art. It is easy to make certain mistakes.
Taking Too Few Notes	Sometimes information covered in class will be obvious. When this happens, students sometimes write down very little or no notes. Later when preparing for an exam, many students look at their notes to discover that their notes are sketchy and their memory for what was said is meager.
Taking Too Many Notes	Sometimes information covered in class is complicated. When this happens, students sometimes write down almost every word. They hope that when they read over the many words recorded, it will finally make sense what the professor was talking about. Later when preparing for an exam, many students look at thcir notes to discover that they are too detailed because they realize that their professor is more interested in general principles and less so in a word for word account of his or her lecture.
Recent Information	Class discussion is important for many courses. You are expected to remember the gist of these discussions for term papers and exams. If you forget what was discussed, you are at a disadvantage in the course. Another thing that can be forgotten is work for an assignment. It is not unusual for students to forget to hand in an assignment that they have completed. Drew a blank. You realize that you have forgotten what was discussed in a previous class.
Intentions	Forgot what to do. You know that you were supposed to bring something to class but you forget to do so.

Table 3-2. Your Memory/Study Diary Record

Day and date _____

Description of Kind of Failure

<u>Reading.</u>
What is this about? _____

False starts. _____

_____

<u>Taking notes.</u>
Taking too few notes. _____

_____

Taking too many notes. _____

_____

<u>Recent information</u>
Intention – forgot what to do
Intention – forgot to take something to class _____

_____

Table 3-3. An Example of a Completed Diary Record Sheet

Your Memory/Study Diary Record

Day and Date _Tuesday_

Description of Kind of Failure

Reading.
What is this about? _My mind wanders_

False starts. _I go back and reread, but my mind still wanders_

Taking notes.
Taking too few notes. _I should have taken more notes. When I tune out, I do not make notes._

Taking too many notes _Sometimes writing everything down makes me tune out_

Intention-Forgot What To Do
Intention-Forgot to Take Something to Class _Sometimes I forget to take my notebook to class. When this happens I take even less notes. Conclusion— I have to find reasons why I need to learn something. If I find reasons to learn, my mind will wander less._

Scoring Your Diary Responses

Count the number of memory failures for each task over the period your diary was kept. Before you draw any conclusions from it, consider how often you confronted each memory task. You may have failed most often at a task you faced many times daily; yet, on the whole, your performance at that task may still have been good. For example, your impression of your ability to remember names will differ depending on whether you experienced only one introduction or thirty introductions in the diary period. Thus, it is necessary to change the diary records into a rating that you can later compare to your questionnaire answers. For each of the tasks, rate your study practice on a 7-point scale. A seven indicates that your study practice never or rarely failed during the diary period, relative to the number of opportunities for failure you encountered. Alternatively, a 1 indicates that your study practice failed at almost every opportunity.

Interpretation of Your Memory Questionnaire and Diary

The primary purpose of the Inventory and the Diary was to give you a clearer idea of your study practices. As discussed earlier in this chapter, people are only partially aware of their success and failure at memory and study skills tasks, but their awareness of memory abilities increases after performing the assessment tasks as employed here (Brennan, Winograd, Bridge, & Hiebert, 1986; Falkenberg, 1994; Herrmann, 1990a).

Setting Goals for Study Skill Improvement

After completing the inventory and the diary, you are in a better position to choose those skills on which you would most like to concentrate. In this section, you will summarize the data you have gathered with the memory questionnaires and diary, interpret these data, and determine precise goals for your memory-improvement efforts.

To begin with, consider which of the task categories are most important to your memory goals – your attitude, mental processing, innovative study procedures, remembering ability, study habits, class preparation, use of study procedures, study skill knowledge, or knowledge of self care practices. Which study practices matter the least to you? Recognition of the most important and least important task categories will help you decide which specific tasks you want to devote your energy to improving as you proceed through this book. In setting your goals at the task-specific level, you should review the tasks that you circled earlier on the memory questionnaire. Reconsider, in light of the diary experience and everything that you have thought about while working on this chapter, which specific tasks you want to work on later.

Once you are satisfied which two tasks in each category deserve to be improved, write the names of these in Table 3-4. In the next several chapters, you will be learning information that will help you with all manner of memory tasks generally. In chapter 9, we will show how the knowledge of the intervening chapters can also be used to improve the specific tasks you have listed in Table 3-4 as most annoying to you.

Table 3-4. Specific Study Skill Goals

1._____

_____

2._____

_____

3._____

_____

4._____

_____

5._____

_____

6._____

_____

7._____

_____

8._____

_____

Summary

An accurate evaluation of your memory abilities is essential to improving memory performance, because different methods of improvement work best on different task categories, and because maximal improvement is usually obtained with methods that pertain to specific tasks. Thus, the questionnaire responses and diary responses provide you with concrete data that you can use to select the task categories and especially the specific tasks in which you would like to improve. Your choice of courses depends in part on how you view your memory abilities. Unfortunately, most people are only partially aware of their study skills. Thus, they avoid courses and tasks within courses that they could succeed at, and take on tasks they should have skipped.

A realistic knowledge of your study practices is necessary to work on your abilities that need improvement and to ignore your abilities that already are in good shape.

You can achieve a realistic understanding of your memory abilities by carefully studying your answers on the comprehensive questionnaire and the diary that address these practices.

Section II.

How You Feel When You Study and When You Are Tested

4. Physical State

For centuries, many have thought that the mind and body are separate. Consequently, few people have assumed that the state of their body can affect the state of their mind. This chapter will demonstrate that many aspects of the physiological state of the body can interfere with academic performance. For example, did you know that your physical condition – like whether you get enough vitamins and enough sleep – can have a major impact on whether you remember someone's name or what you wanted to buy at a store? When people are asked about how to improve academic performance, they almost never mention taking care of their health, reducing stress, or adopting a better attitude towards memory tasks. Nevertheless, there is ample research to show that a student's overall academic performance can range from good to poor simply because of their physical and/or mental condition (Davies & Thomson, 1988; Herrmann & Searleman, 1990; Risko, Alvarez, & Fairbanks, 1991). An increase in physical fitness, general health, sleep, relaxation, and realistic attitudes improves memory performance. Certain times in the day are better for registering and remembering information. Changes in one's routine can interfere with your memory unless you take steps to recover from such changes.

Your condition is the single most important factor in how you perform incidental memory tasks – when you are not aware that you are doing a memory task. Your condition is also a major factor in your performance of intentional memory tasks, because your use of mental manipulations is dulled if your condition is poor. If you foresee periods in which you want to be at your intellectual best – taking a test, for instance – take better care of your condition, if only for several days preceding the event. It can work to your advantage.

The recommendations in this chapter aren't quick fixes, but they will help you lay the groundwork for better memory performance. They do involve more of a commitment than taking a pill that promises you a better memory, or memorizing supposedly miraculous memory strategies.

They can even involve major lifestyle changes. If you really want to change your memory performance, they'll be worth it.

The Influence of Physical Condition on Memory Mechanisms

As we've discussed, attention is one key to memory performance. Poor condition lessens memory performance because it robs us of our ability to pay attention. A deal settled over a "two-martini" lunch will seem hazy a day later. A late night spent studying often results in fatigue that interferes with the remembering of whatever was learned. As deficiencies in either physical or mental condition lessen attention, the rate of absorption of information into long-term memory decreases, and the rate at which traces emerge from long-term memory into working memory decreases as well. Some deficiencies may interfere with attention to mental efforts at registration or remembering, leading to omissions and errors in performance. If your condition is poor when good memory performance is desired, the entire memory system clearly will not function well. In terms of the memory model presented in Chapter 1, poor condition may impair memory processes in several ways. The upper panel of Figure 4 presents the memory model of the first chapter, a model of a system in good condition. The lower panel presents a model of the memory system in poor condition. As you can see, poor condition impairs the system in several ways. First, it lessens the ability of the central processor to attend to the contents of working memory. Thus, no idea or image in working memory is likely to be attended to strongly. As a result, no idea or image will produce a salient trace in long-term memory or will forcefully prod desired memories to emerge from long-term memory. Second, long-term memory's physiological receptivity to absorption or its physiological readiness for the emergence may be reduced by poor condition.

When poor condition has impaired the memory system, manipulations of physical and mental condition are needed to restore the system to proper functioning (Herrmann & Searleman, 1990, 1992).

Manipulations of condition are applicable to a wide range of memory tasks. You can use these manipulations to do better at memory tasks of considerable personal importance: giving a speech, making an oral report, participating in a lab practicum, questioning your professor about what will be on an upcoming exam.

You can also use these manipulations to do better at all manner of memory tasks – often ones you cannot anticipate – which may or may not

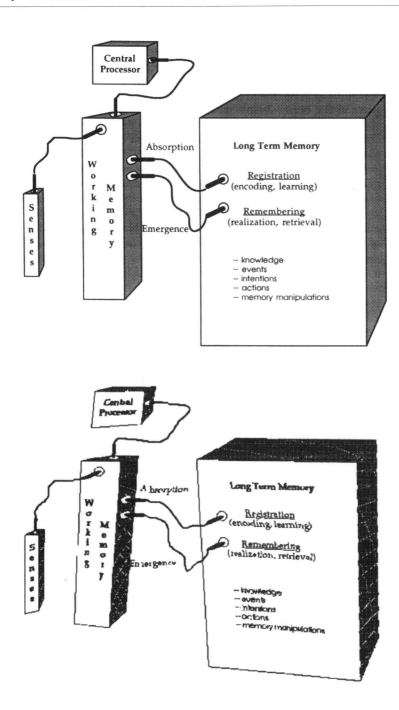

Figure 4. The Memory System in Good and Poor Condition

arise at certain occasions: tasks that must be carried out at a high school reunion (from remembering names to recalling where you put your coat or drink), or tasks that must be carried out during a job interview (from answering questions about your qualifications to remembering to return the interviewer's pen).

Physical Condition

Aspects of your physical condition can critically influence your memory performance (see Table 4-1). In addressing these aspects, the question is not so much how to manipulate your physical condition to favor memory, as it is how to avoid the failures to take care of yourself that impair memory. In some cases, a deficiency is beyond correction. However, the prescriptions that follow mainly address physical concerns most adults encounter and can correct. A heavy dose of common sense combined with a few innovative manipulations can rectify most conditioning problems enough to improve your memory performance.

Table 4-1. Physical States that Impair Memory Performance

Poor Health
minor
major
Poor Nutrition
Overeating
Adverse Substances
Fatigue from Work or Play
Lack of Sleep

Fitness

Exercise helps you maintain your strength and your cardiovascular condition, and thereby keeps you physically ready for memory tasks (Blumenthal & Madden, 1988; Harma, Illmarinen, Knauth, & Rutenfranz, et al., 1988; Powell, 1974; Stamford, Hambacher, & Fallica, 1974). It also helps relieve you of the "blues," lessens stress, improves sleep, and enhances digestion – all of which help memory. Some researchers suspect exercise may be especially effective for facilitating short-term memory performance, but this claim has not yet been fully investigated.

The exercise you engage in to improve memory need not be excessive. A 20-minute walk each day is probably sufficient to improve memory performance if a person has not been exercising previously.

Your Energy Cycles

Time management requires more of you than just making a mental or written note of when to do things (Brandimonte, Einstein, & McDaniel, 1996; Burt & Forsyth, 1999; Ellis, 1996; Luckie & Smethurst, 1998: Macan, 1994). Your strength for memory tasks is cyclical. There are certain times in the day and across days of the week when memory functions best (Folkard & Monk, 1978,1980; Revelle, Humphreys, Simon, & Gilliland, 1980). For most people, the best time to perform memory tasks is between 11 a.m. and 4 p.m. This peak in memory performance probably occurs for several reasons: people get more involved with their activities by mid-day; they gradually lose their sharpness later in the day as general fatigue sets in; and their attentiveness varies with daily biological cycles (such as body temperature, respiration rate, pulse rate; Wyon, Andersen, & Lundqvist, 1979). Memory ability also tends to be at its best on Fridays and Saturdays. A peak in memory performance occurs on these days, probably because the anticipation of the weekend picks up a person's mood (Folkard & Monk, 1978, 1980; Revelle, Humphreys et al., 1980).

Although the typical peak times for memory performance occur in the middle of the day and at the end of the week, some people will have different peak times. You can judge what times are peak for you simply by paying attention to when you are most alert and most able to think clearly. Obviously, if you work the night shift or on weekends, your peak times will be different from those of people who work 9 to 5, Monday to Friday. Generally, people remember to do tasks that they regard as important (Andrzejewski, Moore, Corvette, & Herrmann, 1991), but even important tasks may be forgotten if they occur at an off-peak time.

There is also evidence that your routine time for waking and sleeping affects your daily peaks for memory tasks. If you are a "morning" person, who goes to bed early and rises early, you learn more readily earlier in the day. If you are an "evening" person, you will probably learn more readily later in the day. Because of our natural cycles, the times we choose to schedule events will affect our success or failure at memory tasks. You can make the best use of your reserves of strength by performing memory tasks when these reserves are at their peak. Take on memory tasks in the middle of the day and toward the end of the week. If you have control over the scheduling of an important meeting, schedule it around 10:30 a.m. (a little earlier if you are a morning person, a little later if you are an evening person). Additionally, schedule such meetings, if possible, on Thursday or Friday. Try to minimize or at least decrease the number of memory tasks you must carry out when you anticipate disruptions in your daily and weekly cycles. When life does not allow you to schedule an event at an optimal time, you can at least attempt to be more alert when the event does occur.

Disruptions to your cycle diminish your cognitive capacity. Interruptions to your sleep wear you down considerably. Changes in your cycle, which may be caused by a radical change in your schedule (such as occurs in shiftwork) or by travel that induces "jet lag," interfere with your ability to pay attention and do memory tasks (Idzikowski, 1984). Such shifts make it harder to pick up new information and remember old information. If your cycle is disrupted by traveling, you may find it hard to remember directions on how to get to your hotel, or what room the desk clerk just gave you in the hotel, or where you put your bag just before you asked the desk clerk about your room. Thus, when there is a shift in your cycle, allow extra time to recuperate before taking on major tasks that rely on your intellect and your memory.

Sleep and Sleep-Learning

Proper sleep obviously makes a person strong and alert for studying and tests. Getting sufficient sleep before an exam or an interview is essential in order for you to remember quickly and accurately. We all can recall occasions when we were forced to stay awake much longer than usual and fumbled for our words and struggled to remember answers the next day that normally we would have remembered easily. You can ensure getting a good night's sleep if you avoid eating and drinking in the evening, avoid thinking about your troubles prior to bedtime, and if you go to bed at approximately the same time every night. Also, avoid using sleeping pills. The sleep they induce is usually not as refreshing as natural sleep. Sleeping pills often have a carry-over effect the next day, making you less able to register new memories and less susceptible to stimulation that will help you remember.

There is some evidence to show that going to sleep immediately after learning leads you to remember what you learned better than if you put off going to bed after learning. Apparently, playing cards or going out to eat after a study session does not help your memory as much as going to bed directly after the study session. Thus, if you can arrange it, study until lights out, dive into bed, and go to sleep!

It has often been claimed that a person can learn while asleep, and that "sleep-learning" makes a deeper impression than learning while awake. A great deal of research has been done on this topic, and the conclusion is very clear: people do not learn while asleep. If you play a record or tape during the night and learn some of what is played, you are remembering what you heard while actually awake. When you are truly asleep, you learn nothing. If you need to learn something, get a good night's sleep and use your waking hours to study it.

Eating Habits

Diet has been suspected of affecting memory and cognitive performance for centuries. In the 15th century, roasted fowls and young hares, as well as apples, nuts, and red wine were recommended for improving one's memory (see A. E. Middleton's Memory Systems published by G.S. Fellows in 1888). Similarly, today's nutrition experts also say that poor nutrition places added limits on memory performance. Some experts say that a normal diet supplies sufficient vitamin levels to guard against deficiencies that produce memory deficits. Others claim that certain foods must be included in everyone's diet or that vitamins must be supplemented to prevent memory-related deficiencies. The rationale usually offered for why vitamins may help memory is that they are believed to enhance brain chemistry. This remains to be proven, largely because too little research has been done on the effects of vitamins on the chemistry of the normal brain.

The foods that experts recommend as "memory nutritious" include: beef, pork, kidneys, liver, fish, shellfish, milk, eggs, cheese, vegetables, kelp, and onions. Recently, it has been reported that drinking lemonade right after studying facilitates later recall, apparently because sugar aids the absorption of information into long-term memory (Benton, 1993; Foster, Lidder, & Sunram, 1998; Gold, 1987; Manning, Stone, Korol, & Gold, 1998). Whatever you eat, moderate amounts are recommended before you perform memory tasks. Large amounts of food make you sleepy and unable to pay attention during registration and remembering.

"Memory nutritious" vitamins and minerals include choline, B-complex vitamins (especially Bl, B6, and B12), iodine, manganese, folic acid, and L-tyrosine. At least one vitamin pill is sold explicitly as a facilitator of memory ("Memory Booster," produced by Puritan Pride). However, vitamin supplements probably won't improve the memory performance of most people.

If you feel that your diet or eating habits are so irregular that you might have a mild vitamin deficiency, you might try a supplement. But don't expect it to work like a magic pill, and be careful not to take too much: vitamin overdoses can be dangerous. If you suspect you have a nutritional disorder, you obviously should consult a physician. But you should also recognize that how much you eat can be as important to memory performance as what you eat. Specifically, you should be careful not to eat a great deal before an exam or a special academic challenge, such as a speech in class. Overeating will diminish your ability to concentrate and remember (Smith, 1988).

A lot of attention has been paid to the supplement ginko biloba. The vitamin industry claims to have investigated the effects of ginko biloba in a sound manner. The research suggests that it may have a positive effect, not because of any specific properties that target memory function, but because it acts as a blood thinner that facilitates blood circulation to the brain and hence affects memory.

Sensory Difficulties

Poor eyesight or hearing can prevent a person from performing memory tasks well because such difficulties slow the initial registration of information and make it harder to notice cues that can help remembering. The sensory difficulties may also lead others to conclude that a person has memory deficiencies. People draw this erroneous conclusion because they assume that unsatisfactory memory performance occurs only because of memory problems. Since many people try to conceal sight or hearing problems, it is not surprising when others attribute an unsatisfactory memory performance to memory alone rather than to the sensory problem. Unfortunately, when a person with a sensory deficiency explains frankly that a memory failure was due to such a deficiency, the explanation may be regarded as an excuse rather than the truth.

If you believe that one of your senses has suffered a partial loss, do not hesitate to get yourself examined by a physician. If your loss is sufficient, you will probably be advised to use either an occasional corrective device (magnifying glasses or phone-loudness boosters) or to use a permanent corrective device (eyeglasses, hearing aid). Either kind of device may impose some inconvenience, but the improved performance they enable you will more than compensate for the inconvenience.

Illness

We all get sick from time to time. When we do, we perform mental tasks less well, including memory tasks such as studying (Matthews, Davies, Westerman, Stammers, 2000). Illnesses, major and minor, interfere with memory performance because discomfort diminishes attention. When our ability to pay attention is lessened, we do not register or remember as well as when we are healthy. Even a minor illness can impair memory performance. Did you ever come down with a bad cold the day you had to give a speech from memory? Chances are that you had difficulty remembering much of what you had to say.

Taking steps to reduce discomfort and control symptoms will improve memory performance during an illness. If you have a big exam when you're sick, ask for a deferral or postponement – there's no way you'll be at your best. If you can't, make sure that you're as well rested as possible. If your illness is chronic, there are other things you can do to minimize the distractions to memory performance caused by your illness.

Table 4-2. Potentially Toxic Drugs That Impair Memory and Cognition

Psychiatric Drugs	General Medical Drugs
Barbiturates	Digitalis
Bromides	Analgesics
Benzodiazepams	Antihypertensives (especially Beta-blockers)
Phenothiazines	Antidiabetics
Lithium	Methyldopa
Antidepressants	Inderal
Antipsychotics	Antibiotics
	Antihistamines
	Eye drops for glaucoma

It is wise to check whether the side-effects of your treatment or medication impair memory (Bowen & Larson, 1993; Idzikowski, 1988; Parker & Weingartner, 1985). Medicines are rarely identified explicitly as interfering with memory per se. But, if a medicine diminishes your capacity to pay attention, it is routinely pointed out on the box and label.

Any medicine that lowers your attentive powers will reduce how much you register and remember. If a prescription medicine lessens your ability to pay attention, you should discuss with your physician whether you should take it.

Memory Illnesses

Certain illnesses impair memory so severely that they are known as "memory illnesses." These include Alzheimer's disease, Korsakoff's (alcoholic) syndrome, mini/major strokes, and low blood pressure (Khan, 1986; Mayes, 1988; Wilson, 1987). Alzheimer's disease (1907) is the most widely known memory illness (Aronson, 1988). Articles on this disease occur frequently in news magazines and on TV because it has a devastating effect on the memory abilities of its victims.

Korsakoff's syndrome involves a progressive and eventually severe loss of the ability to register new memories (Birnbaum & Parker, 1977). The victim recalls knowledge and events of the past prior to the onset of memory difficulties. The cause of Korsakoff's syndrome is excessive drinking of alcohol over a prolonged period. A stroke is produced by a blood clot that enters the brain and causes some cells to die. Mini-strokes involve many tiny clots that are dispersed throughout the brain. They render a person confused and less able to focus attention. Unless you arc a senior citizen who has returned to school, students will almost never have to worry about their memory ability being impaired by a major memory illness. There are, however, other serious conditions to which everyone is potentially vulnerable.

Very low blood pressure, a life threatening condition, reduces a person's ability to register and remember. Apparently, low blood pressure impairs memory because it lessens a person's ability to pay attention. Fortunately, the medicines that are used to treat low blood pressure restore attentive powers and alleviate the memory problems that accompany the condition.

All of these illnesses require a physician's care. If you believe that you (or someone close to you) have developed a serious memory problem, you should consult a physician.

Adverse Substances

Several substances impair memory performance. Perhaps the best known is alcohol, sometimes called the "amnesia food." Drink can mask sorrows and diminish memory for events that occur under its influence. Conversely, frequent and extensive memory loss from drink foretells the onset of a severe drinking problem. Extensive memory loss may come about because a drinking bout impairs brain chemistry or because drinking itself provides an excuse to "forget" antisocial acts performed during the bout. As mentioned under the memory illness section above, prolonged use of alcohol causes permanent and obvious damage to a person's memory system (Birnbaum & Parker, 1977).

Marijuana has effects on learning and remembering that are similar to those produced by alcohol. Research has examined the effect of a pill form of marijuana that induces a high comparable to several drinks. People who were given this pill learnt a list of words more slowly than sober people. When asked to recognize whether a digit was in a digit series presented moments before, people under the influence of marijuana recognized the test digit more slowly than people not under the influence (Block & Wittenborn, 1984; Darley, Tinklenberg, Hollister, & Atkinson, 1973). Because of such research, our government advises the public that marijuana impairs memory.

It is sometimes held that mind-altering substances and stimulants have a state-dependent effect on memory (Swanson & Kinsbourne, 1979). According to this theory, a memory registered when sober can be more accurately recalled when sober, and events observed when under the influence of a drug or alcohol can be more accurately recalled later when under the influence again. Conversely, this theory predicts poorer performance when a memory is remembered in a state different from the one in which it was registered. This theory underlies some claims that people make about the effects of alcohol or marijuana on memory. For example, some people say, "When I'm sober I can't remember things I did at a party the night before, but if I have a drink or a joint I recall the party better." Despite such claims, research has not provided clear support for the state dependency of any mind-altering substance or stimulant. Research on alcohol has suggested a small effect of state dependency. Some research has suggested that memories formed under the influence of marijuana might be state dependent, but again the effect is very small.

Thus, remembering still appears to be best accomplished when in a state of sobriety. Some students study while under the influence and some people in business plan strategy over several drinks. Usually the justification is that learning is more effective when relaxed. However, the student will often later complain that an exam was scored unfairly low and the business person will lament that certain aspects of a project were poorly presented at the meeting. In fact, the exam was probably scored fairly, and the presentation at the meeting was clear and complete. The real basis of these complaints is that the memory task was performed under the influence. If you are serious about performing a certain memory task well, the message of memory research is unambiguous: alcohol and marijuana will impair your memory performance.

Stimulants

Who hasn't used a cup of coffee to help themselves stay alert while studying? Mild stimulants commonly found in tea, coffee, sodas, or tobacco supposedly make you more attentive and, thus, better able to register and remember. However, you should know that stimulants are as likely to have adverse effects on memory as they are to be beneficial. Even if they could enhance performance at some level, the ideal doses are currently unknown. If you are wide awake and well-rested, mild stimulation from caffeine or nicotine can do little to further enhance your memory performance. Indeed, if you have too much of a stimulant, you will become jittery, find it difficult to sleep, and your memory performance will suffer. Additionally, if you are a habitual or addicted user, having to go without a stimulant will also make you jittery and affect your memory performance. However, if you are likely to fall asleep and you must learn information by a certain deadline, a mild stimulant may help you stay awake and pay attention, at least somewhat. Surprisingly, little research has been done with humans to explore the effects of stimulants on memory. Some studies have found that coffee had a facilitative effect on memory but other studies found a detrimental effect. No studies have examined the effect on memory of non-prescription stimulant products, based on caffeine, such as NoDoz and Vivarin.

It has sometimes been assumed that nicotine facilitates memory, presumably because it may make a person alert while performing a memory task (Peeke & Peeke, 1984; Wittenborn, 1988). However, recent research indicates very clearly that nicotine can impair memory performance considerably, as much as occurs from a couple of alcoholic drinks (Spilich, 1986). This research has shown, for example, that non-smokers were quicker than smokers at performing a task requiring temporary remembering of a list of digits. Moreover, nonsmokers scored higher on the four tests that make up the Wechsler Memory Scale (Wechsler, 1945): memory for a written passage, digit span, reproduction of a visual pattern, and learning pairs of words. The research indicates that if you smoke, do not do so before a memory task. And if you worry about your memory performance in general, you might consider quitting.

Some people believe that amphetamines enhance memory. These drugs will keep someone awake for a memory task. However, they are highly addictive and dangerous. Avoid them. Any short-term gain they offer can quickly turn to tragedy.

In general, you're better off not using stimulants or, at least, using them moderately. Stimulants may come in handy for fighting fatigue, but they may exact a cost. While stimulants keep you awake, they also make you more distractible – putting you at a disadvantage for memory tasks. If you need to stay awake, some relatively safe stimulants (like coffee and tea) may be useful. But what might help you the most is a dose of motivation.

Finally, a word of caution about so called "memory medicines." Presently, no such substances exist. All of the medicines reputed to facilitate memory actually facilitate attention. Perhaps an "attention medicine" may be regarded as good enough because attention is so important to memory. These medicines are, among others, magnesium pemoline (Cylert), Piracetam (not sold in the U.S.), vasopressin, and naloxone (Martinez & Kesner, 1986). All these medicines require a prescription and would not be prescribed to you unless you have one of the serious memory illnesses described earlier in this chapter (Rosenzweig, 1998). If you do not have one of the memory illnesses, you really do not want one of these medicines. The effect they have on performance is negligible. People who have taken one of these drugs typically recall one more word out of a list of 30 words than they would have without the drug. Additionally, these drugs induce various side effects, such as increased tension. For some of these medicines, the side effects can even be fatal.

Memory medicines are like the fountain of youth. They promise something that we know can never be delivered. But even if a miraculous medicine could be developed to give you a perfect memory, would you truly desire it? We think not. A fully effective memory medicine would make you remember everything. Suppose you took a memory tablet before studying for an exam. You would register the material perfectly, but you would also register every time you picked up your pencil, every cup of coffee, every belch, and so on. When taking the exam, not only would the relevant material emerge into memory, but so also would everything else registered. In short, your recall would be distracted by an endless stream of petty details irrelevant to a memory task. Maybe, at some future time, a memory drug will be developed that could overcome such a problem, but science is presently a long way from such an accomplishment.

Physiological State Checklist

Clearly, good physical condition is one of the necessary ingredients for good memory performance. To avoid lowering the level of your memory performance, you should follow some common sense guidelines:

1. Promptly treat or seek treatment of major and minor illnesses. Discomfort distracts.
2. Avoid the use of adverse substances. They impair your ability to pay attention.
3. Eat a well balanced diet, and do not overeat before memory tasks. A well balanced diet ensures strength and optimal brain chemistry for when you attempt memory tasks. Moderate eating avoids the sleepiness that comes with overeating.

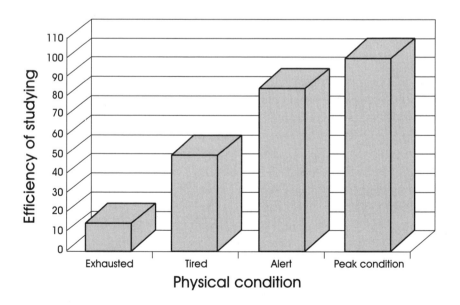

Figure 5. The Effect of Physical Condition on the Efficacy of a Person's Studying (hypothetical data based on the research literature)

4. Get enough sleep and keep to your natural cycles of wakefulness and sleep. Sufficient sleep and consistent cycles keep you strong and alert to register and remember.
5. Take account of your peaks (whether you are a morning or an evening person) when you schedule important or demanding memory tasks. If you can arrange it, perform memory tasks when you are at your strongest and most attentive.
6. Everyone gets tired. Rest when time allows during the day so that you will be up to your memory commitments.
7. Stay in shape. Physical vigor is necessary for mental vigor. Physical weariness is always coupled with mental weariness. If you are physically fit, you will also be fit for memory tasks.

Summary

This chapter has described a variety of ways to manipulate your physiological state to enhance your performance of memory tasks. These manipulations are designed to focus your attention in a manner that helps you acquire and retrieve information.

Physiological manipulations are important because they are one of the only ways of ensuring improved performance of memory tasks that you either "can't see coming" or do not recognize until they have "come and gone." For example, if you have an instructor who gives you pop quizzes, you will do better on them if you are in good physiological shape. If you know you have an important memory task coming up, do one or more of the several physiological state manipulations discussed here to enhance your condition. Consistent care of your physiological state will improve your memory widely across all manner of tasks.

Manipulations that alleviate inadequate emotive states can have a marked influence on your ability to study. Your emotive state can make you more ready to pay attention to memory tasks and prepare your long-term memory to absorb new traces or to produce old traces. The next chapter will present you with manipulations to improve memory by facilitating your emotive state.

5. Emotional State

Everyone gets upset sometimes. We may be upset by a snide remark or by being told to do something by our boss. Everyone is emotionally moved on some occasions. When emotions are stirred, it is difficult sometimes to concentrate, and we may find that we do not think as clearly as usual. In addition, we may discover we are unable to focus on what we are reading, what others are saying, or even on what we just said. Since disrupted concentration and disturbed emotions impair attention, these states will affect how much information we register and remember. Additionally, because emotive states affect the physical state of the brain, they may reduce the absorbing and emerging powers of long-term memory (see Figure 6).

Alternatively, manipulations may be used to restore normal emotive states and thereby return learning and remembering to normal function-

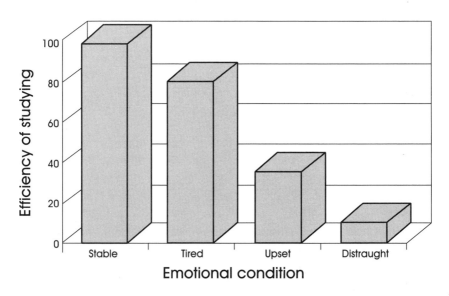

Figure 6. The Effect of Emotional Condition on the Efficacy of a Person's Studying (hypothetical data based on the research literature)

ing. Emotive state manipulations have a more general effect than the manipulations of physical states. Table 5-1 lists some of the mental states that affect your efficiency at studying.

Table 5-1. Mental States that Impair Memory Performance

Confusion
Being in a Rut
Anxiety
Excessive Ups
Downs
Preoccupation
Excessive Relaxation

Diminished Concentration

A hectic and harried lifestyle can leave otherwise fit people occasionally disoriented. Whatever its origin, confusion hampers performance. It lowers the level of attention we give to our immediate surroundings, and it lowers our ability to focus attention. Sometimes the things we do when we do not concentrate are comical as well as annoying. Who hasn't, with some embarrassment, done something like stepping in the shower with your socks on or saying thank you to a Coke machine when it delivers a can of soda?

Alternatively, a very predictable and routine lifestyle can also lower attention and the ability to concentrate. Sometimes we become so relaxed and adept at our tasks that we can do two tasks at once (for instance, preparing a meal while thinking about some problem at work). Proficiency is usually admirable and rewarding. However, proficiency sometimes backfires. Research has shown that a great deal of experience and practice at a task leads performance to become automatic, sometimes so automatic that we cease to pay full attention to the task at hand. As our attention wanes or wanders, errors increase. These errors can have drastic consequences. Some airplane accidents have been found to be caused by very (perhaps overly) experienced pilots having inadvertently thrown a switch in the wrong direction (Reason & Mycielska, 1983).

Your ability to concentrate is affected by how well your environment allows you to pay attention to what you are doing. Research has found that there are optimum levels of noise and physical comfort for performing memory tasks. Total silence and maximum comfort are probably not the best conditions for your memory. Neither are tight-fitting clothes, uncomfortable furniture, or extremely loud noises. Whether a situation provides you too little or too much comfort is a matter of personal taste. Some people enjoy wearing tight clothes. If a person truly functions best with rock 'n roll blasting in the background, then it should blast on: it would be a mistake to put on Bach or to turn the stereo off altogether.

In general, slight discomfort will make a person more alert than will coziness. Slight discomfort ensures that you will not be drowsy. Coziness gives a feeling of safety, but it may lead you to fall asleep. Slight discomfort will make you ready to pay attention. Thus, to ensure that you will pay better attention to memory tasks, choose environments and modes of dress that are not too comfortable.

Stress

College life is typically very demanding. It is impossible to go through college and not experience stress that can interfere with memory and cognition (Hammand, 2000). Most students carry a full load and incur workload stress. In order to complete all assignments on time, the student must keep track of multiple responsibilities. At times, students feel "conflict stress" because they are competing with other students to get a good grade. Sometimes these conflicts erupt into open disagreements, with anger producing additional stress. Typically people are painfully aware that they are stressed. Other times people are so involved with what they are doing that they do not recognize they are stressed until they consider the possibility.

The most common stress for college students is that experienced when taking exams. "Test anxiety" distracts a person and stifles their ability to recall information (Williams, 1996). On the other hand, indifference to the importance of a test will make them try too little to remember and to overlook clues to appropriate answers. Again, some anxiety will ensure the student is alert during a test. Simply put, you should view the test as an important component of your education, but not as one that determines your later success or failure in life.

Although stress can interfere with memory and cognition (Hammand, 2000), we need an optimal level of it to survive (Spielberger, Gonzales, & Fletcher, 1979; Spielberger & Vagg, 1995). Too little or too much stress makes us vulnerable to illness. A proper level of stress keeps us alert and active as we cope with the problems of everyday life. Likewise, too little or too much stress lessens memory performance. Stage fright can cause one to forget lines in a play. Conversely, total complacency will lead an actor to fail to recognize a cue. Some stress will at least keep an actor alert.

Students are not the only ones whose performance is impaired by stress. Nurses who work in high-stress situations, such as on an intensive care ward, manifest more memory failures than those who work on routine wards (Broadbent et al., 1982; Reason, 1988). Women scheduled to have mastectomies manifest a greater number of memory and absent-mindedness errors than usual in the period just prior to surgery (Reason, 1988, 1990; Reason & Lucas, 1984).

If you suspect but are not sure whether you are stressed, ask yourself these questions. Do minor problems upset you more than usual? Do you find it hard to stop thinking about your problems? Do you doubt your ability to do everything that you have said you would do? Have you changed your sleeping or eating habits? Are you experiencing more headaches and other aches?

If you feel that you are overstressed, here are some things to do. Give yourself a break and at least temporarily drop your desire to be super-successful. No one is perfect, so do not try to make yourself perfect. Take one step at a time. Avoid trying to do everything at once. Take care of your health: eat well, get enough sleep, exercise regularly, limit the amount of coffee and alcohol you drink, and remember that all work and no play makes Jack/Jill dull. If you have some heavy problems, find someone to talk them out with. Be flexible. Take time out for relaxation.

Moods

Normal ups and downs affect academic performance because they affect how we feel physiologically (Cacioppo, Petty, & Morris, 1985), as well as altering motivation. When things are going our way, we feel positive about life. Positive moods dispose us to pay attention to whatever happens and, thus, to perform memory tasks more efficiently (Matlin & Stang, 1978). However, extremely positive feelings may interfere with memory performance. When we are deliriously happy, such as when deeply in love, we may pay more attention inwardly to our deliciously positive feelings and less attention to other important things in our life.

Negative moods, whatever their intensity, impair memory performance. A slightly negative mood, such as the down we feel after someone insults us, diminishes our ability to pay attention. Normal depression weakens memory performance because a preoccupation with unhappy thoughts lowers a person's level of attention and reduces their capacity to focus attention (Erdelyi & Goldberg, 1979; Hertel, 1992; Yesavage et al., 1989). Attentive powers may also be lowered by depression because it can alter brain chemistry in a way that slows absorption and emergence.

An intensely negative mood, such as might occur after a big argument with someone we care about, will impair memory performance (Zarit, Gallagher, & Kramer, 1981). If the intense mood is an active one – such as anger or rage – it energizes us too much and makes us too distractible to perform memory tasks well.

Researchers suggest that our success at remembering depends, in part, on the similarities in conditions between when the registering took place and when we are trying to remember (Bower, 1981; Tulving, 1983). This proposal is the "state dependency" issue discussed in the last chapter with respect to certain substances (alcohol, marijuana). As with substance use, research suggests that remembering may be enhanced sometimes by striving for mood comparability. However, it is not yet clear just how to create the comparable mood that might facilitate remembering.

Depression

Students are people, so it is to be expected that they will get depressed sometimes. Sometimes people become depressed, because of stress and other factors. Other times people are so involved with what they are doing that they do not recognize they are stressed until they consider the possibility. Several factors can indicate the presence of depression. A depressed person may have a persistent sad mood and feel hopeless. They generally appear uninterested in activities that once were seen as fun. A depressed person exhibits fatigue and irritability. If a person experiences several of the foregoing factors and has thoughts of suicide, they should see a doctor to cope with the depression as soon as they can. Depression is especially hard on students because the student's main job is learning and depression makes learning very difficult.

If the depression is intense, it will render a person extremely withdrawn. Severe ("clinical") depression weakens memory so much that some doctors regard memory failure as a major indicator of clinical depression – even when the patients themselves do not complain of depression. Treatments that relieve depression (such as antidepressant drugs or psycho-therapy) also restore memory abilities (Watts, 1988).

A great deal has been written in recent years to indicate that depression can come from flawed thinking. It might be questioned why this would happen to students who are so busy learning how to be especially good at thinking. However, many people can be successful at thinking on the job and not have any energy left to deal with the flawed thinking that produces personal unhappiness and depression. Research has shown that some depressed people engage in: all or nothing thinking; overgeneralization; filtering out positive and optimistic thoughts; forecasting only disaster and minimizing successes; emotional inferences where bad feelings indicate flawed thinking; imperative thinking that they should have done something; hasty generalizations such as "I am a failure" instead of "I made a mistake." The remedy for such depression is to identify why the flawed thinking is defective and then in its place substitute a valid conclusion.

Relaxation

Relaxation relieves stress and decreases the distractibility that interferes with memory performance. You know, of course, a variety of ways to relax: a snooze on your sofa, reminiscing with a friend, listening to music, watching TV. Exercise, as discussed in the previous chapter, reduces stress and improves your mood.

Perhaps the form of relaxation best known to facilitate memory is yoga. Hatha yoga teaches a series of exercises or body postures (separate from yoga philosophy) that can be conducive to memory. The movements involved are similar to those in traditional calisthenics, but they are executed in slower and more graceful ways. Yoga's effectiveness for producing physiological states of relaxation – states that are beneficial to memory in general – is widely accepted. Yoga masters regard certain body postures as particularly beneficial to memory performance. One group of such postures places the head lower than the rest of the body. This group includes the headstand, the "candle" (where you prop up your back and feet with your hands as shown in Figure 7), or simply hanging one's head down over the edge while lying on a bed. The rationale for the supposed effect of these postures is that, by driving more blood to the brain than usual, they facilitate memory performance both immediately following the exercise and for an indefinite period beyond (because the exercise presumably helps brain functioning in general). One study found that the head inversion technique did help the memory performance of older subjects.

Another group of yoga postures that may help memory concern the spine. These postures gently twist the spine, as would happen when you lock your knees while touching your toes with the opposite hand. Spinal exercises supposedly make a person feel better overall, and hence more ready for memory tasks.

The yoga procedure for muscle relaxation is also held to facilitate memory. In this posture, you lie on a firm surface and gradually relax the muscles of the body. Considerable research has shown that regular muscle relaxation diminishes your susceptibility to stress-related illnesses. Yoga masters suggest the posture aids memory itself. They advise engaging in muscle relaxation until the body is extremely flaccid. Once in the relaxation state, you may study (often with a tape recorder, because lifting a book or notes would disrupt the relaxation of the arm involved), or you can attempt to remember something you found hard to recall in a normal or less relaxed state.

by amanda Herrmann (at age 9)

Figure 7. The Yoga Position Called the "Candle," Claimed by Yoga Masters to Improve Memory

Intuitively, the rationale seems plausible. If you have been anxious about a memory task, muscle relaxation may facilitate your performance. Relaxation techniques have generally been found to facilitate the memory of the elderly (Yesavage, Rose, & Spiegel, 1982; Yesavage et al., 1989). More research is needed to explore and validate all the various claims of Hatha Yoga for improving memory. To the extent that the exercises help you relax, they can certainly provide some benefit.

In the past two decades there have been numerous systems of relaxation developed that presumably facilitate memory performance. Perhaps the best known is Transcendental Meditation (TM). TM teaches a person to engage in the yoga method of muscle relaxation, just described, while repeating a word or sound (called a "mantra"). The repetition also helps to induce a relaxed state and reinforces the effects of muscle relaxation. Other relaxation systems include methods for: creating and dwelling on comforting imagery (sometimes called "positive imaging" or "creative visualization"), for experiencing sensory deprivation (the Lily tank), for learning to control your brain waves (Alpha wave control), for learning to control your blood pressure and pulse rate (Biofeedback), for controlling what you say to yourself (neurolinguistic programming), and others yet.

Presently, the effects of relaxation systems on learning and remembering are still under evaluation. Properly used, these relaxation systems can reduce stress and thereby facilitate your memory performance at in least the short-term. However, it is important to know that some people have claimed these systems had a negative effect on them, including nervous breakdowns. Until the effects of these systems are better researched, we cannot endorse any one of them as effective or safe. If you decide to undertake training to use one of these systems, we advise that you do the following. Talk carefully with a few people you know who have gone through the training. Do not take the training if you have been going through a rough emotional period. If your nature is that you occasionally get very upset over life's problems, check with a psychologist or psychiatrist about whether the system might have a bad effect on you.

Many psychologists will tell you that you need not pay a lot of money for a system to relax. Stretching out on your sofa, listening to music, playing ball, reminiscing with friends – any of these will relax you sufficiently to achieve better memory performance.

Attention Training

Condition manipulations improve memory performance because they remedy deficiencies that lower attention. All condition manipulations improve our capacity to pay attention. However, the improvements are essentially temporary. They will disappear when we begin to neglect our condition. It would be very helpful if there were manipulations that could produce permanent increases in your capacity to attend (Plude, 1992). There have been, in fact, a number of proposals for training people to have greater powers of attention.

Four kinds of attention training have been proposed. One kind attempts to increase your ability to sustain attention. It is commonly known among sentries in the military, police officers on stakeout, and security guards that experience is necessary to maintain sensitivity to detecting intruders and potentially dangerous people. Some researchers believe you can develop such experience through practicing to listen for faint, unpredictable sounds or looking for dim, unpredictable lights. For example, you may practice by watching and listening for planes in the sky (or for squad cars with radar on the highway). A second kind of attention training attempts to increase your ability to divide your attention. Research indicates that practice at doing two things at once can improve your ability to pay attention to two things simultaneously. For example, you may practice watching TV while maintaining a conversation. A third kind of attention training attempts to increase your ability to notice details. Research shows that practice at picking out a detail in a scene or a sound in a mix of sounds results in improved performance. A fourth kind of training attempts to increase your ability to resist distraction. Research has found that practice can improve your ability to pay attention to something despite distractions.

Most research that demonstrates attention training to be effective has been done with brain-damaged patients. This research requires a patient to perform one or more of the kinds of training just mentioned. Often the training is done with a desktop computer, which presents the patient with a perceptual task requiring some kind of attentive process (Wilson, 1987; Wilson & Moffat, 1984). For example, a patient might attempt to either detect a spot on a screen, keep track of the position of two or more moving spots, pick out details from a complex pattern, or keep track of a single spot while the background changes randomly. Patients often show improved performance on tasks such as these, and this seems to help in performing everyday memory tasks. However, it is not clear that these practice tasks improve a patient's general attentive capacity. Rather, they increase a person's confidence in being able to cope with challenging tasks. Once a patient recognizes that performance at a computer task has improved, he or she feels more able to tackle some routine memory tasks.

Research with normal adults indicates that the ability to pay attention in general cannot be improved by training with the procedures just described. But research does indicate that the ability of normal adults to pay attention can be improved for particular tasks. If you desire to improve your attentive powers, you are advised to practice paying attention in situations where you want your memory to succeed. For example, suppose you want to improve your ability to pay attention to what a speaker says during a meeting. You can improve this ability by paying attention to what a person says in a different situation – at a party or even on television. Please note that for practice to work, you have to engage in a lot of it, perhaps over a month or two. Attention training is no simple proposition, and you may wish to influence your attentive powers by manipulating your condition in the other ways described in this chapter.

Attitudes

Whenever a study task or a test arises, you have an attitude towards it. The attitude may address the content of the task – what you have to register or remember. For example, the attitude may be related to your views on studying French or Greek. The attitude may also address the kind of memory task. For example, the attitude may reflect your views on studying a foreign-language vocabulary or grammar.

Your attitude may facilitate or impair your performance because it affects your inclination to try to perform the task and your ability to sustain attention while performing it (Forrest-Pressley et al., 1985). Since memory performance is affected by your attitudes, one way that you can improve your memory performance is by improving these attitudes. Attitudes about one's memory abilities for different tasks are typically deeply rooted. The origin of your attitudes comes from your upbringing and how you have observed yourself performing memory tasks. Hence, we cannot change them easily. But they can be changed (Herrmann, 1982, 1990a).

Components of an attitude. An attitude has three characteristics that may or may not be appropriate. An attitude conveys a belief about something, such as "foreign languages are easy to learn" or "foreign languages are almost impossible to learn." The belief is valued positively or negatively. We are attracted to the study of foreign languages or we are repelled by it. And we value a belief with a certain strength. We are attracted or repelled by the study of foreign languages weakly, moderately, or strongly. If you decide that certain attitudes are damaging to your memory performance, you can change them by changing the belief, its value, and/or its strength.

Changing attitudes about task content. Your attitudes about the content of a course may be inappropriate. It might be that, with your background, the content would be more interesting and easier to learn than you think. If this is the case, your performance on a task will be inefficient and possibly in error. On the other hand, the content of certain courses are especially difficult to register and remember. Each kind of task requires a special approach so that the attitude can facilitate memory performance. These problematic kinds of task content are as follows:

Uninteresting Information

Boring information is obviously hard to register and remember. Unfortunately, we often are unaware of how uninteresting something is to us until it is too late. We will often forget something that someone said or something that we were to do because we were uninterested. To avoid such difficulties, you need to decide ahead of time whether it is important that you remember something. Then, if you recognize that something is uninteresting to you, beware. Take extra steps (described in the following chapters) to ensure that you will remember it.

Negative Information

Memories connected with strong negative emotion are usually easy to remember. In fact, they are often so easily remembered that they intrude into consciousness when you would rather forget them. But memories connected with only moderately negative emotion may be more difficult to recall. The emotion can lead us to suppress the memory. Suppression is a common reaction to negative feelings. As Scarlett O'Hara preferred to say, "I'll think about it tomorrow." Unfortunately, suppression often leads to forgetting other obligations (like meetings or chores) and gets us into trouble.

There are two ways to protect yourself against suppression. The first way is to convince yourself that the content of the memory should really be viewed positively. Obviously, this is not always possible or appropriate. If the boss fires you, positive feelings will be hard to come by. When using this manipulation bear in mind that, even if you can convince yourself of some of the good aspects of a memory's content, negative feelings will still accompany the memory. Thus, while adopting a positive view may diminish the likelihood of suppression, it will still be possible.

A second way to protect a memory against suppression is to develop plans to force yourself to think about the memory when necessary. For example, to enable yourself to remember to attend a meeting that you would dearly like to miss (but should not), set two alarms and ask someone to give you a timely reminder to go. Or if you know that you will be asked to discuss some unpleasant topic at a meeting (such as a bungled project for which you were responsible), review the details before you attend. Make a special effort to look knowledgeable about the incompetence. If you take deliberate steps to face up to the negative memory prior to an occasion for its use, suppression will be less likely to occur. As a not too incidental benefit of this approach, it will appear to others, including your employer, that you have learned from your mistakes and are less likely to repeat them.

Personally Upsetting Information

Some negative memories are so threatening that they are repressed (Erdelyi & Goldberg, 1979). While suppressed memories can be remembered with effort, repressed memories cannot be remembered at will. Repression removes any awareness of the information, blocking it from our normal means of remembering. The classic example of repression is the soap opera character who, after some traumatic experience, becomes unable to remember it at all. Some psychologists believe that everyone represses some memories; others believe that repression occurs less commonly and that it may indicate a serious adjustment problem. Access to repressed memories comes only after recalling many related memories (a process Freud called "psychoanalysis" and made central to psychotherapy). If you suspect yourself of repressing part or all of an important memory (or memories), consult a clinical psychologist about the problem. The recovery of a repressed memory is something we cannot expect ourselves to do alone.

Disturbing information that is not suppressed may be distorted instead.

The distortion may occur either during registration or later during retention, to make it consistent with our self-image and goals (Greenwald, 1980). Distortions are difficult to detect because they protect our view of ourselves. Some distortion in memory is normal, but an excessive amount can lead to maladjustment. When a memory has become distorted, others are often first to recognize and point out the distortion to us. By being open to the possibility, we are more likely to discover and correct distorted memories.

Changing Attitudes about the Kind of Memory Task

Most people think their attitudes or beliefs about which memory tasks they do well are correct. They feel as confident about their notion of how well they register and remember as they do about other abilities, such as vision or hearing. However, as discussed in Chapter 3, the truth is that most of us have only a slightly accurate view of how well we perform different memory tasks (Cavanaugh et al., 1998; Herrmann, 1990a; Hertzog et al., 2000; Morris, 1984). When people are asked how well they perform memory tasks in everyday life and in the laboratory, their answers agree only somewhat with how well they actually perform these tasks.

Sometimes people hold an incorrect attitude because they believe they have observed their memory to succeed when it failed or to fail when it succeeded. Sometimes they hold an incorrect attitude because they have been given an incorrect report about their memory. "Knowing thy memory" is neither easy nor common (Klatzky, 1984).

Since attitudes about the difficulty of memory tasks are often flawed, your decisions about which tasks you should tackle or avoid are often wrong. Thus, you can improve your handling of memory tasks by correcting inappropriate attitudes about the processing requirements of memory tasks. Note that a correction does not necessarily mean that these attitudes should be made positive. Positive attitudes that are untrue will only lead us astray, making us try tasks we should avoid or not trying hard enough at tasks we incorrectly suppose we are good at. What you need are attitudes that are correct, so you do the tasks you are good at and avoid the tasks you find difficult (or that you work at becoming better at performing difficult tasks). To ensure that your beliefs about memory tasks are correct, you need an assessment of what tasks you are actually good and bad at, an assessment such as was discussed in Chapter 3.

Ironically, people may have a negative attitude about having to perform certain memory tasks that they know they are good at. For example, some good students report disliking the process of studying. Unfortunately, negative task-attitudes have negative consequences. These attitudes will lead you to pay less attention during studying and to respond less quickly and efficiently while taking exams. The obvious manipulation needed here is to develop reasons for believing that the task is worth performing. Often it is difficult to think of positive reasons, whereupon you should ask someone else for help.

It also happens that people value positively having to perform tasks that they are poor at. For example, some poor students report they regard studying as important and wish they were better at it. Fortunately, positive task-attitudes will facilitate paying attention while studying.

Emotive State Checklist

The information reviewed above on mental condition and memory performance makes it clear that a good mental condition is necessary for good memory performance. Therefore, to avoid lowering the level of your memory performance, you should – as Mom and Dad would advise generally – do the following:

1. Maintain an optimum level of activity (avoid a hectic lifestyle, and avoid getting in a rut). Too little or too much to do lessens your capacity to pay attention.
2. Try to keep stress at a manageable level. A little stress keeps you alive and alert to perform memory tasks, but too much of it makes you distractible.
3. Engage in recreational activities (such as hobbies, sports, and socializing). They relieve the stress that may hinder your memory performance.
4. Relax (daily, on weekends, and on annual vacations). It will also reduce stress and renew your strength.
5. Rest (by taking catnaps). It will also renew periodically just before having to do a memory task.
6. Exercise. You will be less stressed, stronger, and have a more positive viewpoint when you perform memory tasks.
7. Try innovative ways of relaxing (such as yoga exercise and yoga meditation).

8. Talk out your problems. Alleviation of depression and a more positive outlook will make you more able to register and remember.
9. Choose harmonious environments for studying (ones that set the right noise level, and do not contain overly comfortable furniture) and wear comfortable clothing. Discomfort decreases your concentration for studying.
10. Maintain appropriate attitudes towards memory tasks (prioritize information to motivate yourself and establish the level of effort that will be required).

Summary

This chapter has described a variety of ways to manipulate your emotive state to enhance your academic performance. Emotive manipulations are an important part of your memory skills because they are one of the only ways to ensure improved performance of memory tasks that you either "can't see coming" or do not recognize until they have "come and gone." If you know you have an important study task or test coming up, carry out the several manipulations discussed here to enhance your condition. If you wish to improve your memory widely across all manner of tasks, consistent care of your condition will give you much of the improvement you desire.

We appreciate that few of you will follow all of the preceding recommendations, but each one will improve your ability at recall, so try to develop the habit of doing one or more of these manipulations as you approach a memory task. The following chapters will present you with other manipulations to facilitate your memory. Like condition manipulations, these manipulations are designed to focus your attention in a manner that helps you acquire and retrieve information. However, the manipulations you will learn about next involve doing things with the environment or with your thoughts.

Manipulations that alleviate inadequate emotive states can have marked influence on your ability to study. Your emotive state can make you more ready to pay attention to memory tasks and prepare your long-term memory to absorb new traces or to have old traces emerge.

Section III.

Storing Information and Remembering It

6. Memory Manipulations and Study Skills

Ever since the time of the ancient Greeks, memory experts tried to find simple mental tricks that would help them overcome the limits and inconsistencies of memory (Herrmann & Searleman, 1990, 1992). The techniques they developed go by a number of different names: mnemonics, mnemotechnics (both words deriving from Mnemosyne – the Greek goddess of memory), memory strategies, or "artificial memories." We refer to them as "mental manipulations."

Almost everyone has tried to use an outline, mental trick, or some key to help him or her memorize information. Some of the more popular techniques include repeating lists to ourselves, quizzing ourselves on material we need to memorize, organizing information so it will be more meaningful and memorable, restating fundamental ideas to be remembered, relating key ideas to a familiar pattern that will help us retrieve them, and visualizing the scenario in which our memory will have to perform. Over time, these mental manipulations have become almost the sole focus of memory training courses and books. As a result, most people think of them as the only way to improve their memory.

Unfortunately, memory isn't that easy to control. Research shows that learning a single mental technique helps your memory only for a specific situation – and that you can't substantially improve your overall memory without mastering a broad assortment of techniques (Herrmann, 1990a; Herrmann, Rea, & Andrzejewski, 1988). As discussed earlier, mental manipulations aren't the only factors determining your memory performance. Your condition, attitude, environment, and the social context all strongly influence your performance, and their effects must be addressed in any conscientious effort to improve your memory.

Still, mental manipulations can play an important part in a program of memory improvement. They all have a common goal – to help you learn, retain, and retrieve information. If you use the right technique properly, you can improve from 100 to 200%. For example, suppose you had to attempt to learn as many items as possible on a 30-item list but were not given much time to do so. In a limited time period, you may only be able to remember 10 items. If you had used certain mnemonics, in the same amount of time, you could have learned 20 items (a 100% increase). And if you had used yet another kind of mnemonic, you could have learned all 30 items (300% of unaided recall).

What is in This Chapter?

Unlike most books on memory improvement, we won't claim to show you a few general procedures that will work for all readers and all situations. As you'll see, the sheer number and diversity of mental manipulations are strong evidence that a single foolproof, all-purpose technique doesn't exist. This chapter will introduce you to a wide variety of mental manipulations. Some of them were devised as long as two thousand years ago, and some were developed through research during the past two decades. Most of us will have used one or more at some time, but it's likely that we did so without much forethought or consistency. These manipulations are designed to help you learn, retain, and retrieve information. Out of the many techniques that are presented here, you're sure to find several that you can adapt to your own needs and abilities.

The chapter will also explain how mental manipulations differ from each other. Some manipulations emphasize rehearsal, others embellishing information, and others associating what is to be learned or remembered. Knowledge of the nature of these different kinds of manipulations will enable you to choose the right manipulation for the task confronting you and to customize mental manipulations to serve you better. The manipulations covered here are intended to prepare you for a wide variety of situations, especially for unexpected learning and remembering tasks. Chapter 8 will propose additional manipulations designed to serve specific tasks and will propose modifications of manipulations advanced in this chapter so they can be applied to certain tasks. But often you will not know in advance that a certain memory task will arise, in which case you will need to know at least four or five of the broad, non-specific manipulations taught in this chapter.

Below you will be acquainted with a little more theory of how we learn and you will be presented with a range of learning manipulations. Then you will read about the factors that lead us to forget and the manipulations we can use to ensure we retain information we need. Finally, you will be presented with explanations of how remembering occurs and manipulations to retrieve information when it is not forthcoming.

How Do Mental Manipulations Work?

First, mental manipulations are relevant only to intentional learning tasks, in which you are conscious of the information you must learn or retrieve (Ericsson, 1985; Morris, 1977; Pressley & Levin, 1983). When your boss asks you to remember something, you are aware of what is asked of you and you intend to do it. Incidental tasks, in which information is automatically encoded into or emerges from long-term memory, cannot be handled with mental manipulations. Often we are asked to recall something that happened at an event we attended but did not pay attention to. When this happens, all we can do is to try to remember what we registered incidentally. At that point, it is too late for us to have intentionally learned what is asked of us.

Mental manipulations work by intensifying your attention to information during the learning, retention, and retrieval phases of the memory process. A manipulation causes you to process – in some way – that information, and your increased attention leads to either or both of two mental processes that affect the memory traces in your long-term memory. First, new information can be absorbed from working memory into long-term memory. Second, your attention can activate existing traces in long-term memory that have similar informational content.

Once an existing trace is activated, its activation can spread to other associated traces. When a trace has received enough activation – either directly or indirectly – its contents will emerge into consciousness (Carlson, 1997). Therefore, when you want to learn, you should use mental manipulations that make you pay enough attention to the information you want to remember to form traces to constitute an adequate record of the information.

Once the trace has been formed, the memory system retains it. Unfortunately, this system has its shortcomings much like other systems of retaining information and experiences (film, newsprint). As the retention period increases, it becomes harder to find what you want in storage. It is hidden amidst everything else, and the physical record is disintegrating. Because memory traces become less accessible with time, it is necessary to refresh memory in order to be sure you have retained it.

When you want to retrieve information, you should use mental manipulations that make you pay enough attention to the informational "clues" you've been given to activate secondary traces. Once these traces are sufficiently activated, this activation spreads and converges on the desired trace, causing it to emerge from long-term memory into consciousness (see Chapter 1 or the glossary for definitions of many of these technical terms).

When You Should *NOT* Use the Mental Manipulations Taught in This Chapter?

The boost in memory performance that mental manipulations can give comes with a price tag – it takes both time and effort to use a mental manipulation. If you have time to execute the manipulation and/or the task deserves the effort, a mental manipulation can be your best way to deal with a particular memory task. However, in many cases, you may not have the time, or you'll decide that the particular memory task isn't worth the effort.

As useful as the mental manipulations taught in this chapter *may* be, they are not as powerful as mental manipulations *can* be. Mental manipulations that have been modified to be used for a specific memory task are usually more efficient and more effective than the non-specific manipulations discussed here. If you want to prepare yourself to respond better to a particular memory task, then you will need to acquire manipulations designed specifically to deal with this task. However, task-specific mental manipulations require extra preparation before the task arises and there are far too many tasks for which it would be possible to prepare task-specific manipulations. Thus, as a foundation – as insurance – it is wise to know several of the mental manipulations discussed in this chapter. Additionally, knowing about these non-specific mental manipulations will help you appreciate and develop the task-specific manipulations.

Your intellectual style and tastes will also be important in your choice of mental manipulations. There is no sense in trying to learn a manipulation that seems foreign, weird, or stupid to you. So choose manipulations that suit you.

Ultimately, the best way to be sure that a manipulation will help you remember is to try using it. Compare the effort and effectiveness of different manipulations. Generally the best manipulation is one that both meets your goals for effectiveness and fits your intellectual style. The remainder of this chapter will present you with manipulations for each phase of memory: learning, retention, and retrieval. Take note of which manipulations appeal to you as you read through the chapter. By its end, try to have identified three or four manipulations for each phase of memory. Knowledge of several non-specific manipulations will prepare you to cope better with a wide variety of memory tasks, especially ones that occur unexpectedly or infrequently.

How We Learn

Learning occurs when you intentionally pay attention to the contents of working memory, leading it to be absorbed into long-term memory. Mental manipulations influence what is absorbed into long-term memory in one or more of four distinct ways.

- Firstly, a mental manipulation can increase the strength of an item's trace. Repeating an item, for example, will keep it in your working memory longer, possibly increasing the intensity of your attention. As a result, a stronger trace will be absorbed into your long-term memory. The way an increase in attention can increase the strength of a memory trace can be compared to how much clearer a photograph will be if it's taken in bright light than if it's taken in dimmer light. The stronger the trace, the more familiar we are with an item. Consider when you attempt to register a person's phone number in memory, at least long enough to dial it. Rehearsing the number by repeating it to yourself or out loud boosts the strength of the number in memory.

- Secondly, a mental manipulation can foster the encoding of attributes of the information that would otherwise probably not be included in the memory trace. Examples of the attributes of information would include whether the idea is an object, an action, or a quality. Examples of the attributes of an image would include the size, shape, and color of the image.

You can make a memory trace easier to retrieve by incorporating surprising or interesting attributes. For example, you can improve your ability to remember the name of a person you've just been introduced to by analyzing the national origin of their name, or by determining the number of vowels and consonants in the name.

In both cases, your analysis of the name increases your attention to the name. Most people don't pay much attention to attributes like this, but the additional attention will definitely help you register the information in your memory.

- Thirdly, we can use mental manipulations to establish an association between two or more items we wish to learn, or between items we need to learn and more familiar items already in our memory. Sometimes the associations are conventional; other times they are idiosyncratic. In attempting to learn someone's name, you can associate it with someone else you know with a similar name or you may associate it with the town, county, or state they are from.

Associations are established by any manipulation that makes you attend jointly to items that are separate in consciousness. Paying attention separately to two items will not result in their being associated. Suppose you are studying vocabulary for a foreign language. You will not learn which foreign terms go with certain English terms simply by reading through the list of foreign words and then the list of English words. Joint attention to the corresponding foreign and English items is necessary to produce an association of the appropriate translations.

Associations differ from each other (Bellezza, 1981, 1983). An association can be bi-directional – if item A reminds you of item B, item B will also remind you of A. Or they can be unidirectional – A reminds you of B, but not vice versa. For example, if people are asked to say what word comes to mind ("free associate") when they hear another word, what they say reveals the directionality of associations. If they hear the word "smart," they often think of the word "intelligent"; and if they hear the word "intelligent," many think of "smart." Thus, "intelligent" and "smart" share bi-directional associations. On the other hand, if people free-associate to the word "hot," many will say "dog," but when asked to give a word association for "dog," almost no one will say "hot."

As the number of associations between an item and other items in memory increases, its trace is said to become "more meaningful." The more associations, the easier the trace is to retain and retrieve from memory.

Associative patterns may occur when an item's associations number more than one (Anderson, 1983). Patterns are important because they affect retrieval. For example, we may not be able to remember a poem, prayer, or song if we start with one of the middle lines – because our associations form a line-to-line pattern starting from the first line of the text. Try singing the Star Spangled Banner from the middle. Or try recalling the Pledge of Allegiance from the word "indivisible." Our bet is that in either case you will have difficulty unless you start at the beginning.

- Fourthly, a mental manipulation can establish a framework that facilitates the retrieval of the memorized items. By exploiting certain characteristics of each item, we can devise a retrieval structure for finding all of the items in memory (Chase & Ericsson, 1982; Ericsson, 1985). One such manipulation is the "first letter mnemonic" for learning a short list. To remember a list of grocery items – milk, eggs, bread, and Alka-Seltzer – you could arrange the first letter of each item to form the word "beam." When you go to the store, you could recall one item for each letter of the word until you retrieved the entire list.

Figure 8 shows that a list learned using a retrieval structure has twice as many avenues for retrieval from long-term memory as a list learned without a structure. The top panel shows a memory trace for a shopping list that was learned without a retrieval structure. The trace is remembered in two steps. The physical situation (the setting you are in, the people you are with, what others say) elicits your memory for this situation when you originally learned the list. Your memory for the situation elicits, in turn, your memory of the information (in this case, the shopping list).

The lower panel shows a memory trace for a shopping list that was learned by forming a retrieval structure. This trace can be remembered by the physical situation eliciting your memory of the learning situation and therefore the shopping list. In addition, the memory of the learning situation can *separately* elicit the retrieval structure, which can also elicit the desired information.

For some people, and for some tasks, retrieval structures may seem like excess baggage – too much work for too little reward. In fact, retrieval structures are eventually forgotten. The structures fade in memory because the direct association between the situation and the trace increases sufficiently with use to make the retrieval structure unnecessary. However, until the association is well established, the retrieval structure is invaluable. Besides giving you a second path to successfully retrieve the memory, retrieval structures augment the learning process itself. The added process of forming a retrieval structure causes you to pay more attention to the trace, making it stronger, embellishing it with more attributes, and activating its associations with other traces.

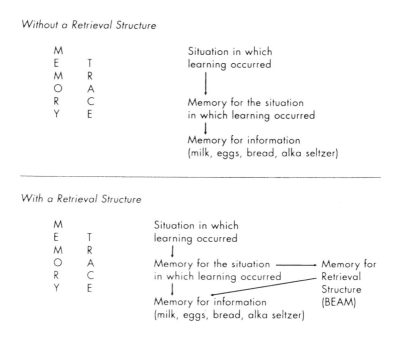

Figure 8. Memory Learned with or without a Retrieval Structure. The top panel shows how situational cues elicit information that was learned without a retrieval structure. The bottom panel shows how this process works for information that was learned with a retrieval structure. Note that in the bottom panel, the retrieval structure provides a link to situational cues.

Figure 9 illustrates the importance of these four effects. To simplify the illustration, the figure depicts a simple memory trace without showing the association with the situation in which the learning occurred.

Panel A shows the trace as it would be registered in long-term memory when the trace information has not been subjected to a mental manipulation. Panel B shows the trace after it has received a strength-building manipulation. Stronger traces will emerge from long-term memory into consciousness more readily than weak traces.

Panel C shows the trace after it has been subjected to an attribute manipulation. Thinking about an attribute tends to activate a trace bearing it, and leads the trace to emerge into consciousness. For example, the attribute "white" may activate "milk," and "stomach remedy" may activate "Alka-Seltzer." Thus, a trace with many attributes is easier to remember than one with few attributes.

Panel D shows the trace after association with another trace. There are two kinds of possible associations: one kind involves pre-existing asso-

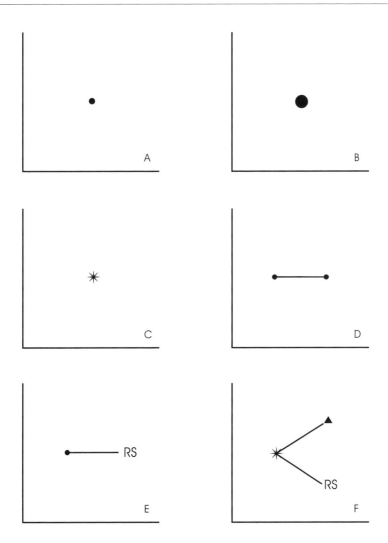

Figure 9. Illustrations of the Different Effects of Mental Manipulations on a Trace. Panel A: registered trace before a manipulation. Panel B: a trace after a strength manipulation. Panel C: a trace after an attribute manipulation. Panel D: a trace associated with another trace. Panel E: a trace associated with a retrieval structure. Panel F: a trace after all four manipulations.

ciations, like the one between "milk" and "shake." The other involves new associations, like the one formed here between "milk" and "Alka-Selt-zer." In either case, the information associated with the target trace affects the trace in the same way as attributes do: the associated information tends to activate the desired trace and leads it to emerge into consciousness. Panel E shows the trace associated with the retrieval structure described above. Finally, Panel F shows a trace that has been subjected to all four effects of mental manipulations – strength, attribute, association, and a retrieval structure.

Most of the mental manipulations covered in this chapter will improve your ability to register information in memory in more than one way – usually in some combination of the four categories we've discussed. The more effects a manipulation produces, the better it will work. Retrieval of the memory in Panel F is considerably more likely than in any of the other panels. In the final case, the trace is more familiar to memory (due to added strength) as well as more likely to be activated and to emerge (due to the presence of relevant attributes, associated information, and the activation of the retrieval structure).

Most importantly, the relationship between categories tends to be hierarchical, with the manipulations in each category also producing the effects typical of the categories that come before it in the strength-attributes-associations-structures hierarchy.

Thus, while strength manipulations affect only strength, attribute manipulations also increase the strength of the trace; association manipulations also increase both strength and the number of attributes; and retrieval structures also provide greater strength, more attributes, and more associations. If you want to remember some information only briefly, strength manipulations are what you need. For example, an idea may occur to you during a conversation that you want to bring up before the conversation is over. You want a manipulation that will enable you to remember the idea long enough to bring it up, but not necessarily to remember the idea forever. As the need for durability of the memory increases, you should use increasingly more powerful manipulations in the hierarchy of attributes, associations, and retrieval structures. If you want to remember something critical that someone said at a meeting so you can relate it to your boss later, you are going to want to use one or more of the more powerful manipulations.

An Inventory of Learning Manipulations

The inventory that follows presents you with a variety of learning manipulations to be used when studying. The inventory is organized according to the category of the manipulations' dominant effect – that is, whether it operates primarily through building the strength, attributes or associations with the trace, or retrieval structures designed for the trace. Within each category, the different kinds of manipulations are generally presented in alphabetical order.

In order to illustrate for you how these manipulations are used, we will discuss the manipulations and then we will make use of a story – told below – that involves many routine memory tasks. The story and examples have been concocted solely to illustrate the use of the manipulations. Don't worry about having to remember the details of this story. Please realize that the examples of mental manipulations given below don't reflect the range of complexity of the actual memory tasks to which you could apply or adapt them, but they should give you a good enough idea of how the manipulations are used. But first, let's consider the mental manipulations that can be very helpful.

Strength Manipulations

Manipulations that augment the strength of a trace are of two kinds: those that foster paying attention and those that involve rehearsal. If used with unusual intensity, both attention and rehearsal manipulations can also lead to registration of attributes and associations with secondary traces. However, as normally used, the principal effect of these manipulations is to increase trace strength.

Attention

These manipulations focus your attention on the details that should be registered. They are important in situations where remembering only the gist of information will not be sufficient.

Mental snapshot. When attempting to remember a scene, scan it systematically, then close your eyes and question yourself about the scene; open your eyes and note what you missed. Repeat the cycle until you are satisfied that you have registered the scene in memory. – To etch in memory the time your bowling team won a trophy, take a mental snapshot.

Multisenses. Perceive or imagine what you must register in memory with as many of your senses (or "sensory modes") as possible: how does it look, how is it said, how does it feel. – In order to remember what happened at a conference you attended with Bill, register the various events there multimodally.

Reflection. Think back on information just noticed or understood. Many recommend a daily practice if your work makes it important to remember routine details or if you place great importance on reminiscing. – You will remember better the things you do with daily reflection.

Rehearsal

Rehearsal is particularly useful for two kinds of situations: when you want to keep information in consciousness, but are not concerned about establishing a long-term memory; or when you are not motivated to use a more challenging or elaborate manipulation to establish a long-term memory.

Acting out. Act out the information you want to register. – For example, when studying history with George and Arlene, you can imagine key events you should know and then, like an actor, overtly act out the interactions as you imagine them.

Simple rehearsal. Repeat the items to be learned to yourself over and over. – For example, on being introduced to Bill, say to yourself "Bill, Bill, Bill, Bill, ..."

Articulatory rehearsal. Repeat the items while carefully enunciating each syllable and noting the placement of the tongue in your mouth as you pronounce the words. – On learning someone's name, rehearsing the articulation of the name will stamp it into memory, such as, "B, B, B, ih, ih, l, l, l."

Cumulative rehearsal. Repeat the items in successively larger groups. – For example, in learning several names, say to yourself "Bill; Bill, Sarah; Bill, Sarah, George; Bill, Sarah, George, and Arlene."

Rhythmic rehearsal. Repeat the items in a rhythmic pattern, either in syllables or with a certain beat. – For example, in learning a name, say to yourself "Bill – Bill, Bill, Bill – Bill, Bill."

Spaced rehearsal. Repeat the items to yourself at increasing intervals in which each successive interval is twice as long as the preceding one. – For example, after having been introduced to someone, such as Bill, say his name to yourself once, wait a second, say it again, wait two seconds, say it again, wait four seconds, say it again, and so on (Landauer & Ross, 1978).

Attribute Manipulations

Anything that may be registered in memory can be characterized by a set of attributes. People, for example, can be characterized as large or small, rich or poor, bright or dull, and so on. Objects can similarly be described as large or small, rounded or angular, light or dark. Ideas can be analyzed as interesting or uninteresting, simple or complex, and positive or negative. Attribute manipulations are designed to foster your registration of more attributes than you would otherwise register.

The more attributes you include in a memory trace, the better. Each additional attribute provides one more way to retrieve the trace. There are several learning manipulations that are designed to increase the number of attributes you would normally incorporate in a trace. Registering more attributes leads you to deepen your comprehension of the details and implications of the information to be learned. These manipulations also increase trace strength. They are useful for learning information that is initially difficult or uninteresting, or that must be remembered in particular detail.

Affect elicitation. Attend to your feelings concerning what is to be learned, or dredge up such feelings as you rehearse. – If, when you first meet George or Sarah, you find something pleasing or repugnant about them, dwell on this.

Attribute judgments. Make judgments related to the nature of the items. – For example, judge how "rich" each name to be learned sounds (as "Abercrombie" sounds more affluent than, say "Smith").

Description. Verbally describe to yourself what you plan to learn, and study your description. – For example, to learn someone's face, describe for yourself the shape of the eyes, nose, mouth, etc. Notice that George has a gray beard, blue eyes, and slender build.

Meaning analysis (semantic). Consider the information's meaning and subtle variations of the information's meaning. – For example, to remember that Bill is a mechanic, analyze the meaning of the word "mechanic" (one who repairs mechanisms, usually automotive but also other machines).

Phonetic analysis. Consider the sounds that make up the stimulus. – To remember that Bill is a mechanic, sound out the syllables of the word (me-can-ik), rather than just repetitively.

Prioritize. Judge the importance, i.e., the priority of information to be learned. – If going bowling with the gang is more important than returning your neighbor's cake tin, realize and remain aware of this.

Question. Ask whatever can be asked about the information: If? Who? What? Where? When? Whose? Whether? Why? To what purpose? Under what conditions? How? In what manner? How much? How many? How often? For how long? By? Of? In? If you want to be able to remember what Bill and Arlene tell you about their jobs at the chemical firm, ask them a lot of questions about their jobs. Both the asking and the answers build up a durable memory.

Self-referencing. Judge how an item to be learned might relate to you as a person or to some aspect of your past. For example, in learning about Sarah's and George's jobs, you might decide how you regard the newspaper they work for – how well it is laid out, or whether you feel it gives fair and balanced coverage of the news. Doing so makes it "your" newspaper and thereby ties in what Sarah and George tell you.

Temporal ordering. Describe, or even imitate, to yourself the relative intervals between successive things to be learned. – For example, in learning the names of some people you met, take note of how much time intervened between each meeting (such as two minutes between meeting Bill and Sarah, and five minutes between meeting Sarah and Arlene).

Understanding. To learn information, come to know it from several perspectives (as would result from using the different forms of analysis presented in this section). – Thus, if you needed to make a presentation at work, you will recall your ideas most easily if you concentrate on understanding rather than memorizing only key phrases.

Visual analysis. Consider the visual characteristics of what is to be learned. – To remember that Bill is a mechanic, visualize the printed structure of the word "mechanic" (m – two upside-down "V's" joined; e – a pattern similar to Pacman; c – an "o" with a bite out of it; etc.).

Association Manipulations

Association manipulations enable you to relate different traces with each other. Both traces may be new or may have already been established in memory. Association manipulations are called for when it will be necessary to remember that a trace is related to certain information, or when the material taken by itself is difficult to learn. Associations are often necessary to successfully carry out certain tasks. For example, suppose that while traveling you stop and ask someone for directions. For the directions to lead you to the right place, the steps must be registered (thus, associated) in a proper order.

The process of forming associations can also enhance the strength of the items you associate and foster registration of the attributes of the items. Even if the association between items is unnecessary, the process of associating makes your registration of the items themselves easier. Finally, associations with old information may function as a casual retrieval structure for the new trace.

Simple Associative Manipulations

The simplest associative pattern involves just two traces. The manipulations below apply to this kind of association. These manipulations are helpful for situations in which a desired trace can or must be activated by a very restricted piece of information.

Verbal. Determine whether one item to be learned possesses direct or indirect verbal associations in the language with another item to be learned. Then rehearse both the items and the associations between them. For example, suppose you had to buy some items at the store before getting together with George. In trying to remember milk, eggs, bread, and Alka Seltzer, you may recall that milk and eggs are associated, as are eggs and bread. Alka seltzer seems to be on its own here.

Present with past events. Determine similarities between a current and a past event; you may attempt to remember a certain story you have read by likening it to a different story you read previously. You may better register in memory a conference you attended with Bill and Arlene if you identify how the conference resembles others you have attended.

Relations (meaningful). Judge whether there are meaningful relations between two items to be learned. You might look for synonyms, contrasts, or category labels. For example, to register in memory that a certain country was mentioned in a newspaper as being in a state of anarchy, generate the synonym or antonym of "anarchy."

Relations (phonetic). Judge the ways that two or more items to be learned sound similar to each other. To remember the names of obscure countries mentioned in a textbook, you might note that the sound of one is similar to the sound of the other country.

Relations (visual). Judge the ways that items to be learned may or may not be visually similar. To learn the names of obscure countries reported in a textbook, you can also judge whether the letters in one country look like the letters in another country.

Organization Manipulations

Organization manipulations increase the strength of items in a trace and the associations between these items. They are used when the information you must learn conforms to a specific structure. The varieties of animals and plants, for example, are organized according to a system of subspecies, which you would learn separately in order to associate particular animals or plants. These manipulations are also extremely useful when you must acquire a great number of items or pieces of information (Miller, 1954; Tulving, 1983). Extensive research has shown that organized information is learned as much as four times faster than the same information devoid of organization.

Clustering (meaningful). Organize items into clusters, so that each cluster contains items with similar meanings. For example, group the names on a list by gender: (Bill, George) (Sarah, Arlene).

Clustering (phonetic). Organize items into clusters, so that each cluster contains items with similar sounds. For example, group names by their similarity in sound: (Sarah, George, and Arlene all have an "r" sound).

Diagram. Sketch the relationship of items to be learned. For example, if you know certain people are friends, note and review this link on paper: Bill–Sarah, Arlene–George.

Sequence. Arrange stimuli mentally in the sequence of presentation or in the sequence that you feel is most natural. For example, to learn the names of several people you just met, take note of the order in which you met them: such as Bill, then Sarah, then George, and finally Arlene.

Spatial arrangement. Notice the spatial arrangement of stimuli. When learning the names of several people you just met, take note of where they were standing or sitting. Bill, for example, was standing next to Sarah, and George next to Arlene.

Retrieval Structure Manipulations

Retrieval structures are most useful for important information that you need to remember perfectly or almost perfectly (Bellezza, 1981; Ericsson, 1985; Higbee, 1988). The manipulations that create retrieval structures fall into one of four categories: elaboration, reduction, transformation, and technical.

- Elaboration manipulations create a retrieval structure that builds on the information to be remembered.
- Reduction manipulations create a structure that relies on part of the trace information.
- Transformation manipulations change the information to be learned into secondary information, which is different in form but related in a meaningful way to the primary material.
- Technical manipulations manipulate information according to a scheme that you must memorize ahead of time. (Schemes memo-

rized to facilitate learning are sometimes called "mnemonics", "artificial memory" or, less often, "mnemotechny.")

The easiest manipulations to learn and use fall in the elaboration and reduction categories. Transformation manipulations are somewhat more difficult to learn and use, and the technical manipulations require the most effort. There is also, presently, no evidence that one category of retrieval-structure manipulations is more effective than another (although, generally retrieval-structure manipulations have been shown to register more effectively than strength, attribute, and association manipulations). It is perfectly sensible for you to apply more than one manipulation to the same task, because remembering is enhanced by each manipulation used. The multiple manipulations applied to a given task may come from the same category or from different categories.

Each of the four retrieval-structure categories is discussed in separate sections below. These sections are ordered from the least to most challenging categories.

Elaboration Manipulations

Elaboration manipulations build a retrieval structure that combines the information to be learned with additional information. The elaboration of the information provides you with a code that leads retrieval to the desired information because the code incorporates the information. People who learn to read music are often advised to remember the notes on the upper part of sheet music by learning this elaborative structure: "Every Good Boy Does Fine." This structure indicates the notes on the lines of sheet music with the first letter of each word in the structure: E, G, B, D, and F. If you decide to use a retrieval structure, you must learn it well because a forgotten or partially remembered elaboration is useless.

Acrostic. Form a poem or free verse in which each line describes something of what is to be remembered and the first letter of each word beginning a line forms a word. For example, to remember Bill's name elaborate by saying that "Bill" is a Brave Intrepid Lovable Lug or Bumbling Idiotic Lumbering Lug.

Ad hoc. Cast information to be learned in the form of a limerick. For example, to learn the name of four people on a bowling team (Bill, George, Sarah, and Arlene), you might form the limerick, "There once was the greatest of all bowling teams, made up of Bill, Sarah, George, and Arlene."

There are dictionaries of customary ad hoc mnemonics for learning certain information (Pugh, 1970) (see Figure 10).

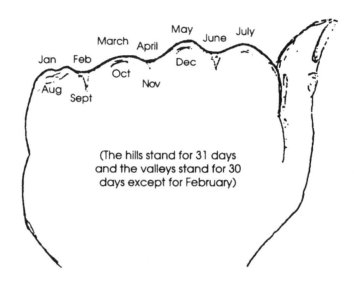

Figure 10. Ad Hoc Mnemonics for Remembering the Number of the Days in the Months

Image (color). Imagine that the item to be learned appears in one color against a different colored background. Use colors that catch your attention. For example, to remember the name of a product sold by Bill and Arlene's company, imagine it in bright purple against a violet background (if you prefer harmonious colors) or purple against a bright green background (if you prefer clashing colors). The same process could be used to register a person's face or an object you wanted to remember.

Image (color with affect). Imagine that what is to be learned appears in a color that is symbolic of how you feel about it. For example, suppose Bill introduces you to an acquaintance of his. If you like this person, register his facial features in silver or gold; if this person annoys you, use red paint; if you dislike this person, use paint with a muddy color.

Image (graphic). Form an image of a word's letters in print or of the way they were spoken to you. On being introduced to Arlene, visualize the letters of her name.

Mediation (image). Integrate the items to be learned into a visual image. For example, to register that the name of the newspaper Sarah and George work for is the Sentinel, imagine a one "cent" coin was mailed to someone named Nel –"cent-ta-nel."

Mediation (verbal). Associate items to be learned with a word that has established associations with the item. For example, to register that Bill pitches a baseball with a curve, you might discover a mediator such as "baseball-round-curve."

Number elaboration. If you have to learn a number, state it to yourself in the form of money (or in minutes, years, phone numbers, zip codes, dates). For example, suppose you decided to learn Sarah's phone number (733-3121). This number might be coded as the price of a meal: one for your dish ($7.33), and one for the total bill ($31.21).

Principle stating. Describe a pattern or regularity that is apparent in the material to be learned. For example, after attending a play, state to yourself whether the story was a tragedy or a comedy.

Ridicule. Turn the item to be learned into an amusing or ridiculous name or pun. For example, when you first meet Sarah and learn that her last name is "Smith," change it to "Smithiewithy" or to "Smoothie Smith" or any combination that strikes you as funny.

Sentence generation. Generate a sentence that contains the items to be learned. For example, to learn Sarah's last name, embed the name in a sentence, such as, "I just met Sarah Smith, a resident of Des Moines." The sentence need not be true to serve as a retrieval structure, but a true sentence has the advantage of supplementing the targeted information with other useful information. Also, if the generated sentence is false, try to make it blatantly so, or over time you may be inclined to remember it as a fact.

Story generation. Generate a story that contains the items to be learned. For example, "Once upon a time, Bill lived in the city. To make his living, he worked as a mechanic." You may choose to make a story on the same bases given above for the sentence generation manipulation. However, false stories may be easier to generate than true ones.

Reductions

Reduction manipulations extract and apply part of the information in the trace to form a retrieval structure. You may prefer them to elaboration manipulations because reductions are shorter and usually easier to remember. The reductions yield a structure that relates to the information to be learned much like shorthand does to dictation. However, reductions tend to point more ambiguously than elaborations to the information you want to remember. Nevertheless, if the reduction is naturally memorable to you, it will be more manageable.

Abbreviation. Form a smaller word by using a few letters from a larger word. For example, to remember the name Bill, form a smaller nonsense word. In many cases, a ready-made abbreviation can be found in standard sources (White, 1971).

Bleaching. Imagine the item to be learned in black and white. For example, to remember Arlene's face, an object, or a scene, imagine it devoid of color.

First letter coding. Form the initials in a list of items into a word (often by adding other letters). For example, to learn three names (George, Bill, and Arlene), form the word GAB. (First letter coding results in an acronym and may be viewed as a form of an acrostic.)

Sentence reduction. Form a word or words from the first letters of some of the words in a sentence. For example, suppose you wanted to quote Lincoln in a presentation you have to make at work. To learn "Four score and seven years ago," form the word combination of "fassyago."

Summary stating. Identify key words in a passage or story that will stand for the overall issue or theme.

Transformations

These manipulations generate a retrieval structure by transforming or translating the trace's primary information into secondary information. The secondary information bears a conventional relationship with the primary information you wish to register. A well-known transformation is an acronym for remembering terms. An acronym is helpful when a person has a set of terms to memorize. Suppose that you had to remember to pick up some things at the grocery store, such as milk, eggs, asparagus, and bread. The acronym of beam can be constructed from the first letters of these four things to be bought. The resulting retrieval structure (beam) tends to be about the same length as the individual terms. By exploiting conventional relationships of meaning, transformations remain closer to the meaning of the trace than do elaborations or reductions. This more direct significance may make them more effective for you.

Transformations were made the cornerstone of one of the most popular memory systems in the last century (Loisette, 1896) because these transformations lead to a meaningful trace. Indeed, it may be argued that transformations provide one of the best ways of helping yourself to comprehend information, as well as to register it.

Synonym generation. Determine the best synonym for the word to be learned. For example, to register that a certain country mentioned in the Sentinel is a democracy, rehearse also that it is a "free state."

Contrast generation. Determine the best contrast for the word to be learned. For example, to register that a certain country mentioned in the Sentinel is a democracy, rehearse that it is "not a totalitarian state."

Class-member generation. Determine the words that are in the same class as the word to be learned. To register that a certain country is a democracy, rehearse that its people enjoy the same freedoms as, say, Canada, Great Britain, and the United States.

Homophonic generation. Determine the word(s) that most sounds like the word to be learned. For example, to register that a certain country is a dictatorship, rehearse that this form of government sounds something like "dictate or ship."

Comprehensive generation. Determine the set of terms that reflect all the possible relations of sound and meaning with the word to be learned. This judgment combines the previous relation-generations of synonym, contrast, class, and homophonic determinations, applying each manipulation to the trace.

Technical Schemes

These manipulations are called "technical" because their use requires more involved instructions and preparation (Bellezza, 1981, 1983). To use them, you need to memorize an encoding scheme long before you attempt to register new information. Technical manipulations depart from the preceding retrieval-structure manipulations, which make use of knowledge implicit in the information to be learned. Instead, technical schemes relate the information to special material that you have learned previously.

Technical manipulations have a long history. The method of loci, discussed below, was devised over 2000 years ago (Herrmann & Chaffin, 1988). The other methods presented here were devised somewhere between the Renaissance and the 18th century (Yates, 1966). Because the technical manipulations have been around for so long, they are the kind of mental manipulations most often equated with memory improvement.

Technical mnemonics are probably the most powerful of study techniques (Bellezza, 1982; Higbee, 1988). Although technical mnemonics are known to be the most powerful, these techniques are also the most demanding to use. Considerable effort is necessary to learn and use them well. Many people find they do not want to invest the effort. And those who do learn these manipulations tend to stop using them, apparently because of the continuing effort needed to apply them (Bellezza, 1983; Higbee, 1981, 1988, 1999; Lapp, 1983; Park, Smith, & Cavanaugh, 1990). Nevertheless, if you feel highly motivated to make the effort these methods require, you should pay special attention to Chapter 7. Generally, some knowledge of technical mnemonics is good for a student. You can also consult one of the many books that concentrate on them to supplement the brief account given here. A thorough and clear account of technical mnemonics can also be found in *Improve Your Memory Skills* by Bellezza (1982).

Link. When learning a list of ordered or unordered items, form an image involving the first and second terms, then an image of the second and third terms, and so on. For example, to learn the bowling team's names, form an image of Bill handing a bowling ball to Sarah, Sarah throwing the ball at the pins set up by George, and George giving the score sheet to Arlene.

Loci. The method of loci was invented by a poet named Simonides more than two thousand years ago. When learning a list of items, imagine a familiar building (such as your home), and then imagine placing each item in a different room. For the bowling team example, leave Bill in the foyer, Sarah in the living room, George in the kitchen, and Arlene in the dining room. It is sometimes recommended that a person have several loci locations in mind: buildings, churches, golf courses, car, town, or terrain. Later the user of the loci method simply conjures up an image of location used when learning. The user merely takes a mental stroll through the location and recalls the list items as each one is encountered. (Figure 11 presents an example of the use of the method of loci by a student in preparation for an exam. It is not necessary to sketch the loci as this student did; a mental image of the loci is sufficient.)

The method of loci can be used to remember long lists of items. Ross and Lawrence (1968), for example, asked students to remember 40 items using the method. The places they used in their experiment were different parts of a university campus. Ross and Lawrence found that 37.5 out of 40 items to be learned were remembered immediately after they had been presented. This is considerably more than would be expected when not using a visual imagery method. De Beni (1988) found that the method of loci even helped in the retention of orally presented passages.

Peg (alphabet). You must first learn a system of letter-to-word peg pairs, in which each pair represents one letter of the alphabet. For example, you might assign the following words to the first four letters: a = ace, b = bee, c = sea, and d = deed. To use this system to learn names, you mentally "peg" the person to the word. For example, you might imagine Bill hold-

House of Memory Floor Plan

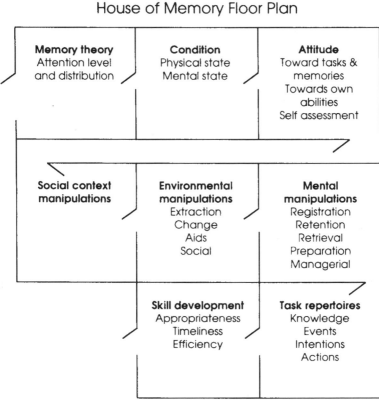

Figure 11. An Example of the Method of Loci as a Student Applied it to Studying the Principles of Memory Involvement Advanced in this Book

ing an ace, Sarah being pursued by a bee, George standing in the sea, and Arlene performing some good deed.

Peg (image). You must first learn a peg system consisting of number/ word pairs that may be used for memorization on many occasions. In memorization, each word to be learned is associated with each peg word by constructing an image that contains both (see mediation image above). To use this system it is necessary to first learn the following rhyme (note that the numbers rhyme).

1 = bun	6 = sticks
2 = shoe	7 = heaven
3 = tree	8 = fate
4 = door	9 = wine
5 = hive	10 = hen

As with the method of loci, visual imagery is used to relate new words to be learned with the peg words. If for example, the new words to be learned are (1) dog, (2) pen, (3) carpet, then a dog might be pictured eating a bun (1); a pen might be pictured sticking out of a shoe (2); and a big carpet might be covering a tree (3). The advantage of the peg system over the method of loci is that the learner can recall words in any order, so if you were asked to recall word 2, then 1, then 3, you would first picture a shoe (2) associated with a pen, then picture a bun (1) with a dog, then a tree (3) with a carpet. Like the method of loci, there is considerable evidence that this method is an effective way of learning word lists. Bugelski (1968) for example, presented six lists of 10 words to one group using the peg system and to another group with no instructions on how to learn what was given. The peg system group recalled at a significantly higher level than the control group. Furthermore, studies such as those of Higbee and Millard (1981) have found the peg method to work for memory for ideas. The image peg system is also useful for learning lists (see Bellezza, 1982).

Letter similar pegs. Another way that image-pegs are constructed involves peg words whose first letter visually resembles the number. For example, you might assign this system: 1 is Ice, 2 is Zoo, 3 is Beer, and 4 is Ant. In yet another variation, the "rotten peg" system uses displeasing or offensive peg words: 1 = Limburger cheese, 2 = dog feces, and 3 = sour milk. As you have probably guessed, you could devise an alternate peg system around some topic that pleases or fascinates you (such as food, movies, or rock stars).

Peg (verbal). This peg system is also learned beforehand for use on many occasions. The pegs are adjectives that provide additional meaning in a fashion analogous to how image pegs provide an imaginary visual context for information to be learned. The adjectives should be ones that intrigue you. For example, a person might learn the system: one is smart, two is exciting, three is cunning, and four is cocky. This system may be used to learn a list of items by conceptually linking the peg word and the word to be learned, as is done using the mediation manipulation (verbal).

Elaboration technique as described above. For example, to register chores to be done at the library, gas station, grocery, and involving George, you might form the following sentences. The library is for the smart. The gas station sign was exciting. The grocer sets out the specials in a cunning manner. And George is very cocky when things have gone well.

An Inventory of Retention Manipulations

After memory records are registered in long-term memory, they almost always become harder and harder to remember as time passes. After a long period of time, we remember them only faintly and often we cannot remember them at all. It is true that some of our memories are easy to remember throughout our lifetimes, especially ones that carry personal significance. But memories that are always accessible are not of concern to us here. Our concern is memories that become harder to remember with time, despite our wishing to remember them whenever we want.

The Causes of Forgetting

Forgetting information already registered in long-term memory comes about by brain processes that have one of two effects. Some processes destroy part or all of memories and, thereby, make the original information no longer available in memory. Other processes allow traces to remain intact in memory, but make them less accessible to retrieval processes (Baddeley, 1990; Higbee, 1981).

Loss of availability. There are several ways that memories become unavailable or inaccessible. Several processes are believed to be involved in the loss of information from memory. The best known such process is that of decay – in which the trace erodes physiologically. Brain cells are known to die due to drinking alcohol and to high temperatures that come with illness. The loss of such cells can be expected to hinder memory.

It is not necessary that a trace disappear for it to become unavailable in memory. A trace may become selectively altered by one or more of several processes. Traces may be intentionally revised to change the original memory for personal reasons. Our renditions of our recent triumphs (at work, in sports, in social relationships) are usually presented by us in a way that casts our behavior in the best light. Similarly, traumatic events may be retold to ourselves in a way that protects us from the full pain a complete account would elicit. Traces may be unconsciously distorted. The information we hold about ourselves, others, and issues is rendered more consistent and favorable (as described in Chapter 11 on social context). Because these processes occur unconsciously, the alterations are not usually detected by us. Finally, some new experiences may write over the traces of related past experiences and lead us to unlearn the past experiences. In a manner similar to how tape recorders erase a prior recording as a new recording is made, unlearning destroys prior traces. It is doubtful that the mind works just like a tape recorder, but there is considerable evidence that we do occasionally unlearn past information and skills.

Loss of accessibility. There are several processes that lessen accessibility of traces that remain available in memory. This may come about through willful inattention to the memory trace, i.e., not rehearsing the trace when possible. Willful inattention is useful in avoiding the later remembering of trivial information or mundane events. Lessened accessibility may also occur because a memory trace, already well rehearsed and encoded in memory, has been deliberately suppressed. Suppression is a normal process that is often necessary to survival in an information-loaded world. For example, as you start up a new project, it is natural to put out of mind the activities you have just been concerned with. Some people believe that your tendency to forget will increase if you are in the habit of acquiring trivia. Finally, accessibility to emotionally threatening memories may be unconsciously lessened to almost zero by repression. This loss in accessibility is often normal as well because it may be adaptive for us not to dwell on such memories. However, if a person engages in repression so much as to be unrealistic, it may be a sign of adjustment difficulties.

Often only part of a memory trace becomes inaccessible. When part of a trace is lost, retrieval may become error prone. The loss of trace information, if sufficient, interferes with our ability to remember accurately. In some cases we may be aware that our memory is inadequate to the task, such as when we are uncertain whether to give credit for an idea to ourselves or someone else. In other cases, we are not aware that part of the trace is inaccessible, such as when we accidentally recognize a fact as relevant to another topic (a "case of mistaken identity"), like confusing the properties of chemical elements or attributing some historic act to the wrong historic figure.

Accessibility may also be thwarted simply because testing conditions do not provide enough cues for successful retrieval. A desired trace may not be retrieved because the cues present when remembering is attempted are inadequate for the job. According to this view, if the cues that were present during learning are present at some later point, the memory will emerge, even if we do not intend to retrieve it. But if the situation provides too few of the cues present at learning, you will forget what the cues are calling for.

Pseudoforgetting. It is important to note that what seems like forgetting is not always the case. Neither a loss of availability or accessibility is involved. For example, you may appear to have forgotten something requested of you because you never properly registered the information in the first place. You probably have had experiences when someone has asserted that you must remember a certain meeting or social engagement whereupon, on reflection, you realize that you never attended the event. You may also appear to have forgotten because you did not understand a request for you to remember something or did not grasp the cues that might elicit the desired memory. This situation was mentioned in Chapter 4, when it was noted that people may appear to forget some information or past experience because poor eyesight or hearing prevented them from noticing relevant cues.

Manipulations that Forestall Unavailability and Inaccessibility

There are only a few manipulations that focus just on retention. Each of these manipulations act on one or more of the different causes of forgetting described above. The manipulations currently known come largely from common knowledge about memory and a small body of research on retention. Different kinds of tasks have different rates of forgetting. Skilled actions are remembered indefinitely (you never forget how to ride a bicycle, as they say), as are some forms of knowledge acquired in school. Events may or may not be remembered for reasons that researchers are just beginning to investigate. Intentions appear to be retained poorly, but they too have only recently been subjected to investigation (Harris & Wilkins, 1982). Research has yet to systematically compare retention rates for different kinds of information and to develop manipulations of retention that are sensitive to the kind of information involved. Figure 12 shows the retention rates for three kinds of information encountered in school.

The retention manipulations now known address four general retention situations that cut across many memory tasks. Using these manipulations requires discipline. Once registration has been carried out, most people are happy to trust a memory to retention until retrieval is required. But when the task is sufficiently important to you, and you lack confidence in your eventual ability to remember, one or more of the manipulations will prove well worth the effort.

The following inventory first describes situations in which you might expect retention problems, and then lists its potential safeguards.

If you fear that the information will not 'stick' because it is uninteresting or foreign to you: *review periodically*. Retention begins anew each time a memory is fully registered. Review often until you recall at the level of accuracy required; subsequently, you may review less frequently as long as you continue to recall adequately. It is wise if your review involves some of your original registration manipulations (strength, attribute, association, and retrieval structure). – Prevents loss from decay, distortion, interference, suppression, and unlearning.

If you sense that information just learned may be confused with other similar information that you might encounter: *avoid similar information*. If possible, avoid having to learn material that is similar in content to the material you wish to retain. For example, if you can avoid it, do not attempt to learn simultaneously, or in succession, two foreign languages or the details of two highly related projects at work. – Prevents loss from interference, suppression, and unlearning.

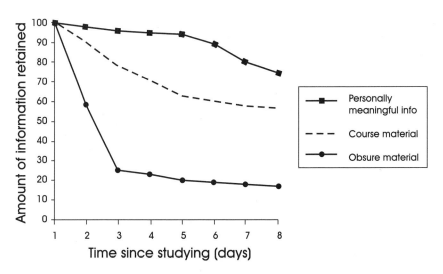

Figure 12. The Amount of Obscure Material, Meaningful Information, and Well Studied Course Material Retained after Initial Learning (hypothetical data based on the research literature).

Sleep or rest. If the retention interval is brief (say, one or two days), sleep as much as possible during the retention interval. Sleep allows you to avoid encountering new information that could interfere with what you learned or could lead you to suppress what you have learned in order to consider the newly encountered information. – Delays decay and prevent forgetting due to interference, suppression, and unlearning.

If you worry that you might not be able to retrieve the desired information when you need it, or will not retrieve it fast enough: *anticipate re-*

membering situations. Try to imagine situations in which you might be called on to remember. Doing so will help to prepare you to recognize, when in the remembering task, the cues that were present during learning, and thereby stimulate the memory to emerge when it is needed. Prevents forgetting due to not noticing retrieval cues.

If you recognize that you may forget something because you find the topic unpleasant to think about long enough for registration to occur: *make moderately unpleasant memories salient.* If you have an unpleasant memory task that you do not want to forget (for example, writing a thank-you note to an obnoxious person with whom you must remain on good terms), take steps that will lead you to not suppress thinking about the memory. Such steps might include thinking of reasons why you want to remember the unpleasant information or consequences that will ensue if you fail to remember. (For a discussion of such steps, see the section on mood in Chapter 5.) Such steps prevent repression, revision, intentional forgetting, and suppression.

When forgetting is what you want. In some cases, you might prefer a memory loss to perfect retention. At one extreme, spies, members of organized crime, and some politicians often wish they did not know or could forget certain information. At a more common level, the rest of us occasionally have bad days that we would like to forget. Like retention manipulations, manipulations for intentional forgetting have yet to receive much scientific attention. Thus, these manipulations are few in number, unsophisticated, and obvious – including taking one's mind off the undesired memory by distraction, changes of scene and time, and mind-altering substances (whose effects are usually more onerous than the offending memories).

An Inventory of Retrieval Manipulations

Sometimes we are certain that we could recall everything about some topic or event if only we were presented with the right cues. At other times we doubt that we could recall some information or some event, even if we spent the rest of our lives trying. In order to remember information that eludes us, it is necessary to try one or more manipulations to retrieve information from memory. The more retrieval manipulations we try, the better our chances for success. Although long-term memory has an enormous capacity (Landauer, 1986), there is no guarantee that even a prolonged interrogation of memory with retrieval manipulations will dig up the desired memory. Nevertheless, the use of retrieval manipulations will generally come up with more information than if no effort is made at all to retrieve (Adams, 1985).

The Inventory below describes several potentially effective retrieval manipulations. These manipulations make the desired trace emerge from long-term memory into consciousness by stimulating either surrounding traces or part of the trace itself. A trace or part of a trace is stimulated in long-term memory whenever information that makes up the trace is attended to in consciousness. Thus, retrieval manipulations involve attending to information in consciousness that is related in some manner to the four effects of learning manipulations on traces: strength, attributes, associations, and retrieval structures.

Retrieval Based on Strength

This is the weakest retrieval manipulation. When you cannot retrieve a trace on the basis of attributes, associations, or retrieval structures, you must carry out a strength search as a last resort. For this search, you examine the trace strength of potentially appropriate memories. The trace that possesses the level of strength you expect the memory to have is regarded as the trace required. The fact that a trace possesses the requisite level of strength does not necessarily prove that you have remembered fully or correctly. Occasionally, the strength search has the side effect of activating specific trace information and thereby providing access to the trace itself.

Retrieval Based on Attributes

Most of the known retrieval manipulations access a trace through one of its attributes. These manipulations assume that traces usually emerge fully into consciousness once a person is aware of one or a few of its attributes (Herrmann, 1990c). This assumption proves correct often enough to make attribute manipulations the best and most likely to retrieve a trace.

There are two kinds of attribute manipulations. One kind attempts to gain access by dwelling on an attribute of the trace you already *know* to be true. The other kind of manipulation gains access by dwelling on an attribute that you suspect is probably true of the trace. The likelihood that an attribute manipulation will be effective depends upon the number of at tributes you generate and on the importance or relevance of a given attribute to the memory.

To retrieve the entire trace from a part (that is, from an attribute) of the trace, one can use *known attribute manipulations*. Examples of these manipulations are numerous: remembering when an historic event took place but not where; recognizing that you have met a person previously but failing to recall when or where; recalling how you felt about an issue while being unable to remember all of the reasons why you felt the way you did. Whenever you know you are remembering less than all of a trace, you can assume that just a few of the trace's attributes are available to you as well. Once you do retrieve a known attribute of a trace, focus attention on the attribute until the full trace emerges. This attention acts to activate the attribute in long-term memory. The attribute's activation then spreads to the desired trace, causing it to emerge into consciousness.

A critical process in using known attributes to retrieve a trace is reconstruction (Neisser & Winograd, 1988; Schank, 1982). When considered separately, the attributes you do know are often insufficient to make the trace emerge. In such cases, it is useful to reconstruct (or "piece" attributes together into) a plausible, albeit incomplete, account of the event or information desired. Often the reconstructed memory, or the pattern of known attributes, leads to educated guesses of other attributes. For example, knowing when you met someone can often allow you to guess likely places where the meeting took place. Sometimes, a reconstruction (such as when and where the meeting took place) leads the full trace to emerge from memory. There are different ways that attributes may be manipulated for reconstruction.

Associate attribute. Recall as best you can the key attributes you know of the memory trace. Then, reconstruct. This manipulation is the first one to attempt when dealing with known attributes. If it is unsuccessful in making the trace emerge, then try one or both of the following manipulations.

Part reconstruction. Recall as best you can the key attributes that pertain to the part of the memory you do know. For example, in recalling an event, concentrate on remembering where the event occurred, then attempt to recall the whole memory. Continue alternating between attempting to recall the parts of the memory trace and attempting to recall the trace entirely.

Sequential reconstruction. Recall attributes according to the time of occurrence or time of registration. For example, try to recall recent information, then initial information, and finally the information in between.

Probable-attribute manipulations. Often, we vaguely sense which memory trace we want to recall, but still are unable to recall enough attributes to stimulate it to emerge. In such cases, we have no chance of retrieving the desired memory except through guessing an attribute of the memory. If you are lucky enough to guess an actual attribute of the trace, the attribute may cause the rest of the trace to emerge. Of course, a guess that comes up with an attribute that is irrelevant to the trace will not facilitate retrieval and may diminish your chances of a successful retrieval even further.

Retrieval Based on Associations

These manipulations access the memory through associations between the trace and other information. The secondary information may have been present during registration, or it may be conceptually associated with the content of that trace (Kolodner, 1984; Schank, 1982). An associative manipulation is usually most useful when you recall very little or none of the trace and, therefore, cannot attempt to access the trace by using attributes. Additionally, this manipulation is often used when attribute manipulations have been tried and failed.

Causation. Recall the circumstances or agent that produced, or was produced by, the memory you wish to remember. *Reinstate situation.* Imagine the surroundings you experienced when the memory was registered, and ask yourself what you were doing, saying, or thinking. *Retrace.* Remember chronologically the memories that preceded or followed the one you wish to remember. *Return to the scene.* Go to the surroundings where the memory was registered, and try to spot features of the room or site that pertain to the trace. *Recall registration manipulation.* Recall any registration manipulations that you may have used when you acquired the memory.

Retrieval Based on Retrieval Structures

You can also attempt to gain access to the trace by first retrieving any retrieval structure you may have used during registration. If the retrieval structure has been retained well, it will almost always generate the desired memory. If the retrieval structure is only partially remembered, it will function like any other association with the trace and, therefore, will be about as effective as any of the other associative manipulations.

Choosing Retrieval Manipulations

The retrieval manipulations presented here are intuitively obvious, yet many people employ just a few of them. Although we may recognize these manipulations, they probably do not come readily to mind when memory requires them. You can increase your use of these manipulations by copying them on a three-by-five card and keeping the card in your wallet or purse. The next time you are stumped, pull the card out and run through the manipulations. There is no guarantee that you will succeed in retrieving a given memory trace, but your success rate over a series of different attempts will increase.

Potential Use of Learning and Retrieval Manipulations

As we have seen, mental manipulations are numerous. Indeed, there are so many learning and retrieval manipulations that it would take tremendous ambition and a great deal of time to memorize them all. Few people are likely to ever try. This surplus can be put to your advantage, however, if you take time to comb the wide range of manipulations and choose the ones that suit you. Even the most suitable mental manipulations will still clearly require a great deal of time, knowledge, and effort to produce new memories and retrieve old ones.

Guessing Schemes

The manipulations below constitute different guessing schemes. They provide ways of guessing the attributes that probably make up a trace (Reder, 1987). As last ditch maneuvers, they are tried when surer manipulations have failed and you are desperate to achieve retrieval. These manipulations can be especially helpful on exams.

Alphabet search. Ask yourself whether the information you wish to remember began with an A? a B? a C? and so on. For example, you may attempt to remember the name of a person by generating names beginning with A, then with B, and on through to Z. If you are lucky, you will generate the appropriate name and recognize it as the correct one.

Free generation of attributes. Recall everything you can that is in some way associated with the information you are trying to remember, and then try to recognize any actual attributes of the memory trace among the indirect association you generated. For example, in trying to remember directions, you might freely associate the names of streets, or of stores or landmarks, and then see if you recognize any of the streets, stores, or landmarks as being on the route you are trying to recall.

Question. Ask as many relevant questions you can about the information to be retrieved: If? Of? By? In? Who? What? When? Where? Whose? Whether? Why? Whence? While? How? How much? How many? How long? How often? How manifested? This manipulation is useful when you are trying to remember the nature of a complicated event or information (such as from work). Rarely can people remember all of the necessary details without a multi-question approach.

Reinstate mood. Imagine the mood you experienced when the memory was registered, then try to recapture that mood.

Tip-of-the-tongue. Guess the length, first letter, unusual letters, doubled letters, or other unusual features of the word or words to be remembered.

Limitations of Retrieval Manipulations

The manipulations discussed here are definitely useful in many situations. One practical limitation of these methods is time. They require you to diagnose situations before deciding which manipulation is appropriate. Often, there is not sufficient time, or you are unprepared or unwilling to undergo the diagnosis and selection process. In Chapter 8, we will discuss ways of preparing more direct manipulations for specific tasks (Herrmann, 1990b; Weinstein & Mayer, 1986). Even if you choose to concentrate on mental manipulations for memory improvement, applying them with a task-specific repertoire in mind will make your use more timely and appropriate.

Summary

Mental manipulations have been used for centuries. It takes a lot of practice and discipline to make them work effectively. Different kinds of manipulations are used for learning, retention, and retrieval tasks. There are four basic kinds of learning manipulations: building strength, attributes, associations, and developing retrieval structures. Use of all four kinds when studying for an exam will yield knowledge in memory that is easy to access.

Forgetting renders traces unavailable (due to decay, distortion, intentional revision, and unlearning; or less accessible due to willful inattention, suppression, repression, interference, and retrieval failures). Consideration of what forgetting can do to memory for knowledge may alert you to when you should study a little more before an exam.

Retention manipulations keep a trace available or increase trace accessibility through periodic review, making unpleasant memories unforgettable, protecting the memory from interference with new memories, and anticipating situations in which you will have to remember. If you anticipate not having much time for studying prior to an exam, retention manipulations may save you.

Retrieval manipulations make the desired memory trace emerge into consciousness by a search for the trace with the appropriate strength; attending to potential attributes of the unretrieved trace; attending to associations of the unretrieved trace; and making use of a retrieval structure. Different kinds of mental manipulations will work for different people and for different memory tasks.

7. Technical Memory Manipulations

The last chapter introduced you to the idea of technical mnemonics such as the method of loci and the peg systems. This chapter presents more technical mnemonics. Some of these methods rely on imagery and some rely on words. The invention of the first technical mnemonic is attributed to the Greek orator Simonides. His method involved using visual imagery in order to associate one item to another.

Visual Imagery Techniques

Visual imagery techniques considerably enhance memory for word lists. There are a number of practical uses to which these methods can be put. Research has demonstrated many times over that imagery works. Many investigators, such as Paivio (1969), have shown how effective the method is for improving recall. These techniques can be best described in terms of mental filing systems used for remembering speeches and exam material.

A Mental Filing System

One everyday memory problem that students experience is when ideas come to you and you cannot write them down. Everyone has had the experience of waking up in the morning, having had a good idea overnight, only to discover that the idea or ideas have gone. The same experience is sometimes true if one is driving to a meeting or is sitting in a train without a pen and paper. Suppose, for example, you are going to a meeting and want to raise the question of (1) appointing an assistant, (2) paying your expenses, (3) arranging the date of the next meeting, and (4) opening a new bank account, then the mental filing use of the loci or peg system can come into its own. You can use the peg system, described in the previous chapter, to remember the items in the following manner.

(1) Bun – assistant (picture bun and assistant together)
(2) Shoe – expenses (picture shoe and expenses together)
(3) Tree – date of meeting (picture a tree and date together)
(4) Door – bank account (picture a door and bank account together)

One problem with remembering ideas such as those above is that you need to make everything into an object that can be visualized. So you would need to picture say, a previous assistant; then picture, a large envelope with your expenses inside; the date could be a packet of dates; and for the bank account you could imagine your bank, so that:

(1) you imagine someone else's assistant eating a bun
(2) you imagine a brown envelope with money stuffed into a shoe
(3) you imagine a tree with dates on it
(4) you imagine banging your head on the door to your bank.

Of course this mental filing use can be applied to situations such as trying to give speeches or presentations, and it does work well for such situations. However, prudence is advised when using the system in public, since under the stress of a public presentation, forgetfulness can occur. It is sensible to make a written note of the main points of your speech, so you can refer to it if the worst comes to the worst. Often having a written note gives you the confidence to remember without having to use extensive notes.

The same method can be used for examination preparation, where key points can be linked one at a time to the pegs of the peg system. This can be useful if names of authors are to be remembered. For example, if the first three names to be remembered are (1) White (2) Davidson (3) Bahrick, you might picture (1) a white bun; (2) King David's son throwing a shoe out of a sling; (3) a tree falling on military barracks. Keogh (1999) illustrates the use of the peg-word system in revising for chemistry examinations. The colors of a universal pH indicator with different numbers are:

3– = Red
4   = Orange
5–6= Yellow
7   = Green
8   = Blue
9+ = Violet

There are of course other methods of remembering, but this example of Keogh's shows how easy it is to adapt old methods to new problems.

One situation where it is probably *not* worth using the peg system is when going shopping, since it is much less effort to write down a list, at least for most people! The peg and other systems are best used when writing something down is impossible, or when you want to make an impression in public by appearing to know what you want to say without referring to notes.

There is one more major limitation to the use of the peg system. If information is coming in too fast for you to make a picture, then the method will be ineffective. If, for example, you are given material to learn so that a new image has to be made at a speed greater than one every 4 seconds, do not try to use it.

Foreign Language Learning

One of the most extensively investigated uses of mental imagery is in foreign language learning. At least 50 studies have shown that using visual imagery to relate an English word to a foreign word facilitates recall. In one of the first studies, Raugh and Atkinson (1975) found that a group learning 60 Spanish words by the keyword method recalled 88% of words, compared to 28% for a control group. More recent studies, e.g., Gruneberg and Pascoe (1996), have found facilitated effects of the method for elderly individuals, and Merry (1980) found that 11-year-old children benefited when learning French.

The keyword/linkword method involves linking an English word to another English word which sounds like the foreign translation (Gruneberg, 1985, 1987). For example, the French for "tablecloth" is "nappe." In order to remember this, the learner is required to imagine him-/herself having a nap on a tablecloth.

Recent research (Thomas & Wang, 1996) has shown that testing immediately after a series of keywords has been presented is critical for long term retention. Other studies have shown that the keyword method is most successful when combined with learning in context. Courses that combine the keyword method with immediate testing and context learning (i.e., using words in sentences), provide evidence of students learning large amounts of material in short periods of time. Gruneberg and Jacobs (1991) reported on the use of courses employing these principles (Gruneberg, 1987). They report on one case study of executives who were taught 400

Spanish words and basic grammar in 12 contact hours, and who made a total of four mistakes. Although no direct comparison of speed of learning is possible, Milton and Meara (1998) have found that British school children appeared, on average, to pick up about four words per hour, and that 25% of children appear to pick up no vocabulary at all! (see Gruneberg, 1992 for a review of the literature on the keyword method).

Perhaps of equal importance to the evidence that the keyword method enhances recall, is the evidence that users found the method to be more motivating (Gruneberg & Jacobs, 1991; Kasper, 1993). Gruneberg and Jacobs (1992), for example, found users to report the linkword courses to be faster, easier and more enjoyable than normal language learning methods, a finding reported by Higbee (1999) for other mnemonic strategies. Motivation is clearly a barrier to language learning, and this aspect of the keyword method is, therefore, clearly of considerable importance.

Spelling

Correct spelling is hard for many individuals to achieve. It is possible, however, to use imagery to overcome at least some of the problems that you encounter.

> First make a list of all those words that you find troublesome to remember.
> Perhaps you can't remember whether "professor" is spelt with one "f" or two.
> Imagine *one* professor who is a complete *f*ool. (This should not be too difficult.)
>
> Perhaps you can't remember whether "across" has one "c" or two.
> Maybe seeing only one *sea* (c) *ac*ross to Europe.

What you should do is prepare four to five such images each night. Spend 10 seconds making a vivid picture of each, and then test yourself to make sure you have got this correct. The following day test yourself again to make sure you still remember the correct spelling, then learn another five. On the third day, test yourself on the ten words you have previously learned before carrying on to the next five words, and so on. If you are helping a young brother or sister or child, get them to tell you to join in thinking about a good image to remember the spelling with.

This "story-telling" strategy is not the only strategy which has been shown to help spelling. Kernaghan and Woloshyn (1995) found that using analogies helped to remember how words were spelt. For example, if one wants to remember the spelling of "carefully" as having two "ls", then remembering that dutifully, successfully, and peacefully also have two "ls" is helpful. The researchers have also shown that using visual imagery to imagine yourself painting the letters of a word on a large movie screen, and segmenting words into phonemes helped spelling. Rankin, Bruning, and Timme (1994) also demonstrated that better spellers attribute their better spelling, not to native ability, but to their making a greater effort than poor spellers. The work by Kernaghan and Woloshyn indicates that there might be some truth in this. Using effort to apply strategies has been clearly shown to improve spelling.

Digit/Letter Strategy

The digit/letter strategy was invented in order to extend the peg system, so that imagery could be used to remember thousands of words. Since, however, very few people have a need to remember thousands of words and time has to be spent preparing the pegs, it is more practical to use it in remembering strings of digits. Remembering digits is of course a major everyday memory problem, as we have to remember bank pin numbers, telephone numbers, dates, anniversaries, etc., and numbers themselves are usually meaningless. The digit/letter system makes them meaningful by substituting each number with a letter:

        1 = t   (there is one down stroke in t)
        2 = n (there are two down strokes in n)
        3 = m (there are three down strokes in m)
        4 = r   (r is the last letter of four)
        5 = L (L is the Roman letter for 50)
        6 = sh (the "sh" sound, sounds like six)
        7 = k   (the number 7 is embedded in k)
        8 = f   (f and 8 resemble each other in shape)
        9 = p   (p is 9 the wrong way round)
        0 = s   (s is a zero sound)

In order to remember a number, for example 12, 1 becomes t and 2 becomes n, so 12 is TN. This is made into a word by adding any vowel(s) you like, so that TN could be T*I*N or T*O*N or even T*U*N*A*. Suppose you wished to remember that your mother's birthday was on the 12th, you could imagine your mother balancing a TIN on her head. When you see your mother with a tin on her head, you will remember that T = 1 and N = 2, so her birthday is the 12th.

Larger numbers can be treated in the same way. 835741 is FMLKRT – which could be – Female Kart. If this was your brother's phone number, you might imagine your brother pulling a female kart. Obviously you have to use your imagination. Morris and Greer (1984) showed that using this method significantly increased the probability of remembering number sequences.

There are, however, a number of potential limitations to the method. First it can take some time, especially with large numbers, to make up words that can be remembered. It is therefore advisable only to use the method for numbers that are likely to be important in the future. Secondly, forgetting does occur if the number is not used for some time. This fact was experienced by one of the authors when he had not used his bank pin number for some time. However, it is an effective method for remembering in the short term when a particular number, such as an anniversary date, is important. It is also effective if a number is likely to be used repeatedly or for exam purposes. Keogh (1999), for example, illustrates how it can be used to remember wavelengths of colors. Red is 656: SH L SH. This could be red *sh*aw*l sh*e wore. Green is 486 – R F SH – green-*r*aw *f*i*sh*, and so on.

Verbal Mental Manipulations

First Letter Mnemonics and Examinations

Students frequently use memory aids to help themselves remember in examinations. Gruneberg (1973) found that one of the most frequently used methods was the first letter method, where the first letters of facts to be remembered were made into a phrase or sentence. A common example of this is *R*ichard *o*f *Y*ork *g*ave *b*attle *i*n *v*ain to remember the colors of the rainbow – *r*ed, *o*range, *y*ellow, *g*reen, *b*lue, *i*ndigo, *v*iolet.

There is evidence that using this method increases recall. For example, Gruneberg (1978) found that students who learned a large number of lists of related words (such as lists of flowers, birds, etc.) with the first letter strategy, recalled significantly more words and recalled them in their correct order significantly more frequently after a 20 minute delay than the group who were given no strategy suggestion. Since learning large amounts of related materials, where recall is delayed, is similar to the task required for many exams, it can be reasonably argued that this is good evidence for the value of the first letter strategy in examination preparation.

One reason why the first letter strategy might be effective is the evidence (Gruneberg & Monks, 1974) that being supplied with the first letter of an item you know but cannot get back can give a 50% chance of retrieval. In other words, first letter cueing results in overcoming memory blocks – a likely occurrence under the stress of examinations.

For examinations, where the use of the first letter strategy is appropriate, i.e., where a large amount of factual or conceptual material has to be remembered, the following strategy is suggested for remembering important points. First, use the study strategies outlined in Chapter 8 to understand and assemble material relevant to a particular topic.

Second, after you feel you have read enough on the topic, think about what you think about a topic – how do you feel the evidence points, for example.

Third, organize an answer to a wide range of possible questions on the topic, giving careful consideration to the introduction, the evidence for and against each argument, the main conclusions that can be drawn, and so on, finishing with a concluding paragraph.

Fourth, make a note of all the main points you want to make, with all the names of the major figures/experiments/events, etc. that you wish to discuss.

Fifth, once you have a list of six to ten names/topics, etc., make a list of them, and make the first letter of each name/topic into a word or a phrase. For example, if the points you want to discuss are:

Crime
Punishment
Death Penalty
Mistakes

You might make up the sentence, Crime (and) Punishment Don't Matter. Don't make the sentences too long. If you have more than about six letters, split them into two and make two phrases.

Sixth, once you have prepared first letter phrases for a question, make sure you remember what the phrase stands for. Ideally the answer should be prepared at least a month before the examination.

Seventh, go over your entire exam answers a week before the examination to make sure you remember what the first letters stand for.

Eighth, go over your entire exam answers a day before the examination to make sure you remember what the first letters stood for.

Ninth, go over the entire relevant exam answers the night before the examination.

Tenth, get to the examination at least half an hour before it starts. Do not talk to anyone, but go over the first letters again to make sure you remember what they stand for.

Eleventh, as soon as you get into the examination, choose your answers and write down the first letter phrases and what the first letters stand for. That way you can relax, knowing that you will remember the points you wish to make.

It is often argued against this kind of approach that it is trivializing the examination process. The authors' response to this is that this method ensures that you will not forget to put down what you know. You cannot do well if your original answer and understanding is poor, but often people who know their work really well forget important points under the pressure of exams. What is sillier, to fail to do yourself justice because some people think that this approach is trivial, or to show yourself to your best advantage because you remember to write down all that you want to?

The First Letter Retrieval Strategy

As noted above, cueing with the first letter of a missing item has been shown to be a very effective way of overcoming memory blocks (Gruneberg, Monks, & Sykes, 1976). Recently a number of reports have investigated the value of self-generating first letter cues by getting individuals to go through the alphabet themselves when they have a memory block, in order to see whether sounding out each letter in turn will cue the missing item. The findings on a number of experiments point to the strategy enhancing retrieval (Gruneberg, 1992), although the strategy appears to work more successfully for females than for males. In the study by Gruneberg, Morris & Sykes (1978), using the first letter retrieval strategy resulted in participants recalling about 25% of previously unretrieved items, where the individual felt that they knew them but could not get them back.

Summary

It seems clear that technical mnemonics have a place in helping students with their learning and remembering problems. Provided they are used sensibly, problems ranging from remembering examination topics, foreign language vocabulary, phone numbers, mentally filing ideas which come to you when you are driving, and remembering speeches can all benefit from these methods or their derivations.

Technical mnemonics are useful for people who want powerful methods and who are willing to exert a lot of effort in learning how to use these techniques. You probably would not want to go through the effort to learn all the mnemonics in this chapter. However, it will be worth your while to learn one or two. Having a large repertoire of memory skills is likely to equip you for many of the important memory problems you will meet, even if the really challenging problems do not occur frequently.

8. Task-Specific Manipulations

Applicability of a Manipulation

A manipulation involves one or more steps that are intended to achieve an end. In this book, all manipulations are intended to improve memory. Manipulations vary in how applicable they are to different memory tasks (Baddeley, 1982). General manipulations apply to many memory tasks. Specific manipulations apply to one or a few memory tasks, and often to the situation in which a task is performed (Brent & Myers, 2000; Greeno et al., 1993; Lave, 1988; Scribner, 1984).

Manipulations vary in applicability because of the number and kind of steps they involve. Those involving one step will apply to more tasks than manipulations involving several steps. Additionally, manipulations that use simple steps, requiring little prior learning, will apply to more tasks than manipulations involving complex steps, requiring considerable prior learning. Simple rehearsal, for example, involves the repetition of one step: saying to yourself repeatedly the information to be learned (Tulving & Craik, 2000). This can be applied to many (although not all) memory tasks, including learning pairs, lists, sentences, stories, words, numbers, or melodies. In contrast, the first letter mnemonic requires five steps: identifying the first letter of words to be remembered, organizing the letters into the skeleton of another word, filling in the vowels of the scheme-word, rehearsing the letters to be learned, and rehearsing the words to be learned. The first letter manipulation is widely regarded as most applicable to learning relatively short lists of words. It can be used for longer lists or other material, such as sentences or passages, but not as easily as it can be applied to short lists. It might be adapted to learn numbers and melodies, but the adaptation would probably require more effort than the task deserves. Thus, the generality of a manipulation is a function of its intrinsic properties.

A manipulation's specificity has straightforward effects on memory performance. Many have supposed that the general manipulation, applicable to many or all memory tasks, is preferable to specific manipulation. A general manipulation has the advantage of versatility. However, a specific manipulation is often more effective than a general manipulation applied to the same task (Herrmann & Searleman, 1990).

A manipulation is executed sequentially in four stages, as shown in Figure 13. The utility of a manipulation depends on how easy it is to execute, how much time is necessary to execute it, and how effectively each stage is executed (Miller et al., 1960).

Advantages in the Selection Stage

General and specific manipulations function differently at each stage. In order to use a manipulation, you must think of it before or while a task confronts you. The probability of a manipulation being elicited (or brought to consciousness) by a situation is directly related to the manipulation's specificity (Baddeley, 1982). A general manipulation, which is associated equally with all tasks, will not be strongly associated with any given task. Conversely, a specific manipulation will be most strongly associated with the task to which it applies and unassociated with other tasks. Thus, specific manipulations are more readily elicited than general manipulations by a task or by a situation that foretells a task.

For example, consider the task of remembering to water your plants. A specific manipulation will be more likely to elicit the intention than a general one (Meacham & Leiman, 1982; Morris, 1992). A mental manipulation in which the intention to water a plant at a certain time is rehearsed by imagining or physically acting out the watering will be more effective than rehearsal in which the intention is repeated only verbally to oneself.

In addition, when a task elicits two or more manipulations, you must choose between them (Herrmann & Searleman, 1990). Preferably, you would use the manipulation that is most appropriate for the task. Such choices are invariably easier with specific manipulations than with general manipulations. Whether or not a specific manipulation is applicable is readily seen; for example, noting the features of a face is clearly useful to registering faces, but not names. However, general manipulations are less readily seen as applicable because of their vagueness. Suppose, for example, you choose to apply a verbal rehearsal manipulation. What steps would you take to rehearse a face or the fragrance of someone's perfume or aftershave?

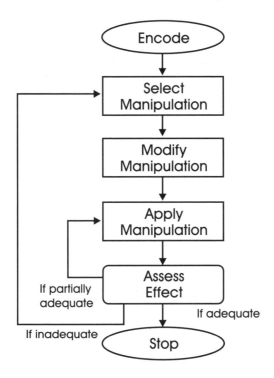

Figure 13. A Flowchart Depicting the Stages of Implementing a Mental Manipulation

Advantages in the Modification Stage

Although it may not be readily apparent, every manipulation must be modified or adjusted to the particular task. The amount of mental effort and time expended in such modification depends on the generality of the manipulation. For example, suppose you need to learn someone's name (say Armandstring). Even if you already planned to learn the name by association, you must decide which type of association will be most appropriate for "Armandstring." Unless you have modified the manipulation and are prepared to associate the name with certain key kinds of information – such as the names of other people "Armandstring" reminds you of his occupation or his regional background – you will probably spend too much time thinking of proper associations. Modifying a general manipulation on the spot requires more time during the execution phase than using a planned specific manipulation.

Advantages in the Application Stage

The effectiveness of an application also appears to depend on whether the manipulation is general or specific. Since general manipulations involve fewer steps than specific manipulations, it might seem that general manipulations are easier to execute. If the issue were solely the number of steps, this would be true. However, the ease of application depends on the general manipulation's appropriateness for the task. A great deal of research now indicates that each manipulation has its greatest benefit for certain tasks. Many manipulations, including most of the mental manipulations presented in Chapter 6, are less general than they have been claimed to be. For example, technical mnemonics are often promoted as useful for any and all tasks (see Chapter 7), but they in fact are most useful for certain tasks (Herrmann, 1987). If the general manipulation does not lend itself readily *to* the task at hand (as in the example of applying rehearsal to remembering the fragrance of a perfume or aftershave), the general manipulation may be considerably harder to apply than a specific manipulation.

As people become proficient at performing memory tasks, their abilities become more specific (James, 1890; Herrmann et al., 1988; Herrmann, 1990b; Schacter & Glisky, 1986). Many studies have found that advanced memory ability transfers to new tasks. Chess experts (who have spent over 10,000 hours developing their expertise) reproduce with great accuracy – after just a glance – the positions of pieces on a partially played-out chessboard. Given the same task, novice chess players reproduce the board with considerable inaccuracy. Nevertheless, the same chess experts recall the board positions no better than the novice players when the pieces are randomly ordered on the board (Simon & Gilmarten, 1973). Thus, the dramatic short-term memory ability of chess experts applies only when pieces are positioned according to the rules of the game.

Practice has a similar effect even with a simple task such as remembering numbers. When most people are presented with a series of digits and asked to recall them in the order presented, they can usually recall no more than seven consecutive digits correctly. With diligent practice over several months, their recall at the task increases substantially. Some people have been found to increase the number of digits they can recall by 10 times! Interviews with these people indicate that practice allows the person to develop retrieval-structure manipulations from their background and interests. For example, one person developed a scheme to remember digits by identifying sequences as a series of winning times in running events. However, if these same trained individuals are then asked to recall a series of letters, their recall drops from about 80 digits back to six or seven letters (Baltes & Kliegel, 1986; Chase & Ericsson, 1982; Ericsson, 1985). Thus, despite the apparent similarity of the two tasks, the dramatic improvement applies only to the practice task.

This finding also seems to apply to retrieval of facts and knowledge. People who practice recalling examples of categories (such as for the category of "animals") – even without consulting books or other resources during practice – increase the number of examples that they can recall threefold (from an average of 40 to 120 animals; Herrmann, Buschke, & Gall, 1987). Like the subjects who practiced learning a series of digits, these subjects reported that they developed schemes to guide their recall (such as thinking of animals at the zoo, in the wild on different continents, or in certain books). However, the increase in recall for the practice category fails to transfer to recall from other categories (such as for "furniture").

It is accordingly not surprising that educational experience yields abilities that are specific to the discipline studied (Glaser, 1984; Lave, 1988; Thorndike, 1924). Similarly, it is also not surprising that occupational experience usually yields advanced memory abilities specific to the occupation. Bartenders have good memory for remembering what drinks they made. Waitresses are skilled at remembering what patrons have ordered, what they have been served, and where they are seated. Professors are adept at remembering books and articles applicable to their specialty. The evidence now available indicates that memory skills acquired through practice are so specific that a bartender who can memorize new recipes for drinks quickly will be no quicker than the typical professor or car mechanic at remembering appointments.

Finally, even interests or hobbies you actively pursue help you to develop memory skills pertinent to them. What may be surprising is that, again, the skill involved remains specific to the hobby. For example, baseball fans can learn and remember the box scores of a particular game with amazing speed and accuracy. However, when they turn the page to the stock listings, their skill with numbers fades quickly back normal. There is no evidence that memory skills acquired in pursuit of a hobby endows a person with superior memory skills for any and all tasks (Herrmann, 1987).

Advantages in the Assessment Stage

After a manipulation has been applied, its effectiveness can be assessed. Often, assessment is carried out periodically while a memory task is being attempted. The assessment should determine whether more manipulative processing is needed for the task, whether the manipulations were effective, and whether modifications or new manipulations should be added. Even in this assessment phase, specific manipulations have an edge over general ones. If a specific manipulation is ineffective, the reason can be identified in a relatively straightforward manner: most likely, the manipulation was inappropriate for the information. If a general manipulation is ineffective, however, many reasons must be considered. The manipulation may have been inappropriate; it may not have been properly modified to the task; or its execution may have been flawed – particularly if interfered with by other memory traces from tasks to which it had previously been applied. Thus, it takes longer to assess the effectiveness of the general manipulation. Increased time and lowered accuracy in assessment diminishes the overall efficiency and effectiveness of performance.

At each stage of manipulation execution, specific manipulations are more effective than general manipulations. Before execution, however, task-specific manipulations require more preparation and forethought to remain useful. There are hundreds of specific memory tasks encountered in daily life (discussed in Cohen, 1989; Gruneberg & Morris, 1979; Gruneberg, Morris, & Sykes, 1978, 1988; Harris & Morris, 1984; Howe, 1977; Neisser, 1982). It simply is not possible to learn task-specific manipulations to anticipate or prepare for all (or even most) tasks. Therefore, for incidental tasks (which you executed without being aware you were performing a memory task) or for unanticipated but intentional tasks, a general manipulation is necessary. Nonetheless, when a task allows or merits your most effective effort, you should prepare specific manipulations.

The Advantages of Repertoires of Manipulations

Preparing a repertoire of two or more manipulations is better than preparing just one manipulation, because a particular task-specific manipulation may not suit every instance of a certain task. The extent of the match between them affects the efficiency and effectiveness of the manipulation for the task. Manipulations emphasize different attributes of task information, and instances of the same task manifest certain attributes more than other instances. If just one manipulation is used, it may not match the task maximally. The use of two manipulations increases the quantity and quality of registration and remembering, thereby making up for any lacking in effectiveness that might come with the use of just one manipulation.

Consider the example of learning names. One manipulation for learning a person's name involves its ethnic roots. Another manipulation involves analyzing peculiar aspects of its spelling or graphic form, such as unusual length, double letters, or unusual combinations of letters. These two different manipulations clearly emphasize different aspects of the same task. Similarly, names differ in the attributes they present for manipulation. To many Americans, "Jones" is a neutral name, because its ethnic roots are obscure and its spelling is typical. "Maloy" is more identifiable for its Irish ethnic roots, but its spelling is equally typical. "Armstrong" is also ethnically neutral to many Americans, but the name combines two common words in a distinct and fairly unusual way. "Andrzejewski" is more ethnically interesting and identifiable for its Polish roots, and its spelling is unusual in both length and letter combinations.

The manipulations of ethnic and graphic analysis may be applied to all these names, but not with equal effect. The amount of interest and attention generated by an ethnic analysis would increase from Jones and Armstrong to Maloy and Andrzejewski. The amount of interest and attention generated by a graphic analysis would increase across Jones and Maloy to Armstrong and Andrzejewski. Only Andrzejewski draws a maximum reaction from both manipulations. A repertoire that includes both will allow you to match the given name to the most effective manipulation.

Thus, using a repertoire of manipulations allows each manipulation to make up for any loss in effectiveness possessed by the other. Additionally, the use of two or more manipulations ensures that you pay extra attention to what you want to register or remember, thereby making success more likely (Anderson, 1983; Bransford & Stein, 1984; Gagne & Paradise, 1961; Geiselman, Fisher, MacKinnon, & Holland, 1986; Harlow, 1949; Kolodner, 1984; Morris, Bransford, & Franks, 1977; Schank, 1982). Finally, in designing repertoires, you can strategically chose manipulations to enhance your performance in a maximally efficient fashion. Rather than using manipulations that overlap in their effect, as in the name example above, manipulations may be used that overlap little or not at all. There are clearly many ways that manipulations might be selected that facilitate memory in very different ways. For example, you might choose mental manipula-

---

tions of strength and retrieval structures that have clearly different effects; a mental manipulation and an environmental manipulation; a mental manipulation and a social manipulation; or an environmental manipulation and a condition manipulation.

Manipulations that facilitate memory in different ways, if judiciously selected, will lead you to respond flexibly to memory tasks and to have a greater chance of success. Figure 14 summarizes the effects of different kinds of manipulations on the efficacy of a person's studying.

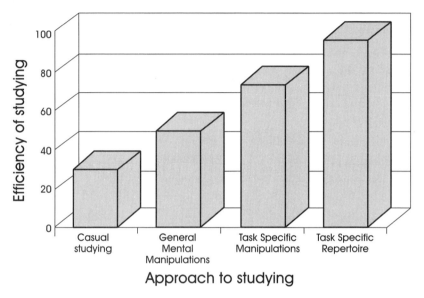

Figure 14. The Efficacy of a Person's Studying as a Function of the Kind of Mental Manipulation Used (hypothetical data based on the research literature)

Method for Acquiring Task-Specific Repertoires

You already apply repertoires of manipulations to memory tasks. For tasks that you are not well prepared for, you fall back on natural manipulations that you have known since adolescence or childhood. Some of your natural manipulations are probably general ones which you apply to many memory tasks. Others are probably specific, such as ones that you developed when in school for studying material or taking exams. After reading the previous chapters, you should now know many more general manipulations. This chapter will expand your knowledge of specific manipulations.

Selection of Manipulations to Make up a Repertoire

Before you expand your use of task-specific manipulations for a particular task, you should decide whether your existing repertoire for this task
may be adequate after all. Figure 15 presents a form to guide you in analyzing your repertoire for a given task. Use this form in the following
manner. For example, you might be interested in learning the vocabulary
for a course. The manipulation categories and chapter references are provided on the form to help you think of the manipulations you use; it is not
necessary for you to classify each manipulation you recall. Begin by recalling the manipulations that you usually use for the task. After you have
exhausted the list of manipulations you have previously applied to the
task, consider whether these manipulations are sufficient. It is possible
that the manipulations you now know would be sufficient if you made a
good effort to use them when you encounter the task. However, it is also
possible that you may judge your natural repertoire as not being up to the
task.

If you feel that the manipulations that make up your current repertoire
are insufficient, then you should develop new manipulations to supplement them. In many cases, some potentially useful manipulations will
occur to you after you analyze your performance on a task.

REPERTOIRE GENERATION FORM

Course: _____

Task Description: _____
_____
_____

Registration:

Physiological Manipulations: _____
_____

Emotive Manipulations: _____
_____

Memory Manipulations: _____
_____

Environmental Manipulations: _____

_____

Social Manipulations: _____

_____

Study-Specific Manipulations: _____

_____

Retention Maintenance: _____

_____

Remembering:

Condition Manipulations: _____

_____

Attitude Manipulations: _____

_____

Mental Manipulations: _____

_____

Environmental Manipulations: _____

_____

Social Manipulations: _____

_____

Study-Specific Manipulations: _____

_____

Figure 15. A Repertoire Generation Form. First, write in the manipulations you now use in whatever space seems appropriate. Second, write in other manipulations that, on reflection, you feel you could use.

You may also discover some useful manipulations in any of the many books that have been published on memory improvement. However, virtually all previous books on memory improvement have stressed a limited number of so-called general procedures and, hence, provide only a little task-specific information. Since no previous book on memory improvement provides much information about them, this chapter presents an in-

ventory of task-specific manipulations to help you in constructing repertoires for the tasks of interest to you. The inventory below provides many
manipulations for everyday memory tasks. For each task in the inventory,
a menu of feasible manipulations is listed. The inventory's form is similar
to a dictionary, with telegraphic descriptions giving you the gist of multiple manipulations. From these telegraphic descriptions, you should be
able to select and implement particular manipulations to suit your task
and preferences.

Fortunately, the nature of most task-specific manipulations is evident
on reading a brief description. The inventory is not intended to be read
like a text. You should simply consult it for potentially relevant manipulations when you have particular tasks in mind. Although the everyday
memory tasks included will be familiar to you, the inventory does not
include all possible tasks. If the task you have in mind is not included in
the inventory, look for similar tasks; they will usually contain some manipulations relevant to the task of interest to you. Each task's menu likewise includes more manipulations than any previous book, but the menus
are not exhaustive. If they do not provide a manipulation that satisfies
you, the menus will still probably guide your thinking and help you devise
a suitable manipulation.

The manipulations you choose to include in a repertoire should meet
certain criteria if it is to be truly useful to you. The manipulation should
seem natural to you. It should be possible for you to imagine yourself
using it comfortably and consistently. Any given manipulation will suit
some people but not others. Where one person will favor visual manipulations, another will favor auditory manipulations. People who enjoy and
collect gadgetry may prefer environmental manipulations, while outgoing
types will be more drawn to social manipulations. Many of the manipulations that you have learned in this book or from other sources are bound to
strike you as implausible or foolish. You should dismiss them. At least
some manipulations will strike you as plausible and prove effective for
you.

Once you have decided to add a manipulation to a repertoire, add it to
the manipulations you listed on the Repertoire Generation Form. When
you add new manipulations, indicate in some way (such as by using a
different color pen) that these are untried manipulations. This marking is
useful when you select the manipulations that you should study in your
preparation of a functional repertoire. Many people forget which manipulations they knew originally and which were obtained from the inventory.
The origin is important to bear in mind because new manipulations need

extra study if they are to become useful; a false belief that one knew the manipulation all along will not guarantee it will be used.

Once you have selected one or more manipulations to add to your repertoire, you can begin to implement them. From the manipulations that you have identified, you should identify one or two appropriate manipulations you do not currently use in the task. Research has shown that prior study of a repertoire can facilitate subsequent memory performance for the relevant task when the number of manipulations is small and manageable. Attempting to acquire many manipulations will lead to worse performance than memorization of a manageable few.

Obviously, a manipulation's apparent difficulty level will bear on your decision to use or to dismiss it. Generally, the more difficult registration manipulations produce a better trace, because these manipulations usually require more attention. But if your time for a task is limited, you will want to pick an easier manipulation. Finally, if the manipulation seems familiar because it is the same as, or similar to, one that you use in other contexts, you will be more likely to succeed at incorporating it into your task repertoire.

After you decide to add a manipulation to a repertoire, you must do some work to make it work for you. It is not sufficient to identify a manipulation and decide to use it. First, make a list of the kinds of situations in which you expect the task to recur (for instance, home, work, or shopping). If possible, specify the particular situations (for instance, with certain people or dealing with certain information). Second, establish a strong association between the manipulation and the task. Simply rehearsing the association will usually not be enough. In addition, you should engage in extended self-association training. This training involves the following steps: Write the name of the task on one side of a card and the manipulation you intend to use on the other side. Then leave the card in a prominent spot, such as next to your bed, on your kitchen table, or on your desk at work. Each time you pass the card, try to recall the manipulations as quickly as possible. At first, you will notice a brief lapse before you recall the manipulation. With practice, it will come to mind immediately.

Once you are confident that you associate the manipulation with the task, you need to take two more steps to incorporate the manipulation into your repertoire. First, use the manipulation whenever you can. If circumstances limit your opportunities to do so, imagine yourself using the manipulation. Second, keep a record for two to four weeks, indicating how often you encountered the task, whether you used the manipulation, and how successful each use was. After you have kept this record long enough to establish a "track record" of performance, analyze the effectiveness of the manipulation. Does it really work for you? If it doesn't work so well, is it because you are not yet skilled at it, or is it because the manipulation does not suit you after all? If you decide the problem lay with the manipulations and not your own efforts, reevaluate whether you really need a manipulation for this task. If you do, find another manipulation that might prove more effective. Note that the repertoires addressed here are those that are most important to studying and college life. For a wider array of repertoires pertaining to everyday life in general, see Herrmann (1990b).

An Example of Developing a Task-Specific Repertoire

To make the foregoing discussion clearer, consider the task of learning and remembering combinations for a lock. Just suppose that you had a job or were in a school where you had to learn a combination from time to time, and forgetting it would get you in hot water. To identify a manipulation for learning combinations, you would first recall for yourself the manipulations that you would naturally apply to this task. Then you would consult the menu of possible manipulations listed in the inventory (under "combinations to a lock"). This menu is reproduced in Figure 15. Suppose that the manipulation for visualizing the numbers in position on the lock seems the most plausible choice to you. Your next step would be to identify situations in which you are likely to be given a new combination lock to use. After identifying them, associate the visualization manipulation with these situations, such as by the card method described above. Once the manipulation is well associated with task situations, practice imagining yourself using the manipulation. Finally, keep track of how often you use the visualization manipulation, and evaluate how effective it is.

> *Combination to a lock.* Registration: visualize the numbers in position; rehearse opening it; associate the numbers with ages of your life and a significant event of each of these ages; notice mathematical properties of the numbers – what they are divisible by, and how the numbers relate mathematically to each other – such as one being about twice the other; write it down and save it; write it in an inconspicuous spot near the lock. Remembering: try to recall the feel of turning the tumbler; consult notes.

Figure 16. A Menu of Manipulations Appropriate for Registering and Remembering Combinations for Combination Locks

Obviously, the development of task-specific repertoires requires a good deal of effort. For that reason alone, there is a limit to the number of such repertoires that you could – or even would want – to learn. Thus, you will want to begin with just one or two tasks that seriously annoy you or that you consider especially important. Once you have improved on those tasks, you may wish to work on a further task. If you can improve your performance on just those few tasks that most trouble you, you will have achieved the memory improvement that most genuinely matters to you.

An Inventory of Task-Specific Manipulations

The inventory that follows presents menus of manipulations relevant to over 40 memory tasks pertinent to studying and college life. The menus have been developed by the authors along with the students who took courses with them concerning memory and/or memory training.

Information in the Task Menus

Each entry in the inventory is unique, although similar tasks will contain some similar manipulations. Two kinds of information may be included in a task menu. First, menus include manipulations from the previous chapters that are especially suitable for a particular task or appropriate modifications of those manipulations. Second, the menus may include manipulations that have been designed specifically for the task. Most of the menus do not mention manipulations concerning condition, attitude, and general manipulations of social context. Condition manipulations tend to be applicable to all tasks and, therefore, specific to none. Attitude manipulations tend to be specific to individuals rather than to tasks. General manipulations of social context, like those for condition, apply to essentially all tasks. Nevertheless, you may need – and should feel free to add – condition, attitude, or social context manipulations to your repertoire for a particular task. By reviewing the assessment procedures and manipulations presented in Chapters 3, 4, and 5, you will be the best judge of whether and which of these areas need improvement.

Menus change systematically with task demands. Some tasks require more manipulations than others. Some tasks exclusively involve remembering (such as when we try to remember the name of someone who we met a long time ago). Other tasks involve only registration (such as most intention tasks in which we register an act we intend to carry out and hope the intention will emerge into consciousness when needed). Occasionally, remembering tasks are based on information acquired in an incidental memory task. For such remembering tasks, registration is past and cannot be altered. However, the remembering in such cases can still be aided by engaging in preparation. Obviously, the inventory will be useful to you to the extent that you have properly identified your task and can match it to the correct task description in the inventory.

Organization of the Inventory

The inventory is divided into four sections, each one devoted to one of the four general kinds of memory tasks: everyday knowledge, events, intentions, and actions. (Knowledge relating directly to study skills will be taken up in the next chapter.) Under every category, a table of contents precedes a series of menus for the specific tasks.

I. Everyday Knowledge Task Menus

Table of Contents

Knowledge Repertoires

1. Combination to a lock
Registration: visualize the numbers in position; rehearse opening it; associate the numbers with ages of your life and a significant event of each of these ages; notice mathematical properties of the numbers – what they are divisible by, and how the numbers

relate mathematically to each other – such as one being about twice the other; write it down and save it; write it in an inconspicuous spot near the lock. Remembering: try to recall the feel of turning the tumbler; consult notes.

2. **Phone numbers**
   Registration: examine the number for mathematical relationships; translate the number into letters according to the dial and then form these letters into a word or phrase; attend to the tones of the numbers while dialing; note the number; record the number in a dialing device.
   Remembering: try to recall how you learned the number (math patterns; letter associations); notes, dialing device, phone book.

3. **Rules of games** (sports, board games, parlor games)
   Registration: identify the winning conditions and the conditions that thwart winning; play with others or with simulator machines; when you are surprised about a ruling, take note; keep notes on rulings that surprised you; buy a book on game rules, such as Hoyle's (see References); review rules before playing the game.
   Remembering: think of the logic of the game and then reconstruct (although, rules are often illogical); notes or a rulebook.

4. **Script for a play or film** (see "Poetry" if learning verbatim; see speeches if learning the gist first; both in Chapter 8)

5. **Special numbers** (Social Security; your own address)
   Registration: note mathematical patterns; translate the number into (a) historical dates of interest to you, (b) your current or previous weight, (c) letters according to a number code and then into a word; record it.
   Remembering: recall how you learned it; reinstate the context of prior use; records.

II. Event Menus

Table of Contents

1. **Actions just performed or recently performed** – remembering whether you did something minutes or hours before (such as brushing your teeth or putting something away)

2. **Birthday** – remembering when someone's birthday is (as distinguished from realizing you have to do something about it – covered under Intentions tasks)

3. **Conversations** – remembering what you just said, such as after being interrupted in the middle of the sentence

4. **Conversation** – remembering what someone said to you at a previous occasion

5. **Date of a past event** – remembering when some event occurred

6. **Dates of future events** – remembering salient future events on your schedule

7. **Directions to perform a particular act** – remembering precisely what someone else told you to do. Employer, teacher, or spouse tells you to do something at home, and when you get there you have difficulty in remembering it

8. **Event** – remembering aspects of an event (such as incidents, course of events, who attended, when it occurred – at a meeting, party, movie, or show)

9. **Face Recognition** – recognizing a person (i.e., remembering that you know a person and why you know the person). "Placing a face"

10. **Finding a file** (Hertel, 1988)

11. **Finding something in a file**

12. **Loans** (to whom you loaned something to)

13. **Location of keys** – remembering where you put your keys

14. **Location of misplaced object** – that was recently misplaced (say from seconds to hours ago)

15. **Location of misplaced object** – that was misplaced some time ago

16. **Long sentence, question, or request** – remembering all of what was said to you in a long utterance (so you can answer it)

17. **Message given on awakening** – remembering what was said to you on awakening before arising or before going back to sleep

18. **Name acquisition** – learning someone's name during an introduction so you will call them by name properly when you see them

19. **Photos** – remembering when and where it was taken and who is in the photo (sometimes who took the photo)

20. **Prior statements in conversation** – remembering the point of view on an issue that you expressed previously (avoid appearing inconsistent, absentminded, or hypocritical)

21. **Prior statement in correspondence** – remembering what you wrote to someone previously

Event Repertoires

1. **Actions just performed or recently performed** – remembering whether you did something minutes or hours before (such as brushing your teeth, putting something away)
   Remembering: think of possible consequences of action or of events that would have been contingent on the action; seek physical evidence of the action if this is possible (for example, to determine if you brushed your teeth, feel your toothbrush).
2. **Birthday** – remembering the date of someone's birthday (as distinguished from realizing you must do something about it, which is covered under III. (Intention Repertoires)
   Registration: Is it close to someone else's birthday? Keep records on birthdays; calendar/diary, commercial aid service (see Chapter 11), appointment books; steer conversation to birthdays/horoscopes. Find association between person and the date; cluster birthdays.
   Remembering: try to recall when this person last celebrated his or her birthday, scan a calendar; try to narrow down to season, then to month, etc.; ask a friend; ask the person what their sign is; say "your birthday is coming up?"
3. **Conversation, current** – what you said just before you were interrupted in the middle of the sentence
   Preparation: anticipate before the conversation what is to be discussed – fosters better encoding; develop an interest for what is discussed – evaluate the conversation: is it interesting, trivial, seditious, salacious, etc.; summarize the conversation to yourself; in some professional situations it is acceptable to record what is happening – if a tape is being made, it is easy to ask for a replay; resist being interrupted; keep focused on the conversation, and treat the interruption as peripheral.
   Remembering: pause, sometimes it will come back; reconstruct the conversation and guess what was probably said; cue eliciting act: Say – "Oh heck, I don't want to say anything wise;" people will usually ask you to finish and mention a key word or two that will trigger your memory; or inquire – "What do you think?"
4. **Conversation, past** – at a previous occasion
   Remembering: rehearsal; remember person; recall counter ar-

guments; recall position where conversation took place; look at paper notes that are written on; rehearsing some of the topics of conversation; ask the person.

5. **Date of a past event** (see entry for "Events")

6. **Dates of future events** – on your schedule
   Registration: associate the date with the event; associate one event with another on the same date; imagine a calendar with key dates marked; associate the date with past historic events; record on your calendar and on your appointment book.
   Remembering: imagine your calendar; appointment book.

7. **Directions to perform a particular act as given to you by someone else** (such as your teacher or roommate)
   Registration: make sure that you have the directions right in the first place – have them repeat the directions (even if you already do have them right, going over them gives you a second rehearsal); notes; if there is another person with you, ask if he or she understood it – the discussion will provide extra review for you and also establish an alternate source should you forget part or all of what is to be done; reflect back on the directions in the interim.
   Remembering: imagine yourself in the situation where instructions were given; consult notes; consult someone who was present when instructions were given; find someone who knows what to do due to experience or knowledge.

8. **Events, general** – (such as incidents, the course of an event, who attended, when it occurred; Herrmann, 1994)
   Registration: describe for yourself the gist of the event just afterwards – select a few key words that capture the event and rehearse these words; self referencing; anticipate the likely way the episode will unfold its script; prioritize – decide ahead of time what things will be worth attending to and remembering; make mental or physical notes about salient aspects of the event; discuss with others right away; discuss with friends immediately afterwards; reflect back on the event as soon as you can.
   Remembering: recall the theme and key descriptors and then reconstruct; check for sensory detail – real memories tend to have more sensory details than imagined ones; check for verbosity – real memories lend themselves to less equivocation than imagined memories; recreate the scene in your mind; re-

call major landmarks at the event; imagine yourself at different spots in the location of the event, looking upon the event from different perspectives; reconstruct the temporal order of the sub-parts of the event (Adams, 1985); question yourself about particular attributes of the event (Herrmann, 1984) – recall of particular attributes will often trigger other attributes; decide which kind of error is least objectionable in the situation (omission, commission) and guess accordingly; recall everything that might be correct to yourself and then pick and choose; recall from different points in the sequence of the event; recall in different orders (start to finish; finish to start); consult notes; find old souvenirs, mementos, photos, or any material associated with the event (Graumann, 1985); consult someone else who was present.

9. **Face recognition**
   Remembering: reinstate a context in which you may have met; imagine people you know who have similar faces; don't be preoccupied with studying their facial features – instead make judgments about them: who do they remind you of; do they seem honest, sensitive, interesting, and so on with whatever characteristics are of value to you (Bahrick, 1984; Hastie et al., 1980; Morris, Jones, & Hampson, 1978; Winograd, 1978; Woodhead, Baddeley, & Simmonds, 1979); sometimes an album or a yearbook will help; take cues from others; if you fail to recognize the person, be blunt but apologetic.

10. **Finding a file**
    Registration: pay attention to the labels on the file; if files are out of order, do not file the new folder until the order is corrected; label files properly; keep a list of labels to files (a directory).
    Remembering: take everything out and go through each folder.

11. **Finding something in a file**
    Registration: pay attention to the organization of the filing system; periodically go over the file and reorganize; label files properly; keep a list of labels to files (a directory); keep notes about reorganization of files.
    Remembering: take everything out and go through each folder.

12. **Loans** – remembering your borrowers
    Registration: imagine yourself handing the person the money or object you loaned; associate the loan with other events of the

day and with who else might have been present, associate the loan with the date it is to be paid back; keep records; note on your calendar and appointment book when the loan is due or when you should ask for its return; when you make the loan, ask the person when the money or object loaned will be returned.

Remembering: calendar; appointment book.

13. **Location of keys**

Registration: put keys in a regular spot, key racks, a special pocket; recheck lock to see key is not left when you enter or leave; keep keys on a string attached to clothing; check to see if you know where your keys are; pat your pockets if you keep your keys on your person or check where you normally carry them.

Remembering: retrace your steps; ask someone else; use a key chain that attaches to your belt or other part of clothing; large key rings; glow in the dark key chain; keep extra keys accessible somewhere, although this practice may make it easier for you to loose a key without being aware of it.

14. **Location of misplaced object, recent**

Registration: be methodical, go step by step; have a routine for the way you lay out things in chores – it may seem boring but use of consistent placement habits makes it easier to find things later; use object organizers at every opportunity; assign standard places to put things; be aware of who is around as you do a task in which things might be misplaced – so you can ask later if necessary; before you have a chance to lose things, make an object check, that is, check that everything is where you had intended it to be; take objects with you on your person if feasible.

Remembering: reinstate what you were doing just before you misplaced it; retrace your steps; develop a search plan; (1) check object organizers and standard places; (2) clear the area in which the object disappeared; (3) turn the place upside down in searching for it; (4) if that fails, pick up the area and put everything back where it is supposed to be and develop a new plan; ask anyone who was around where they think you may have misplaced the object; if you are desperate, ask a friend to help you look for it.

15. Location of misplaced object, some time ago

Registration: rehearse name of object with location; imagine the object in the location; imagine returning and finding the object in the future; put objects in an expected place or visible plan; be orderly – give everything its place; keep a place for priority items; marked storage closets, cabinets; periodically check that things are where they are supposed to be (things can be in their places even in a messy-looking house).

Remembering: recall last use of item; recall probable last use of item; walk to places of possible last use; if all else fails, go through all of your possessions (you may be lucky and as a bonus find something else that was missing); remember ways you found the object before; go out and buy a new one, it will reappear; make sure you have not loaned the object to someone; make sure that someone else did not move the object or put it back in an unfamiliar place; ask a friend; blame someone else and they will help you find it.

16. Long sentence, question, or request – remembering all of what was said to you (so you can answer it)

Registration: pay attention to key words and remember them instead of the whole question or request; pay extra attention to people given to making long utterances or to situations where long questions often occur (in court, class); ignore everything else; note pad where possible; you may, if you like, restate the question or request and confirm it – or ask the questioner to paraphrase the utterance; you may politely ask the questioner to be brief; pick out key terms and rehearse them.

Remembering: recall your key terms; consult note pad if possible; as you recall the answer watch faces of others to determine if you missed a point; after reply, ask if you covered everything satisfactorily (rather than ask if you remembered everything); acknowledge that the statement, question, or request was long and say that you don't have time to deal with all that was mentioned but that you will address the most important points – and then respond to whatever you recall.

17. Message given to you while not fully awake – such as just before falling asleep, when awakened from sleep, or on awakening

Registration: prioritize this situation so that when it occurs you will be more likely to take note of the message; make a note on a pad by the bed; ask the person giving you the message to leave a note for you.

Remembering: reinstate the context, retrieve key words or gist and reconstruct; notes if you made them.

18. **Name acquisition** – during an introduction

Registration: if possible, prime yourself ahead of time by asking someone whom you might meet at a social function – if you know the name before being introduced ahead of time, half the battle is won; if possible arrive before most of the people – this will prevent you from having to meet everyone at once and will give you more time to study the people you are meeting; use the face-name imagery technique; this technique has three steps: (1.) think of a "substitute" word that represents some object that sounds like the person's last name and for which you can form a mental image – such as "duck" for Donaldson; (2.) select the most outstanding feature of the person's face; (3.) form an image of your substitute word on the person's face; use distributed rehearsal; use the SALT method: (1.) say the name out loud; (2.) ask the person a question while using the name; (3.) say the name at least once in conversation; and (4.) terminate the conversation by using the name again; think of a rhyme for the name; decide who the person looks like (either a celebrity or someone else you know); translate the name, with some distortion, into another language; note the person's eccentricities; analyze the national/ethnic origins of the name; take an interest in the person; as you leave the situation look back and see if you can recall the name or names of people met – if you can't recall, ask someone with you; jot down their names at the earliest opportunity – such as in an address book; this practice is especially helpful when encountering several introductions in a row on a receiving line; discuss who you met with others; it is considered socially acceptable to ask someone their name after just being introduced when the introduction situation is hurried and hectic – it is even regarded as a compliment under such conditions that you considered them worth the trouble of asking; reflect on who was met as soon as possible after leaving a social function – including what they looked like and pronouncing their name aloud; review a list you made or which was available for the social function; imagine settings in which you might encounter them in the future and then imagine meeting them and saying their names in this setting; if you cannot recall someone's name after a good effort to recall, ask someone who might know it.

Remembering: reinstate the context of when and where you first met (see also, "First meeting with someone") and how you felt at the time; use the tip-of-the-tongue method; go through the alphabet and ask yourself if the name began with each letter; notes; address book; programs to social or professional functions; rosters by office locations in companies or buildings; ask the person whose name you want to remember cue-gathering questions; ask someone nearby who is out of earshot of this person; ask the person how to pronounce their name, leading them to tell it without your having to admit you forgot it (however, if their name is Jones, this can make you look silly); avoid having to refer to them by name.

19. **Photos** – when and where it was taken, who is in it, or who took it

   Registration: look at your photos when they come back from the developer and attempt to remember who and what is in them; write on back the photo what, where, when as soon as you get it; periodically look over and remind yourself about old photos.

   Remembering: check the photos for notes.

20. **Prior statements in conversation** – remembering the point of view you expressed previously on an issue

   Registration: pay attention to expressed points of view, especially on controversial issues; keep track of positions of others and self after conversations that are likely to recur; in formal situation – notes, recording devices; try to only give points of view that you really believe in.

   Remembering: try to remember your previous positions; use conversation retrieval skills; recreate previous occasion; reconstruct likely position; think before speaking; let the other party begin first; elicit cues from others.

21. **Prior statements in correspondence** – made by you or by someone else

   Registration: keep track of your correspondence, especially important letters; keep notes on correspondence or copies.

> *Remembering*: recall purpose of the last letter; reconstruct what you might have said; look at previously received letters if you have them.

III. Intention Menus

Table of Contents

1. **Appointments and meetings** – realizing you have an appointment
2. **Birthday** – realizing you must honor someone with a card or gift on his or her birthday
3. **Chores** – realizing you have to do chores, as determined by yourself or another (spouse, parent, or roommate): such as cleaning up after a meal, taking out the garbage, feeding a pet, or leaving the toilet seat down
4. **Conversation** – remembering what you were saying after a distraction
5. **Correspondence** – realizing when to send correspondence properly, on time, and with the relevant information (such as thank you notes or business letters)
6. **Deadlines** – realizing that you must meet deadlines or due dates (such as license renewals or sending in forms)
7. **Errands, the nature of** – remembering which errands you intended to do or why you came to a room (see also the retrieval manipulations in Chapter 6 and the entry for "Events, general" in II Event Repertoires)
8. **Hurried message** – remembering something you were told in a hectic situation that you were supposed to pass on to a particular person (for example, relaying necessary information or conveying hot gossip) and delivering the message
9. **Packing for a trip** – remembering to pack all the necessary items to take on a trip
10. **Paying bills** – realizing that you must pay bills by a deadline
11. **Phone calls** – realizing that you must call someone at a certain time
12. **Proper behavior (etiquette)** – realizing that certain statements or actions are taboo in certain circumstances before committing them

13. **Return library books** – realizing that you must return library books before they are overdue
14. **Set clocks when time changes** – realizing that you should re-set your clocks and watch when seasonal time changes occur
15. **Spontaneous idea** – realizing that you must write down or act on an idea that came to you spontaneously when you were busy (for instance, when you were engaged in conversation)
16. **Spontaneous idea while asleep** – realizing later an act you wanted to do or an idea you wanted to use that came to you spontaneously while you were asleep
17. **Starting something on time** – realizing when you have to start something on time (such as when you are timing several items in cooking)
18. **Stopping something** – realizing that you must terminate something (such as stopping a sporting event, taking a roast out of the oven, or turning off lights when you leave a room)
19. **Take-aways, routine** – realizing that you should take routine carry-items with you (wallet, purse, comb, handkerchief, keys)
20. **Take aways, special** – realizing that you must take a certain or unusual item with you when you leave home
21. **Wake-up** – remembering to get up early or on time for a particular purpose

Intention Repertoires

1. **Appointments and meetings**
   Registration: imagine yourself going to the place of the appointment at the appropriate time; imagine what you will be doing just before the appointment and associate that activity with the appointment to follow; imagine the face of your watch set to the time of the appointment alongside of a symbolic image of the action that the appointment involves (such as a piggy bank to represent a trip to the bank; a shopping cart for the grocer's; a hammer for the hardware store); sketch or diagram what you are to do; imagine the consequences of doing the act and imagine the consequences of failing to do the act (Herrmann, 1996).
   Reminding: make a note about the appointment or meeting as soon as you can after arranging it; habitually keep a record of the things you have to do (an appointment book, calendar, di-

ary, bulletin board); transfer notes about new appointments into your appointment book as soon as possible; keep track of your intentions with a two-tier system of recording intentions – a calendar that keeps all long and short range intentions and an appointment book with the same information as well as any last-minute appointments; review your schedule at least twice a day – once at night to make sure that your plans are workable and once in the morning to energize them in your mind; use alarms, clocks, an alarm watch; you can ask another person to remind you; routinely change the environment when you cannot jot down an intention – such as tipping a lampshade, switching your watch to the other wrist, putting something on the floor in a conspicuous place.

2. **Birthday – Giving someone a card or gift**
   Registration: memorize the date and associate it with some other event that precedes it; record birthdays in address book as soon as you find out about them; transfer the date onto a calendar; keep the calendar in a conspicuous spot; post memos to yourself to send the card; purchase cards for everyone you send to at the beginning of the year – address and sign the cards and file them in appropriate slots of an object organizer divided into 12 months.

3. **Chores** – you have to do
   Registration: leave out tools for what is to be done (vacuum cleaner); avoid being deflected from the chores; notes, calendars, memo board; ask someone to remind you, such as the person who required or assigned the chores.

4. **Conversation** – remembering what you were saying after a distraction
   Remembering: retrace your thoughts; ask people you are talking to what they think about what you were saying – their answer will usually cue you to the topic; in a work situation, jot down your last thought as the distraction occurs.

5. **Correspondence** – sending correspondence on time and with the relevant information (thank you notes, business letters)
   Registration: write a note to yourself indicating the gift or topic; as soon after you decide that correspondence should be sent, make notes regarding its possible or necessary content; note on calendar and in appointment book when correspondence should

be written and sent; there is software for intention management and year-round clocks with alarms for pre-set dates on which to do things (see Chapter 10).

Remembering: check calendar, appointment book, or other external aids; you can depend on others to remind you at your own risk, except for secretaries whose job responsibilities often include "reminder services."

6. **Deadlines** – due dates (renewal of license, send in forms)
   Registration: imagine doing something that immediately precedes the deadline and associate it with the deadline – when you perform this associated act, it will then tend to evoke the deadline in your mind; the nature of the manipulations will vary with the kind of deadline involved – exact deadline tasks must be performed on or before a specific time; interval deadline tasks must be performed on or about a specific time; recurring deadlines must be met at routine times; optional intentions may or may not be performed on or about vague deadlines; obligatory deadlines require more preparation than the optional deadlines; exact deadlines invite more use of external memory aids like alarm watches than other kinds of intentions; 1) appointment book, calendar, diary, bulletin board, notes in obvious places; 2) alarms; ask a friend to remind you – risky; review schedule daily (Herrmann & Petro, 1990; Herrmann et al., 1996, 1999a).

7. **Errands** – which errands you intended to do or why you came into a room
   Registration: Carry one of your tools, utensils, or materials with you – it will remind you.
   Remembering: consult list and cross off items as you get them; return to the place where the intention was formed; reconstruct; look around for clues as to what you might have been doing; if list is not available, wander through the store glancing at products.

8. **Hurried message, something you were told in a hectic situation; delivering message on time**
   Registration: prioritize – note value of source and recipient (you may decide to forget the message); rehearse distributively; make up images for the content of message; rehearse aloud; repeat message to source; write message down at first opportunity; turn your watch over on your wrist or switch the watch to the

other wrist to remind you to write the message down later; set an alarm watch to remind you to write it down later; ask source to repeat ("No! Really? How is that again?"); ask source to remind you later to convey message (may not apply often); ask someone else to remind you; refresh often until you record the message on a reliable memory aid.

FORGET IT?

If you forgot
- Toothbrush
- Toothpaste
- Shampoo
- Iron
- Razor
- Hairbrush
- or almost
  anything

Call Guest
Request

HYATT
Thinking of you.

**FORGOT
SOMETHING?**

We want to make sure you're comfortable.
If you've forgotten or are in need
of any essential toiletry items,
check with our front desk
for the items you need.
Dial 503

Holiday Inn

Figure 17. Examples of Reminders Provided by Hotels to Travelers

9. **Packing for a trip**
   Remembering: imagine parts of the body and clothes for those parts; imagine what you will need for every day of the trip; keep a checklist for trips; unpack only those things necessary; keep dirty clothes in a bag near your suitcase.
   Remembering: imagine parts of body and clothes for those parts; make a checklist before you leave; systematically go through every drawer and closet – repeat this process after you have packed the suitcases and have placed them outside your room; ask someone to interview you about which things you may have left behind.

10. **Paying bills** – realizing that you must pay bills by a deadline
    Registration: note the due dates of bills on your calendar; review your calendar at least once daily; keep the bill in a visible place to serve as a reminder that it needs to be paid.

11. **Phone calls** – calling someone at a certain time
    Registration: imagine yourself standing by a phone next to a clock with the hands set to the time the call is to be made; put call in your appointment book; set an alarm; some automatic dialing systems have ability to alert you to when a call is to be made; regular review of your appointment book; leave a note in a visible place to serve as a reminder.

12. **Proper behavior** (etiquette) – realizing taboos before transgressing
    Registration: be sensitive to situations in which you might say or do the wrong thing; note your faux pas, and those of others, so history doesn't repeat itself.

13. **Return library books**
    Preparation: prioritize; consider consequences of failure; write return dates on your calendar a few days before the books are due; place the books by your front door.

14. **Set clocks when time changes** – when seasonal time changes occur
    Registration: mark on your calendar the Sunday in the spring and fall when the time is to change; remember the saying, "spring forward, fall back."

15. **Spontaneous idea, during conversation** – remembering to later write down an idea that came during a conversation
    Registration: during the conversation associate the idea with something you will do later; say little or nothing until you write

it down; continuously rehearse the idea; associate the idea with your prior activity; set wrist alarm to remind you later to make a note of the idea; ask a friend to remind you; place a note in a conspicuous place; if you have to do it shortly, put a memo in your hand; rehearse when you can.

Remembering: if there is a feeling of knowing, think of first letter, syllables, images of the task; brainstorm periodically to recall ideas you forgot; keep pads of paper or 3-by-5 cards with a pencil in a room; change the physical environment in some way (turn a ring; switch the wrists for your wristwatch; position something oddly on your desk, write a memo as soon as possible.

16. **Spontaneous idea, while asleep** – acting on or using an idea that occurred while you were asleep

Registration: dwell on the idea before going back to sleep; change the physical environment in some unusual way (for example, position something oddly on your night table, put your watch on the bedpost); keep a notepad at your bedside.

17. **Starting something on time**

Registration: prioritize task; associate the task with events that immediately precede it; imagine a large clock with the hands on the starting time as you picture yourself about to begin the action; set alarms and timers; remind yourself with increasing frequency as the starting time approaches.

18. **Stopping something** – (a sporting event, taking a roast out of the oven, turning off lights when you leave a room)

Registration: prioritize the task; imagine the things you will do during the interval and determine which thing is likely to precede the time for stopping; make up an image of a large clock with the hands placed at the time for stopping, and picture yourself alongside about to stop things; avoid leaving the scene of the event (for example, don't leave the kitchen); use alarms and timers.

19. **Take-aways, routine** – (wallet, purse, comb, handkerchief, keys, etc.)

Registration: check you pockets or purse before leaving home; use the same pockets consistently for particular items; keep a checklist; connect a chain to wallet, get in the habit of checking for wallet after transactions; leave keys in the car so you won't forget to bring them with you (risky, but some people do this).

20. **Take-aways, special** – certain or unusual items that are necessary
    Registration: prioritize what you must take; imagine act of leaving with the take-away item; placing take-aways in a regular spot (in front of door); periodic check of obligations; review take-aways before you leave; make a note; alarms.
21. **Wake-up** – getting up at a specific time to do something
    Registration: prioritize the next day's responsibilities; rehearse the intention ("I must get up at ___ o'clock to go to the dentist"); think of the consequences of failure; set the alarm clock; set two clocks (or a clock and a wristwatch alarm) if possible; place clocks in an unusual place (such as under the bed); leave the blinds up; put shoes, briefcase, or some other relevant object next to the bed; if at a hotel, ask for a wake-up call; arrange for a friend to check on you.
    Remembering: make yourself jump out of bed the instant you remember what you have to do that day; buy an extra clock.

IV. Action Menus

Table of Content

1. **Actions** – performing an action you have done before and avoid slips during it
2. **Drive to the right place** – remembering your destination while en route
3. **Gas cap, putting it back** – remembering to put the cap back on after getting gas
4. **Polite acts** – performing expected acts of courtesy
5. **Step in a sequence** – remembering where you are in an action that has several steps
6. **Utterances** – avoiding "slips of the tongue"

Action Repertoires

1. **Actions** – remembering what you were just doing (removing a key from a lock; turning off stove)
   Preparation: associate the place you are in with what you have

to do; attend to what you are doing; mentally repeat the name of the action and "done" on completing the action; realize what you are doing is important and concentrate on it throughout the day; imagine yourself performing task, rehearse – keep repeating your intention to do so; link the task to some aspect of where you are – thus, the context will serve to remind you of your task; write it down on a piece of paper and put it in a special place; do tasks on certain days; watch others and imitate them; when you stop, go over in your mind what you still have to do. *Remembering*: look at your surroundings, sometimes they will trigger what you were doing; retrace steps; jot down ahead of time what you are doing and then later refer to this note; use a checklist for common situations.

2. **Drive to the right place** – while en route
   Registration: imagine the destination and the route to the destination before you start out; remember what you are to do there.

3. **Gas cap, putting it back on** – after getting gas
   Remembering: always put the cap in the same conspicuous place, such as on top of the car or on the driver's seat; buy a car that connects the gas cap by wire cord to the car or have such a cord connected to your gas cap; position a memo on the dash reminding you to replace the cap; buy an extra gas cap and carry it with you in the trunk; go to a full-service gas station.

4. **Polite acts** – performing expected acts of courtesy
   Preparation: prioritize and make politeness habitual except for those who do not deserve it; review details of etiquette before events; anticipate the beginnings and endings to events where etiquette is critical – an opened door, someone handing you something, someone holding your coat, someone bumping into you, pauses in conversation; take your lead from others; discuss local customs with a native.
   Remembering: remind yourself of the level of etiquette called for by a situation; prepare by examining an etiquette book.

5. **Step in a sequence** – in an action with several steps
   Remembering: always finish a step and remember that you have done so; review what you have done; notice which steps are already done; observe those participating around you, ask.

6. **Utterances** – avoiding slips of the tongue
   Remembering: be aware of past slips involving words to be used;

in the case of word order problems, get some rest; once your patient has made a slip, be aware of it and the related content so as to monitor his or her speech when the topic recurs.

Summary

Manipulations vary in applicability because of the number and kind of steps they involve. Manipulations that use simple steps, requiring little prior learning, will apply to more tasks than manipulations involving complex steps, requiring considerable prior learning. It is time consuming tying to decide on the most appropriate manipulation to use. Therefore, before certain annoying tasks arise, prepare a repertoire of manipulations that are most suited to these tasks.

A manipulation involves one or more steps that are intended to achieve an end. In this book, all manipulations are intended to improve memory. Manipulations vary in how applicable they are to different memory tasks (Baddeley, 1982). General manipulations apply to many memory tasks. Specific manipulations apply to one or a few memory tasks.

9. Course and Task Specific Skills

We appreciate that you purchased this book to help improve your memory for matters relating to academic work (Mayer, 1998; Weinstein et al., 1989). This chapter emphasizes study-specific manipulations and study skills.

Keep in mind that the best advice is of little assistance if it is not heeded. Doing better academically often involves changing your study habits, and it always involves a willingness to work and to apply yourself. There are better and worse means to improve study skills, but there are no easy means to do so. Your success with the following techniques and strategies should be directly related to the amount of effort you are willing to invest in this enterprise (Hasher & Zachs, 1979).

Effective study skills follow the same rules, as do other memory skills. A person must devote as much attention as possible while employing the most appropriate manipulations and while being in the best physiological and emotive states. The previous chapter especially demonstrates that different kinds of materials require different kinds of study skills. For example, the faculty at a small liberal arts college was asked to suggest the study procedures they recommend that their students use in the elementary course of their discipline. Table 9-1 below shows that the recommended usage for any particular study skill varied across the different academic disciplines. A dramatic difference across disciplines was especially evident in the recommended use of flash cards and mnemonics. The variation in recommended use of study skills was greatest for the physical sciences, social sciences, and the humanities. The least variation in recommended use was for the languages. Clearly, faculties from different disciplines make different recommendations about the way their entry-level courses should be studied.

Table 9-1.   Mean Ratings of Study Skill Usage Recommended for Use in Introductory
Courses in Different Disciplines

Discipline	Skill usage										
	Flash	Out-line	Aloud	Notes	Sour-ces	Cate-gory	Visual	Mne-onics	Dia-gram	Terms	Facts
Physical Sciences	1.4	4.6	2.0	5.6	3.9	5.2	6.4	2.5	3.8	6.5	4.2
Social Sciences	1.1	4.2	2.7	4.2	3.2	6.3	3.6	2.2	2.7	5.8	3.9
Humanities	1.0	4.5	5.5	5.2	4.8	4.9	6.3	4.0	3.1	5.8	5.0
Behavioral Sciences	1.7	6.0	2.4	5.7	2.6	5.6	4.7	3.6	2.9	5.9	3.6
Languages	5.2	3.6	4.7	3.7	2.6	5.9	4.3	5.0	3.0	5.9	3.0

Note. These data are drawn from Herrmann (1987).
A rating of "1" represented "never" and a "7" always.
Physical sciences included at this institution: Math, Biology, Physics, Geology.
Social sciences: Government, History, Art History, Linguistics, Philosophy.
Humanities included: English, Speech, Theater.
Behavioral sciences: Psychology, Sociology, Anthropology, Economics.
Languages: German, French, Classics.

The study just discussed, examined the recommendations of different faculties. In another study, students who got an A or a C in both an art history course and an economics course were asked about their use of study skills. The results showed that students' use of study skills illustrated the same point made by the faculty recommendations – that different disciplines require different study skills. The students generally reported more use of study skills (lower numerical ratings) when taking economics than when taking art history. This result is in keeping with the reputation of economics on most campuses (that it is an unusually tough course). Not surprisingly, the A-grade students reported more use of different skills overall than did the C-grade students. The most used procedure for both A- and C-grade students was last minute reviewing.

One of the most striking differences between A-grade and C-grade students was studying by imagining content and rhyming. A-grade students imagined content more than C-grade students in both courses, but this was especially true when taking economics. Alternatively, A-grade students used rhyming substantially more than C students when taking art history. When taking economics, this difference was much smaller. The principle conclusion of this research is that good students make more use of study skills than average students. A-grade students tend to use certain procedures more than C-grade students. If the A-grade student is regarded as more of an expert in studying, then their ratings suggest the best procedures to use for these two courses.

Table 9-2. Ratings of Study Skill Usage

Kind of Skill	Nature of Course and Performance Level (High, Average)			
	Art History		Economics	
	High	Average	High	Average
Study Procedure				
Categorized	2.5	2.7	4.0	3.6
Imagine content	2.2	3.2	1.1	3.4
Imagine notes	2.8	3.8	2.4	2.5
Rhyme	3.1	5.3	4.0	4.8
Vocal rehearsal	4.3	5.8	5.4	5.7
Time Management				
Cram	3.3	3.8	4.0	4.1
Distribute studying	4.1	4.3	3.6	3.7
Last minute reviewing	1.6	2.0	2.2	2.4
External Study Aids				
Rewrite notes	4.2	4.4	4.4	3.5
Flashcards	5.4	6.9	4.9	7.0
Outline	5.3	4.0	4.7	4.3
Outside Source				
Other people	3.6	5.4	4.5	4.1
Non-course books	6.5	6.7	6.4	5.1

Note. The larger the number in this table, the less often the procedure was used by the students. A rating of 7 represents that the skill was never used. A number of 1 represented that the skill was always used. High represents students who received an A in both courses. Average represents students who received a C in both courses.

Many people do not change their study skills much from when they were in high school. Thus, there is often the tendency to study all courses in the same way. The authors hope that the studies described above will convince the reader that the most effective skills are content specific. Below we present an inventory of content specific manipulations that apply to some common study tasks.

An Inventory of Study Tasks

Table of Contents

1. **Answer to a question** – remembering an answer to a question that a professor asks you, but you cannot presently answer although you are sure you know
2. **Author** – remembering the author of a story, book, or poem.
3. **Class discussion, ill-prepared for** – remembering information to offer in a class discussion for a topic you know little about
4. **Current events** – remembering what is in the news
5. **Dates of events such as in history courses**
6. **Geography** – learning and remembering the locations of countries or states
7. **Grammar** – learning and remembering the rules of grammar
8. **Historical facts** – learning and remembering historical facts
9. **Information read previously** – remembering something that you read
10. **Languages** – learning a new language
11. **Lecture** – learning and remembering what was said in a lecture
12. **Lyrics** – learning and remembering lyrics of songs (see also "Poetry")
13. **Math-problem solutions** – learning and remembering solutions
14. **Melody** – learning and remembering the melody line of music you play or fancy
15. **Poetry** – learning and remembering poetry you wish to recite or quote
16. **Prose** – learning and remembering a passage, either according to its gist or verbatim
17. **Speeches** – learning and remembering the gist of a talk you must give (see also "prose")
18. **Spelling** – learning and remembering how to spell difficult words correctly
19. **Vocabulary** – learning and remembering unfamiliar words

Study Task Menus

1. **Answer to a question** – remembering an answer to a question that a professor asks you, but you cannot presently answer although you are sure you know it
Remembering: reflect on key terms; use the tip-of-the-tongue formula; make notes about related ideas to see if they trigger the answer; ask for a paraphrase of the question – the person's paraphrase will often trigger, if not contain, the answer; stall – the answer may come in time.

2. **Author** – remembering the author of a story, book, or poem
Registration: when you first read a story, book, or poem, associate your reactions to it with the name; note to yourself what other works have been written by the author that you know (if any); analyze the name for unusual characteristics – rare letter combinations, the name's ethnic origins; keep a notebook of works that are of special interest to you; form some "literary" friendships with people who like to discuss reading material of the kind you like.
Remembering: if you have a feeling of knowing, try to recall when and where you read this work; try to remember with whom you have discussed it; also see the entry on learning "names" of people-you-have-met in the Events section.

3. **Class discussion, ill-prepared for** – remembering information to offer in a class conversation for a topic you know little about
Registration: study up on possible topics of discussion prior to getting together with people; keep abreast of events and be well read; consult newsmagazines, encyclopedias; ask an informed friend to prime you on the topic.
Remembering: say nothing if nothing can be recalled; if you remember too little, you may seem naive or foolish; don't jump into the conversation right away, let the conversation elicit what you know; admit lack of knowledge or information before saying anything.

4. **Current events** – in the news or local events for class discussion or just for talking with people around campus
Registration: during reading or listening to the news, note half-dozen key events; test your recall of these events; read

newsmagazines regularly; discuss events with a certain person or persons regularly; associate current news to related previous events.

Remembering: reflect back on your key events; skim through a newsmagazine if it is available; ask others for their impression of a certain event or of current events generally – their answer will trigger your own ideas.

5. **Dates of events such as in history courses**

   Registration: note the century and associate the last two numbers with an age of someone you know; keep a notebook on dates you would like to remember; refresh yourself before situations in which remembering dates will be useful.

   Remembering: try to recall how you learned the date; notes.

6. **Geography**

   Registration: get a visual image of the outline of the geographical unit; verbally describe the shape to yourself (for example, V shaped on the bottom, left and right sides, flat and rectangular protrusion up on the top side = Texas); liken the shape of the unit to something you know (Italy, the boot); make sketches of the geographical unit in relation to other units – and check for accuracy; refresh occasionally.

   Remembering: recall how you learned about the piece of geography; look at a globe or atlas.

7. **Grammar**

   Registration: study a book on grammar; test yourself for the ability to state key rules; assess the logical impact of grammar rules; test your ability to articulate the grammatical deficiencies of poorly formed sentences (most grammar books make drills available with such sentences); test yourself and restudy when you notice yourself forgetting what you learned.

   Remembering: recall how you learned the grammatical point in question – its logic; a grammar book; consult someone who knows grammar.

8. **Historical facts**

   Registration: state the fact; paraphrase the fact; associate the fact with its precedents and consequences; imagine the event; relate past facts to current events; keep a notebook of important historical facts; get books on the historical era you are interested in and read them; find someone with similar historical interests and discuss them; review notebook periodically; make flash cards; highlight texts.

Remembering: reconstruct, retrace, conjure up associated image; if feasible, consult your notes or books.

9. **Information read previously**

   Registration: analyze the author's purpose – is it an expression of fact, opinion, analysis of a problem, or an advancement of a new idea or argument; concentrate; try and remember important points in diagrammatic/pictorial form; try to predict what the author will say as you read it or re-read it; try and summarize (mentally) each paragraph/section after reading; take notes; read in quiet conditions, without distractions; occasionally glance at notes.

   Remembering: imagine the place where you did the reading; reconstruct; look at notes.

10. **Languages – learning a new language**

    Registration: simple rehearsal – repetition in the case of vocabulary words; reviewing rules in the case of grammar; use flash cards; notes; associate or link unfamiliar English words to words or roots of the foreign language; consistently practice reading (silent and aloud) and speaking (alone and with others); listen to tapes (songs included) in the language.

    Remembering: use what you know as often as possible; use two-way dictionaries and grammar books.

11. **Lecture** – learn and remember what was said in a lecture (see also a study skills book, as listed in the References)

    Registration: predict what the speaker is going to say next; attend to summary statements and statements pointing out importance; take notes – but not too many so that it will deprive you of the chance to learn during the lecture; take just enough notes to remind you later; review.

    Remembering: reinstate the context; recall the summary statements.

12. **Lyrics of songs when taking a music appreciation class or just when talking socially**

    Registration: get the message of the lyrics in mind; learn each phrase one at a time; note how rhyming fixes – that is requires – certain words to be said; sing the lyrics, e.g., associate the lyrics with the music; sheet music; recordings; tapes.

Remembering: remember the message of the song; recall which sounds were the basis of rhyming and reconstruct which words contained this sound; consult sheet music.

13. **Math problem solutions** – learning and remembering solutions to math problems
    Registration: rehearse; practice; solve forwards and backwards; flash cards; explain problem to someone else; review.
    Remembering: think of problems you have solved that are similar to the one you are trying to solve (Schoenfeld & Herrmann, 1982; Sweller, 1989).

14. **Melody-lines of music such as in a music appreciation course**
    Registration: play each phrase and attempt to recall from memory (vocally or on an instrument); play successive phrases and note which ones have similar or reoccurring structure; imagine the notes on sheet music; associate with the lyrics – if no lyrics exist, make them up; sheet music; review and practice.
    Remembering: recall the structure of the song – reoccurring phrases, distinctive phrases; sheet music.

15. **Poetry**
    Registration: learn line by line – pick out key words; note patterns of phrase structure that are similar and different across lines; characterize its meter; say the lines with emphasis; rhythmic rehearsal – say the lines with a singsong or tonal variation; get the beat of each line and associate it with the beat of the last line; notes; books; recite to a friend with similar interests in poetry and discuss the reading.
    Remembering: recall the poem's structure and rhythm; notes or book if permissible.

16. **Prose**
    Registration: if learning the gist of a passage: – (1) reduce paragraphs to about six key terms; (2) diagram the paragraph or draw a network of the passage's ideas; (3) note the signposts to content: title, headings, topic sentences of paragraphs, illustrations, or summary; (4) analyze the relations between the key terms; generate synonym substitutes for the key terms, associate the key terms with a memory manipulation; (5) read aloud with emphasis; (6) picture the scene depicted; (7) paraphrase and simplify; (8) write a summary. In addition, you may wish to follow a prose study formula that prescribes the steps of study-

ing prose. For example, the SQ3R (survey, question, read, recite, and review) method has long been recommended to assist one in focusing study efforts (Robinson, 1986). However, recent research indicates that study formulas are usually not effective (Dansereau, 1985) unless the formula prepares one for a certain kind of prose, such as scientific writing. If learning a passage verbatim, follow the learning repertoire for poetry.

Remembering: if for gist, reinstate in your mind the paraphrases, the analyses, the images you used in learning; notes if permitted.

17. **Speeches** – the gist of a talk you must give (see also "Prose")
Registration: identify key terms in the speech and associate them in sequence with the Method of Loci; notes; go over and over the substance; rehearse as many times as you can.
Remembering: recall the key terms; consult notes.

18. **Spelling**
Registration: memorize rules of spelling in grammar or spelling books; practice spelling and checking the spelling of others (you need not challenge them); check books on how to improve your spelling.
Remembering: remember rules; think of a similar sounding word that you know how to spell; use a pocket speller; use a computerized spelling checker.

19. **Vocabulary**
Registration: any of those in Chapter 6; if you know something about the meaning of stems and roots of words, it helps to analyze how the word suggests its meaning; attend to the syllables of the word; routinely attempt vocabulary quizzes in magazines; bookstores carry several books on vocabulary acquisition; also, the VisEd Company makes a set of flash cards for useful English words; make your own flash cards of words you want to be sure of knowing; form friendships with people who value words – especially crossword puzzle enthusiasts; review from time to time; buy a new vocabulary book and see what you still know.
Remembering: 1) think of length, 2) think of the first letter, 3) think of related words; browse through dictionary under suspected letter; browse through a thesaurus under a related word; ask.

A Discussion of Specific Study Skills

The preceding study-specific manipulations should help you to learn and recall various types of academically related information. In an academic setting, these manipulations are most effective when combined with appropriate strategies for study. Below are a series of study strategies that we have developed over more than 40 years of college teaching. We have exposed our students to these strategies in the past, and those who have mastered them have displayed a marked improvement in their academic performances.

As in the case of study manipulations, mastery of these skills will require some attention and effort on your part, but the dividends should be significant and immediate. Accompanying the following text are a series of study guides to which you may refer for a quick refresher on some of the more important skills. Since academic work can involve disparate courses, the following material has been organized to be independent of any particular subject matter – yet to be appropriate for any course.

Study Blueprint

In studying, as in many other endeavors, it helps to be organized and to have a broad perspective on what is expected of you. The purpose of our study blueprint is to remind you of activities that can improve your study performance (Breme & Rosen, 1982; DiYanni, 1997). We will elaborate on these activities in subsequent study guides (see Figure 18).

Strategy. Keep in mind that any course you are taking has been carefully planned by the instructor. Try to develop an understanding of the instructor's objectives. Your biggest asset in this task will be the course syllabus. It is not simply a compilation of assignments. Instead, view it as a road map that displays an intellectual journey on which the instructor wishes to take you.

Try to ascertain the instructor's destination. To the extent that you can do this, you will find that classes make more sense, that you can anticipate developments, and that you may even discover shortcuts, arriving at the journey's end ahead of most and without strain or fatigue. A good sense of the direction the course is taking will enable you to determine better which portions of the terrain are most interesting and important. Do not become so immersed in detail that you miss the general direction of the course. Quite simply, without a sense of direction you can become lost.

Students generally know how to study but because of boredom, fatigue, or anxiety, they often forget to engage in all of the study activites that would be desirable. The **Study Blueprint** will remind you to do all of the activities you should.

Strategy: find your unique challenges of a course the first week of class.

Indepth Reading Procedures:

> *Pre-read* -- your first reading may be your last so make it effective.
>
> Read headings; the summary; identify key words; identify examples; examine figures and tables; read questions at end of chapter; if there are problems - analyze the givens and what is asked of all problems.
>
> *Read* -- generate questions that appropriately ask about what is in the text.
>
> *Post-read* -- skim; generate questions about the gist.

Meaning-Extraction Techniques:

> Outline, hierarchy, key word list, relations table (table shows how one set of elements relates to another, e.g., countries by characteristics, species by attributes, etc.), flowchart, graph, pictograph, historical time line.

Note Taking:

> After class, generate questions that address each paragraph or cluster of notes; continue to condense -- take notes on notes, and notes on notes on notes...

Exam Preparation:

> *Plan your preparation* -- how much to study and when; overview of time, part time; study time; self-test time.
>
> *Gather questions* from notes and texts; identify kinds of questions; design the exam as you predict it.
>
> *Test yourself repeatedly* and/or do problems over; decide what you don't know.
>
> *Study and memorization*
>
>> Rehearse - silent/aloud; act out; cumulative; rhythmic.
>>
>> Associate - with something in your past; with other knowledge; with words or concepts.
>>
>> Make relevant - identify ideas which are similar, different, and in the same class.
>>
>> Make an alternative mental record - transform (paraphrase, restate), reduce (acronym - e.g., NOW = National Organization for Women); elaborate (as on a story).
>>
>> Test again - review material before going to sleep; program self to be relaxed.
>>
>> Take care of yourself - get enough sleep; eat well; relax before the exam; and do **not** review material immediately before the exam.

Exam Strategies:

> Read test; take 1 minute to plan use of time.
>
> *Multiple choice* -- answer what you know first; eliminate wrong alternatives.
>
> *Essay* -- jot down a few key terms or ideas first; then write.
>
> *Problem* -- seek a pattern to the solution; mentally compare with homework assignments.
>
> *Post exam* -- paper; lab; practicum; analysis.

(Remember to take an active, not a passive attitude toward your studying. Don't become so involved in details that you lose the general overview -- that is often the source of essay questions. Good Luck!)

Figure 18. Study Blueprint

Indepth reading procedures. As many students have discovered (often painfully), when an instructor makes a reading assignment, simply turning the pages and reading the words is seldom sufficient for good understanding of the material.

Reading is best viewed as an active undertaking in which you contribute to the outcome, rather than simply passively receiving wisdom. One of the most difficult things for students to realize is that books and articles not infrequently contain errors of reasoning that can be perceived by nearly anyone who is alert for them. Indeed, some of your instructors are likely to choose certain readings that contain weaknesses just to give your critical abilities some exercise. Shortly, we will supply you with some specific techniques to promote your understanding, retention, and ability to deal critically with material you read.

Meaning extraction techniques. As a student, you will experience a large number of assignments from widely differing courses. In the process of completing these responsibilities, you will encounter a formidable amount of information. Accept that you cannot memorize everything you encounter, nor should you. Instead, you should utilize means to identify and extract important information that relates both to the specific assignment and to the more general objectives of the course. There are a variety of techniques we will discuss below that can be employed to extract meaning from readings, lectures, and other formats. However, all of these techniques require you to actively process the information to which you are exposed. Again, an active approach not only helps you to understand material better, it also aids in your retention of that material.

Note taking. Unless you are skilled at shorthand or write remarkably fast, it is unlikely that you can write down everything an instructor says. Indeed, even if you could, you shouldn't. Most instructors will try to make two to three major points in a single class. Everything else is amplification, example, bridging concepts, and context.

You will want to develop the ability to recognize the major points of a lecture and to make sure that you have them properly related to one another (Anderson & Ambruster, 1991). You will also need to include sufficient context, so you can reconstruct the important elements of the class later. Most students do not reexamine their lecture notes until immediately before an examination. They frequently discover that their notes are insufficient and vague, because the information that was in their heads during the lecture has since disappeared.

Until you have developed good note-taking skills, try spending ten minutes immediately after a class reviewing your notes, while asking yourself whether a stranger would understand their importance and the context. At this point, you will still retain the context of the class, and you can easily fill in whatever information may be necessary to establish context and interrelationships. Remember, the next time you look at your notes you will be the stranger you imagined.

Exam preparation. Most students, often with considerable justification, dread examinations. Having taken an exam, many are surprised to discover that they were not as familiar with the course material as they had thought themselves to be. Others find that preparing for an exam takes a great deal of time without yielding appropriate benefits. However, if you have been following the four study guides listed above, you should find that you have less trouble preparing for exams than others, and your performance should reflect your prior organization and active approach to the materials.

Examinations are usually designed to test your understanding as well as your recall of course material. Many instructors will assume that you remember the material to which they exposed you, and they will want to see what you can do with it. Can you manipulate information in meaningful ways to construct answers to questions that you may not have encountered before? As with other study skills, preparing to take an examination benefits from both an active approach and a continuing attempt to maintain an overview on the objectives of the instructor. Additionally, examinations place considerable emphasis on your ability to accurately recall information. In addition to suggestions concerning exam preparation below, we have included a condensed list of four memory strategies that should help you to focus on and retain useful information.

Exam strategies. Many students who spend considerable time and energy preparing for an examination still fare poorly. The difficulty may be due in large part to the dreaded "white-out" – a state of mind (or perhaps better, a state of non-mind) where all facts disappear from consciousness and the brain refuses to focus on anything more than its inability to achieve focus. Physiology often contributes to this condition in the form of elevated adrenaline levels, which can interfere with concentration and cause such undesirable phenomena as "butterflies," indigestion, headaches, etc.

Higher adrenaline levels can easily stem from worry about the exam situation, and they directly relate to perceived stress. In particular, students who are aware they are not properly prepared for an exam are more prone to experience a level of stress that can interfere with effective exam taking. This is a problem you are less likely to encounter if you follow the advice we present in this chapter. However, it is perfectly natural to be somewhat tense before a testing situation. One means to reduce the likelihood of stress-related problems is to take a brisk walk a half-hour before the exam. Your system is prepared for physical activity, and the walk will help to reestablish normal adrenaline levels. It will also give you an opportunity to mentally rehearse the subject areas on which you will be examined, and to reestablish your overview of the course.

The approach for dealing with multiple-choice questions is quite different from that for treating essay questions. We supply some particular advice on taking each type of exam below, but throughout both experiences there are two consistencies. We urge you to take an active approach to the questions, and encourage you to stay in control of your answers rather than letting the questions push you around.

Indepth Reading Procedures

Virtually every instructor will suggest that students read assigned material before the class in which it will be discussed. Perhaps one in two students will heed this advice. Postponing the reading does not make it easier to do. In contrast, coming to class prepared will help you derive more from each session. Doing so also increases the likelihood that you will participate in class discussion, something many instructors reward (see Figure 19).

Pre-reading. The Study Guide on In-depth Reading Procedures contains directions for pre-reading. Despite your probable desire to complete the assignment in a timely fashion, this is worth the time and effort it takes (Anderson, 1985; Nist & Mealey, 1991; Pearson, 1984). It will orient you to the material, give you a clearer understanding of the objective of the reading, and an appreciation of where the material fits into the general course format (Meyer, Young, & Bartlett, 1989). In short, it saves you time in the long run, and increases the likelihood that you will benefit from the reading.

Reading. If you take an active approach to the material you read, you will seek not only the meaning of the work, but also the purpose and plan of the author (Mandl & Trabasso, 1992; McWhorter, 1986; Postman, Keckler, & Schneckner, 1985). Be sensitive to the possibility of errors and shortcomings in the assignment. Pay particular attention to what are termed "unstated assumptions." Few authors clearly state the premises on which their work rests, yet these are frequently necessary for a full appreciation of their position. Identifying premises is equally important for de-

Examinations often occur long after an assignment has been read. Developing good reading habits can save both time and effort when facing an examination. Such habits will also make classes more interesting.

Pre-Read:

Seek the major objective of the reading -- the task is to identify the central topic, argument, or idea of reading and assess how the author supports the position. Keep in mind that any reading assignment usually has only one major objective, though there may be important supporting material.

Strategies for pre-reading -- read headings, summary questions at end of chapters, etc. Identify key words and examples; examine figures and tables. Try to discover the major objective of the author, how it is arrived at, and how supported. The objective is to be ready to begin reading with a good sense of where the author is heading and how he or she will get there.

Read:

Starting to read -- the first two pages of most articles will reveal the goal of the author. Assess this and also try to recognize the premises or propositions on which the article or chapter is based. Identifying unstated assumptions is often an excellent start toward critiquing an author's position.

Taking notes while reading -- do not become immersed in detail. Note major issues, how they relate to each other, and how they are supported. Reduce your outline notes to a two or three line summary including key words. This is what you will commit to memory for examinations, and it will serve to access the broader context of the chapter or article. Remember that the next time you review these notes you will probably be preparing for an examination.

Post-Read:

Generate questions -- appropriately ask about what is in the text. What important principles are illustrated by the reading? Are there words, tables, charts, concepts, or statistics that you didn't adequately understand? (If so, it may be well worth the effort to seek clarification on these points.)

Develop a sense of context -- how does the reading concern other readings you have done for this course? Does it support or disagree with other readings you have been assigned? (If so, it may suggest an essay question that your teacher may employ.) How does the reading relate to the class for which it was assigned - does it integrate with or conflict with material presented by your teacher?

Assess the importance of this reading -- you will want to devote more study time to those readings that are of greatest significance. Are there other readings that cite or are based on this one? Was the reading discussed in class? Was it the focus of a paper assignment? If any of the preceding are the case, the reading is likely to be useful in your examination.

Figure 19. Indepth Reading Procedures

veloping critiques of an author's position. If you can demonstrate the falseness or inappropriateness of a work's premises, you can discredit the entire effort. For instance, we have assumed, without stating it, that many students are interested in improving their memories and study skills. If this assumption can be called into question, the entire rationale for this book is jeopardized. Often your best critiques of readings will employ similar fundamentals, rather than becoming bogged down in concerns about petty details.

Your task is to ascertain what is important about the work and how that relates to the course. Resist the temptation to skip over portions of the book that involve tables, charts, or points that are difficult to follow. It is frequently in such areas that authors synthesize major evidence and/or arguments.

When reading, remember that, unless stated otherwise, the instructor probably does not intend for you to memorize the entire content of the assignment. Identify the one, two, or three major arguments of the assignment, and the best evidence for these arguments. Then make a few clear notes that contain sufficient context for you to reconstruct their significance when you review them for an exam. Do not become mired in detail. Continually strive to identify the major points in a work and view the remainder as secondary. Doing this will not only facilitate an active understanding of the reading, it will also greatly ease your preparation for exams in the future. Finally, it will reduce the volume of material you have to retain.

Post-reading. Having read the assignment, you are in a good position to assess its importance in terms of course objectives. Did the assignment contain pivotal information, or did it supplement and amplify points made by other authors and/or by the instructor in class? There is considerable value in perceiving such interrelationships. First, at the abstract academic level, it will help tie information together into a more meaningful bundle. Second, at the practical level, instructors are aware of such interrelationships – they usually work hard to set them up – and these are therefore fruitful areas for examination questions.

Meaning Extraction Techniques

The amount of information you will encounter in courses requires selective organization. You do not wish to record and to recall all the information you are exposed to, but you will need means to extract and organize that which is most salient (Caverly & Orlando, 1991). There are a variety of techniques that you may employ to accomplish this, and all carry the same benefit. They require you to actively transform the information. Doing so helps you to perceive interrelationships, encourages you to assess the importance of information, and, as we noted in earlier chapters, active processing markedly improves recall (see Figure 20).

Verbal Techniques

Note taking. Many people think that note taking in college is the same activity that secretaries engage in when they take dictation from their boss or that court recorders do when they take down everything that happens in court. However, note taking in a college class is different. A student taking notes should not write down everything the professor says. Instead, the student should take down those details he or she would not remember later. Notes taken in class are not intended to be the same as a dictated letter or court record.

Notes serve to focus your attention and facilitate your registration of key material that you would not be able to recall after class is over. Notes do not replace the need for rehearsal and study techniques. Rather, notes ensure that you go over the difficult information. Additionally, they force you to better organize your mental records (Anderson & Ambruster, 1991; Intons-Peterson & Newsome, 1992).

Intons-Peterson and Newsome (1992) reviewed the evidence on the usefulness of external memory aids. They made the point that no memory aid, whether internal or external, is going to be of value if individuals do not appreciate when, and when not to use them. The evidence strongly points to the developmental nature of the appreciation of memory aids. Beal (1988), for example, found young children poor at assessing the value of memory aids, whereas students were much more aware of when they should be used. Intons-Peterson (1993) reports a study in which students involved in a paired associate learning task were usually able to recognize when the use of external memory aids (note-taking) would be of value. Those students who did not take notes performed considerably less well than those who did take notes.

Note taking in lectures has been extensively studied. In a review of 56 studies, Kiewra (1985) found note taking to be shown to be beneficial in 33 of the studies. Clearly, there are some situations where note taking is less effective than others. These limitations appear where the amount of information given is dense, where presentation is rapid, and where the material presented is not well organized. However, as Intons-Peterson and Newsome (1992) point out, the evidence also shows that high achieving students take more notes, suggesting individual differences in the ability to take good notes from lectures. Of course, 'good' students in one situation may be 'poor' students in another.

As noted earlier, interest and a previous knowledge base make a major difference to the meaningfulness and ease of processing new information. Generally, notes help students the most when they are neither a verbatim record nor just a few words; notes somewhere in between are best. A similar principle applies to the use of highlighters. Students who cover the pages of their book with highlighter learn little; about the same as students who do not use highlighter or who do not underline. Judicious highlighting or underlining leads to the most learning.

After class, a wise student reviews notes soon after class and generates questions that address the material covered in class as well as the reading. Prior to exams, students should take notes on their notes, making them shorter each time. Crib sheets facilitate last minute preparation for exams.

Outline. This is a common means for abstracting and organizing information Properly done, outlines provide a view of a body of information that is organized in terms of more inclusive categories. There are two forms of utility here. We encourage you to recognize the major points of a work and what they are based upon. Also, organizing the material in outline form provides you with a mental flag that you can use to access more specific information. In the Study Guide example, the term sociological theory can help you to recall functionalism and conflict theory, the background to these theories, etc.

Remember that outlines need not be detailed (that's why they're called outlines), but they must be logically constructed. If you discover that you are having difficulty organizing material in outline form, it probably means you are having problems with comprehension and/or overview. It is much better to work at these issues now and solve them, than to re-encounter them when you are trying to prepare for an examination.

Hierarchy. This is a particular type of outline that places even more emphasis on the development of inclusive structures. Hierarchical representations are not appropriate for all forms of information, but they are particularly useful in the sciences, and for those aspects of other disciplines that emphasize vertically structured and logical relationships.

As the example on the accompanying Meaning Extraction Technique Study Guide demonstrates, hierarchies generally present less informational context than standard outlines, but they graphically represent structure relationships in a manner that is easy to assimilate and recall. As in the case of more general outlines, creating a hierarchy is a learning process that will help you to better understand the information you encounter.

Key word list. This is a meaning extraction technique that can be used for virtually all types of information, but its utility is limited. Key word lists provide you with an inventory of terms to which you have been exposed, but they do not ask you for any organization or overview of the material. Thus, key word lists do little to improve your perception of interrelationships. They have little utility in preparing for essay examinations, but are somewhat useful for multiple-choice examinations. They provide a means of assessing your general familiarity with course concepts, and unlike some of the techniques discussed here, you can construct them easily and quickly. Flash cards can improve the rate at which you will

The ability to extract and organize important concepts and propositions from class notes and reading assignments is one of the most important skills a student can possess. This study aid will familiarize you with some of the more effective techniques for extracting meaningful content from your readings and lectures.

Visual Techniques:

Flowchart - emphasizes dynamics of interrelationships, displays processes:

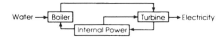

Graph - furnishes an excellent means of presenting complex relationships between two or more variables:

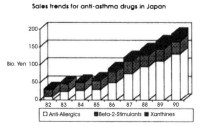

Historical Time Line - provides a convenient means of representing multiple events:

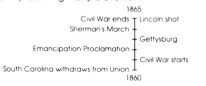

Verbal Techniques:

Outline - one of the most popular and reliable techniques for organizing and abstracting information:

   I. Sociological Theories
       A. Functionalism
          1. basic assumptions
          2. criticisms
       B. Conflict Theory....

Hierarchy - a means of organizing information into progressively more inclusive (and often more important) structures

Relations Table - shows how one set of elements relates to another and allows a quick comparison across the elements comprising the table. Thus:

Figure 20. Meaning Extraction Techniques

learn key words, but they do nothing to promote your appreciation of the framework embracing the terms you study.

Relations table. A table of relations usually represents interrelationships across a range of items. It differs from a hierarchy in emphasizing vertical relations less, while making horizontal relations much clearer. You can employ relations tables to integrate information on a rather wide variety of topics, and doing so yields a significant study benefit.

Creating such a table forces you to seek relations across elements you have encountered in a course. This gives you an excellent sense of the interrelationships among the course's basics, and it promotes the development of the broad overview we are recommending. Not incidentally, a well-prepared relations table is an excellent study device. It provides you with an easily assimilated representation of the information in the course that can be reviewed and recalled in less time than you would need for other techniques. The catch (you were expecting one, weren't you?) is that constructing such tables can be time consuming and difficult. However, if you are willing to invest the time as the course progresses, you will soon discover that examinations cease to be causes for great concern. Indeed, you should shortly find yourself spending much less time in exam preparation, yet performing significantly better. It is a bit like preparing food ahead of time for the freezer. The preparation can be laborious, but at mealtime all you need do is throw it in the oven.

Visual Techniques

There are a variety of visual techniques that can be utilized to represent information and interrelations among elements. The success of these techniques depends to some degree on their appropriateness for the material, and also on the user. Humans rely on vision for the majority of information they process. However, we differ in our ability to develop and retain visual images (Garry & Polaschek, 2000; Richardson, 1991). For some, this is a difficult undertaking. For others, it is both easy to do and easy to recall. You will need to assess your own strengths and weaknesses in deciding the degree to which you will adopt the visual techniques described below.

Flowchart. As the name suggests, flowcharts are particularly good for dealing with process and for displaying the way a system operates and changes over time. They are quite useful for developing an overview of a system and an appreciation of cause-effect relations within a system.

You may find it helpful to color-code some of the elements in the flow-chart to reflect membership in a similar class or category. Thus, in the Meaning Extraction Techniques Study Guide, the arrows linking water to boiler, and boiler to turbine might be in blue representing water. The arrows from turbine to electricity, and from internal power to other parts of the system might be in yellow. This will help you to perceive and recall that these relations are electrical. Similarly, a colored representation of the physiology flow chart might depict the heart and lungs as the same color and different from the body, which is a more inclusive system.

Graph. For certain kinds of information, graphs cannot only usefully represent interrelationships, they may be a necessary means of doing so (Larkin & Simon, 1987). In the sciences and social sciences, you are often asked to perceive and understand interrelationships between two or more variables. Many disciplines rely heavily on graphs to display such relationships. Constructing a graph provides a comparatively simple image of what may be a very complex set of relations. You will also come to better understand the function of graphs, and you will be able to read them more readily. This has a practical value, since many science and social science examinations employ graphs in the construction of questions.

Historical time line. As the name suggests, this technique is used principally to represent a sequence of historical events. It condenses a good deal of information into a visual format that can represent not only the order of events, but also the intervals between them. This technique is not restricted to historical materials. It can be used with any sequence of events, ranging from the steps in developing film to those involved in studying for an examination.

Mind maps. Sometimes information is not so tightly organized and is not easy to represent as a graph, flowchart, outline, relation table, or a time line. Instead the information is more easily represented as a map. Instead of towns and cities on the map, there are key concepts – often put in circles. Instead of roads and highways, there are associations between one concept and another. The circles can be made of different sizes to convey importance. Associations join traces to one another in either a uni-directional or bi-directional manner. Mind maps, sometimes called spider maps, lead you to extract information from class and readings, and at the same time provide material to study for an exam (Gruneberg & Mathieson, 1997).

Exam Preparation

If you use the techniques described above, you will find that you have been preparing for your examinations all along. Nonetheless, you will probably wish to spend time preparing for a specific exam shortly before you have to take it (see Figure 21). Preparing for any given exam requires some forethought, organization, and memory (Wark & Flippo, 1991). Given your prior preparation, you should be able to follow the suggestions below easily – and with less investment of time – than your peers.

One seldom-discussed aspect of preparing for an examination involves assessing the instructor. Good instructors will be interested in your ability to actively manipulate course concepts and information, while poor instructors may simply want you to tell them what they have told you. Regrettably, what prepares you well for the exams of poor instructors won't work for good ones. However, what works well for the exams of good instructors also tends to work for the exams of poor ones. If in doubt about the intent and style of your instructor, it is safer to assume that he or she is good, and is intent on developing your ability to synthesize and criticize.

Plan your preparation. Do not postpone preparing for an exam. Delaying your start doesn't make your work any easier. Instead, it encourages you to see the preparation process as complex and daunting. You will find it very helpful to break your preparation into segments rather than viewing the whole task as one great mountain of information to be clambered over and laboriously mapped. Allocate a given amount of time for each segment and set up a place and time where you can study well. Finally, leave time for integrating the segments prior to the exam.

The process of integration involves developing an overview of the general objectives of the course and how things fit together. Again, relating your specifics back to the syllabus is often a useful means of synchronizing your efforts and perceptions with those promoted by the course.

When you review your readings and lecture notes, do so as an integrated packet, and be alert for interrelationships. Remember that your instructor consciously chose your readings to coincide with specific material being presented in class. Once you have covered each class, seek out connections across classes and between their respective readings. A good instructor will often incorporate such interrelations in the plan of a course

You will develop a good sense of possible essay questions if you can anticipate those aspects of the course that the instructor deems most important. One means of sharpening your ability to forecast exam content is to develop your own questions. In the case of essay questions, strive for

Preparing for an examination should be an active enterprise in order to be effective. You generally have two major tasks: to recall information and to manipulate it in response to questions. The techniques described below will help you to master both these objectives and will, if practiced responsibly, increase your confidence in exam taking situations.

Plan your Preparation:

Time management -- decide how much you are to study, what times of the day and where. Break down what is to be learned into parts and study these as well as the entirety.

Try to develop an overview -- remember that your instructor will be interested in your ability to remember, to understand, and to deal actively with the course material. While details are important, take time to devleop an appreciation of concepts and of how things fit together.

Review your reading assignments and lectures -- examine where and how they integrate. Areas where readings and lectures cross-relate, or where two or more lectures focus on a given concept or particular material, are likely to be the subject of considerable attention, including essay questions.

Anticipate – devise possible essay and multiple choice questions from your notes and from the readings, again paying attention to points of intersection. Design an exam as you think it will be and try it. Even if your choices are mistaken, you will be forced to interrelate the materials for which you are responsible.

Test yourself -- answer questions and/or do problems over and over again. Periodically decide what you do not know, focus on it, and repeat the study cycle.

Study and Memorization: Four Strategies _

Increase the strength of a memory

Take a mental snapshot -- scan it systematically, close your eyes,and question yourself.

Register multimodally -- with as many senses as you can.

Act out -- imagine key events and overtly act them out.

Rehearse simply -- repeat items over and over.

Rehearse cumulatively -- repeat successively larger groupings of items.

Make the memory relevant

Analyze visually -- break down the visual characteristics into meaningful patterns.

Identify attributes -- verbally describe what is to be learned.

Analyze the meaning -- examine all of the implications of the information.

Prioritize -- judge the importance of the knowledge to be learned.

Personalize -- relate information to you or to part of your past.

Associate

Connect present with past events.

Identify meaningful relationships -- such as synonyms, contrasts, or category commonali

Cluster by meaning -- group items with similar meanings and, if possible, group the resulting groups.

Sequence – arrange items in their natural sequence.

Diagram -- sketch the relationship of items to be learned.

Create frameworks for retrieval

Elaborate numbers and dates -- state in the form of years, phone numbers, moneyminutes, etc.

State principles -- describe a pattern or regularity that is apparent in the material to be learned.

Abbreviate -- form a smaller word by using a few letters from a larger word or words

Sentence or story generation -- form a sentence or story that contains the items to be learned.

Imagine items linked -- form an image linking the first and second terms, then the second and third, etc.

Figure 21. Exam Preparation

those that involve a synthesis of course materials, questions that require you to put things together. Do not waste time on essay questions that simply call for a recapitulation of information. Even if you are confident that this is the nature of the task you will be facing, you will get a great deal more out of the material if you prepare it actively. When preparing for multiple-choice questions, be sensitive to areas of the readings or lectures where there may be conceptual confusion. Do not avoid such problem areas; instead, seek them out. They often produce questions that can be quite difficult to manage, unless you have spotted the problem in advance and prepared for it.

Study and memorization. No matter what kinds of intellectual tasks you will be required to perform, you must first recall the information before you can act upon it. Examinations, even the best and most active, always place a premium on being able to recall information. No doubt this helped motivate you to purchase this book.

In preceding chapters, we have presented, often with considerable detail, information and a series of mental manipulations that should help you to develop a better, more accurate memory. On the accompanying Exam Preparation Study Guide (Figure 20) we have created a reference list of the four memory strategies that are apt to be most appropriate for your needs and specific suggestions for exam preparation (Anderson, 1980; Annis, 1983; Nist & Diehl, 1985; Pauk, 1984; Weinstein et al., 1989; Weinstein & Mayer, 1986). These include directions for increasing the strength of a memory by employing a variety of techniques to focus on and manipulate the information you wish to recall. We also include suggestions for making particular memories relevant to particular tasks and to the general objectives of the course. We list means for associating memories with one another and for clarifying sequential and structural relationships. Finally, we suggest means you can employ to create meaningful frameworks to organize more specific memories, so that these may be retrieved in an orderly fashion. Each specific suggestion has been fully explained earlier in this book. These explanations can usually be found in Chapters 6 and 7, or by using the index.

Exam Strategies

The work you have done to this point will have helped you understand and recall the course material. However, in terms of your academic performance, all your previous work may mean little if you cannot effectively perform in an examination setting. Every teacher has encountered exam performances that do not seem to accurately reflect a student's understanding. In the worst of situations, a good student may "clutch" and be unable to recall, organize, and convey information appropriately (see Figure 22).

Common exam catastrophes include answering an insufficient number of questions, overlooking an exam page completely, misreading a question and providing an excellent answer for a question that wasn't asked, and failing to answer. Sometimes the failure to answer involves being unable to answer a question that the student is sure he or she knows the answer to (Gruneberg, Smith, & Winfrow, 1973). On some occasions, students may experience a "white out" in which they "freeze" or have their mind "go blank," rendering the student unable to produce a coherent response to questions. More common problems involve exam performances that display poor organization, that miss major connections between the elements of a course, and that fail to reflect an adequate familiarity with course material. For obvious reasons you will want to avoid these difficulties (Flippo, 1988).

The advice contained in this chapter and earlier ones can greatly increase the likelihood that your exam performance will accurately reflect your familiarity with and understanding of course information. Of course, if you fail to pursue the ideas contained in this book and to work on your studies, that accurate reflection may not be a flattering one.

Preliminaries. A degree of reasoned confidence is one of your best defenses against "white out." If you have followed much of the advice contained in these chapters, you can rightfully expect to be well prepared for any examination.

As you approach an exam, remember that your instructor expects it to be both an opportunity for you to exhibit your understanding of the course's contents, and a learning experience. Recall the overview you have developed on the course, as it may prove very useful in dealing with specific questions. Remember that accuracy is much more important than verbosity.

Most students are nervous about the limited time available for examinations. Consequently, they often begin answering questions as soon as they open an exam book. The idea seems to be, if they are writing, they are performing as they should. Resist this temptation. Spend a few minutes familiarizing yourself with the exam and how it is structured. This will save time later, and will help prevent misinterpretation of the instructions or the questions.

An overview of the exam can greatly assist you in planning how you will apportion your time and effort on specific questions. Some students

Students who have studied faithfully and prepared well for examinations may still encounter significant problems when they actually take an exam. While examinations are probably the most stressful aspect of the student experience, the strategies below should enable you to make the most of your preparation.

Preliminaries:

Keep your confidence. Remember that you are better rested and better prepared than most.

Don't be afraid to spend some initial time becoming familiar with the exam.

Read the exam through quickly. Be sure you understand the instructions and the questions. Don't panic if some of the questions initially seem somewhat obscure.....remember you haven't applied yourself yet.

Plan realistically how you will use your time and note the way examination points are distributed (e.g., if two essay questions are worth half of the exam points, you should spend approximately half of your time on them).

Multiple Choice Questions:

Remember, these questions are usually written very carefully and may be somewhat tricky. Read quickly, but carefully.

Treat each question as if it seeks a precise response (it usually does).

Answer the questions you know first, then return and answer those questions for which you can eliminate at least one wrong alternative.

Eliminate alternatives by comparing one with the others. Don't assume that the first alternative which seems familiar is the correct one. Read them all and watch out for absolutes such as always, all, everyone, etc. These frequently invalidate an alternative.

Essay questions:

Read questions carefully and take time for thought. Try to identify the central issue(s). Generally, an essay requires synthesis or seeks the application of a major concept or method that is prominent in the course. The teacher will normally use essay questions to test your general comprehension and ability to deal actively with the course.

Make a brief outline or at least some notes on your major points. Stay in charge of your answer. Don't succumb to the concept that more words make a better essay. Shorter more accurate answers are preferable to lengthy displays of poorly organized information.

If you include much detail, make sure it is pertinent to the question. You may get marked down for factual errors on information which you never needed to include.

Problem Solving:

Read carefully and identify the nature or class of the problem you are facing. Once you have identified the class of problem, translating it into a familiar formula or structure is much simpler.

Seek for a familiar pattern. If it is a word problem, try to find an underlying structure that you have dealt with in homework assignments, etc.

At the End:

Re-read the instructions. Have you answered all the questions you were supposed to? (A significant number of students lose points because they fail to follow instructions.)

Re-read the major essay questions. Have you interpeted the questions accurately?

(Later, when your exam is returned to you, study it carefully. Try to identify the types of mistakes you may have made so that you can improve your performance next time. Remember -- exam taking is a skill and.continued effort and practice will make you better at it. Good Luck!)

Figure 22. Exam Strategies

take a cursory look and then save the biggest parts of the exam for last. This is frequently a bad idea, especially if the student is left with insufficient time for the section. Obviously, more time should be devoted to those portions of the exam that carry more weight in grading. Your instructor should have weighted portions of the exam to reflect their importance and/or their difficulty. Consequently, such areas need and deserve extra time.

Multiple-choice questions. Multiple-choice questions place a premium on your ability to selectively access information and to make fine-grained comparisons among possible answers. A multiple-choice question poses a question in the *stem* and requires you to recognize the best answer among the *choices*. You are usually confronted with four or five choices. Good multiple-choice questions are very carefully phrased and, properly interpreted, permit only one correct response. A careful reading of the question and the choices can help you to eliminate obvious poor choices. You can then concentrate your attention and memory on those remaining.

People typically make errors on multiple-choice questions even though they know the information that would enable them to make a correct choice. Errors are usually the result of anxiety, fatigue, reading superficially, and not examining the choices carefully.

You can avoid making errors on multiple-choice questions if you use a disciplined approach. This approach involves carrying out five steps on each question. First, read the stem only. If you cannot resist also reading the choices, put your hand or a piece of paper (such as a 3 by 5 card) over the choices. Second, paraphrase the question in the stem to yourself. If the stem is unusually long, read the last sentence in the stem first. The last sentence will often tell you the gist of the question and indicate what the question is about. Third, generate an answer to this question. Fourth, read the choices and grade each choice (A, B, C, D, F) for how well it answers the question. If you have clearly identified a particular choice as an A, you are done. However, if you have graded two choices as the best answer (such as two A's or two B's), more work is necessary. Be prepared for this situation. When two choices seem equally good, reread the stem. If a choice is still not clear, mark one of the choices on the test and put a question mark alongside the question. Rather than spend time trying to "force" an answer that won't come, move on to other questions. Then, if time allows, return to the question later; sometimes, the passage of time will enable you to make a better choice.

With some multiple-choice questions, none of the choices seem compelling. When you encounter questions like this, make a guess, put a question mark on the question, and return to it later. You may well find that the other questions suggest connections that may help you with your earlier difficulties. Even if this is not the case, it is better to concentrate your time on unanswered questions and to improve the likelihood of correct choices than to spend several minutes trying to get one question correct.

Most multiple choice questions ask you to identify the right or best answer that is called for by the question in the stem. Some faculties like to use the diabolical *reversed* question. These questions ask you to select the wrong or worst answer out of the choices. Many students are thrown by the reversed question because this kind of question is encountered infrequently in everyday life, and because the information in class and in reading almost never presents the information this way. If you are stumped by these questions, alter the question in your mind and ask yourself how you would respond if you were looking for the best answer to the question. Often when you can identify the best answer, the wrong or worst answer becomes clear.

Essay questions. Essay questions are the heart of most social science and humanities examinations. They require students not only to recall specific information, but to construct syntheses as well. A good essay question will actively engage your understanding as well as your memory. The instructor will expect you not only to remember the material, but also to be able to manipulate it in meaningful ways. Doing well on essay questions requires recall, understanding, and organization.

Some students approach an essay question as though it is a large flightless bird, and they were armed with a blunderbuss loaded with facts. They blast away at the question in the hope that some facts will hit the target and impress the instructor. We do not recommend this strategy. No instructor finds pleasure in an essay answer that lists reams of poorly related and/or irrelevant facts, even if they comprise tables and lists the instructor has introduced in class. Instructors are much more favorably impressed by succinct, well-organized answers that reflect an ability to select and emphasize important material that is pertinent to the question asked. They also appreciate the parallel ability to omit the peripheral and irrelevant.

In general, fewer words are preferable to many, especially if they are carefully chosen and well organized. Please try to believe this. Overly wordy answers are among the most common shortcomings, even of top students.

A good means of dealing with an essay question is to shape the answer before committing it to paper. It is worth your time to make a brief outline of your answer in which you identify your principal argument and organize your support for it. Outlines help you avoid going off on tangents. They promote good organization and brevity, both desirable qualities.

One final – and somewhat subtle – tip concerns essay questions. A good instructor may use an essay question as part of a learning experience that promotes a new insight into the material on the part of students. In such circumstances, you may be able to gain confidence in your ability to deal effectively with the question by looking for a major connection between elements of a course that are suggested by the question. When you perceive an intended association, you will likely experience an "aha!" sensation, a feeling of certainty that you understand the instructor's objective and are on target. These feelings are usually trustworthy and enable you to begin to construct your answer immediately.

Problem solving. Examinations in the sciences, economics, mathematics, and philosophy frequently require students to apply general principles they have learned to solve classes of problems with which they are familiar (Segal, Chipman, & Glaser, 1985). While the class of a problem should be familiar, the specific problem will not be. However, learning to recognize the class that a particular problem represents greatly facilitates deriving a correct answer. You then know which tools are most appropriate.

You will be better able to deal with specific problems if you have emphasized the nature of problem-classes in your exam preparation (Bransford & Stein, 1984; Pfeiffer, Feinberg, & Gelber, 1987; Whimbey & Lochead, 1999). By learning to recognize distinguishing characteristics of problem-classes, you increase the likelihood both that you will choose appropriate methods to solve a problem and that you will save time while doing so. Thus, while problem solving is a very specific activity, it benefits from the same sort of active overview that we have recommended in preparing for any examination situation.

Thinking skills (Arkes & Hammond, 1999; Bruner, Goodnow, & Austin, 1956; Kahneman & Tversky, 1973, 1982), such as might be needed on an exam, can be improved. However, thinking skills are improved in fundamentally different ways than memory skills are improved. Memory skills are improved by practice skills and by acquiring new skills for learning and remembering. In contrast, thinking skills are improved primarily by learning to avoid natural ways of thinking that typically lead to errors. Learning how to think correctly, more often than not, requires learning the incorrect ways of thinking that must be avoided. In the past decade, there has been a lot said about critical thinking. Unfortunately, many people fail to define what they mean by critical thinking. One common assumption held by scholars interested in critical thinking is that critical thinking stands for careful thinking (Halpern, 1997). Courses on critical thinking can be expected to teach you techniques that will make your thinking more careful (LeBlank, 1998).

Kinds of Thinking Processes

Understanding. In order to respond to the world, it must make sense to us. Making sense out of the world is to understand the world, to be able to recognize the primary forces in our environment, and how they relate to each other. Understanding may fail because a person does not know the essence of a word, a memory, or a concept. Many people often think they understand, when in fact they have accepted the irrelevant as real.

Reasoning. The correct way to reason has been the goal of many scholars and educators. Reasoning can be done from particulars to a generalization or vice versa. Reasoning is in a sense mathematical. If you have all of the pieces of a reasoning problem, it is possible to derive the solution. For example, if A is greater than B, and B is greater than C, then A must be greater than C.

Reasoning may be affected by all modes. It is obviously important to begin with the correct assumptions; many people do not challenge the assumptions on which reasoning is supposed to occur. Emotional overtones can interfere with the reasoning process. Creating a mental model by imagining what the reasoning problem looks like can be fundamental to solving a reasoning problem (Gentner & Stevens, 1983; Johnson-Laird, 1983). External aids, such as diagrams, can be crucial to successful reasoning (Bauer & Johnson-Laird, 1993). Study, practice, and strategies can improve reasoning success (Nummedal, 1987).

Problem solving. Reasoning traditionally involves words and the logical relationships among words. Reasoning has a correct answer to a question. Problem solving may involve words but may also depend on something unstated or perceptual. Convergent problem solving leads to a single best solution. It can get to the solution from two or more paths. Divergent problem solving involves two or more solutions, where each is equally viable. Finding the solution requires the right perspective. Being fixed on certain ways of thinking about the approach to a problem may cause someone to fail to solve the problem. Creative problem solving refers to an unusual solution that only one or a few people would ever think of. There is not a formula for solving problems creatively.

Support Thinking Skills

Unconventional reasoning and problem solving. Some problems resist a solution. When a solution seems especially difficult to achieve, people will resort to problem solving methods intended to give access to unconscious mental powers that are expected to work better. Brainstorming, daydreaming, dreaming, hypnosis, and meditation are used to gain access to unconscious solutions.

Priming skills. Understanding, reasoning, and problem solving are more likely to be successful if a person is well prepared. Reading, note taking, familiarization, and studying prepare a person consciously and unconsciously. They facilitate the accuracy of thought by priming memories and the careful discrimination of what is relevant or irrelevant.

Managerial thinking skills. Solutions to problems require management of time and approaches to the problem. Good managerial skills consist essentially of good work habits. Systematic use of different thinking skills and support thinking skills make it more likely that thinking will succeed.

Communicative thinking skills. People only know that you know something if you can communicate it to them. Many concepts and ideas are very complicated so verbal and nonverbal skills are necessary to convince people you know your stuff. Alternatively, many solutions require the discovery of knowledge that someone else holds. Communication is the key to gaining access to this knowledge.

Academic Thinking

Most college exams test for understanding. Reasoning is sometimes called for, as is problem solving. However, large classes make it difficult to test reasoning and problem solving because tests of reasoning and problem solving are time consuming, and there simply is not enough time to give everyone such tests. Thus, the skills most needed for college are those concerned with understanding.

To the extent that some courses require reasoning and problem solving, the best strategy is to try to learn to determine as easily as possible the kinds of reasoning and problem solving demanded by the course. When it comes down to it, more often than not, the critical factor in academic success is a person's habits of living. Impulsiveness, procrastination, not accepting responsibility for failure, and overloading oneself are more often the reasons why students fail. The ability to think per se is rarely the primary cause.

At the end of an exam. If you have followed the preceding advice, including writing succinct answers, you will likely find that you have some time left at the end of an examination. Use this time to insure that you have not inadvertently misinterpreted either the instructions or the major questions.

If you still have time, review your essay answers for their clarity. You may know the material quite well but, if you fail to communicate your understanding to your instructor, you will not get credit for your knowledge. Remember, the instructor is not a mind reader. He or she can gauge your understanding only by what you commit to paper. Answers that appear vague and ambiguous are vague and ambiguous. It will do you no good to explain later "What I really meant here was..."

Paper Writing

While this is primarily a book on memory and study skills, we do wish to briefly address the topic of paper writing, as this is a major consideration in many courses (Brunning et al., 1999). While many of the preceding memory tips have less relevance here, there are two principles enunciated throughout this book that have continuing relevance: organize your approach to the assignment, and be active in your treatment of concepts and in formulating positions.

The first and simplest rule, which few follow (including the authors), is that papers should be begun as soon as possible. They grow neither easier nor shorter as time passes, and the likelihood that you will perform well decreases markedly with the approach of a deadline. Starting earlier puts you in charge of the process and allows you to utilize your time more flexibly. Few good papers were written at 4:00 a.m.

Second, if the instructor gives you the latitude, a major quality of all good papers is that they have a good topic/question with which the writer is personally concerned. Within the confines of your assignment, try to select a topic in which you are genuinely interested. This will more likely result in a successful paper, as you will find it easier to work and you are more liable to develop it properly. Try also to ask an active question. Do not review the War of 1812. Instead, ask about the role of maritime activities in promoting the War of 1812 or, better still, argue that maritime activities on the part of the British helped to alienate American sentiments.

Third, you must organize your paper. You cannot simply sit down and hope that your pencil or computer has a good idea of what you wish to say.

You need to identify your central theme/argument and then determine how to introduce it to your reader, how to elaborate upon it, how to support it, and where it fits in the general human pursuit of understanding. The last is important to give the reader a reason to read your paper and to value what you are contributing.

Organization is most easily achieved via an outline (see above). These can be the traditional sorts or they can be computer based, such as Acta 7ᵃ by Symmetry Software. While outlines are helpful with all papers, they are virtually essential to the construction of a large research paper. The latter are sufficiently complex and the conclusion sufficiently distant that you must know where you are going, what means you will use to get there, and what routes you will travel before you embark on your intellectual journey.

When you begin the outline, do not try to do each section in detail. Instead use the outline as a means to organize your thoughts and to work on the overall shape of the paper. Thus, your first effort would probably include Roman numerals and perhaps capitals under each Roman numeral, e.g.:

> I. Introduction – The Nature of Explanation
>   A. Science vs. Alternative Approaches
>   B. The Role of Human Nature in Research
> II. Objective vs. Subjective Methods
>   A. Quantification and Replicability
>   B. Contextual Sensitivity

As you may have noted, at this point, it is more important for the outline to be meaningful to you than to others. After you have organized your thoughts you can sweep through the outline again and elaborate each section, adding detail and facts that support your position, e.g.:

> II. Objective vs. Subjective Methods
>   A. Quantification and Replicability
>   1. description is, to some extent, explanation
>   a. Popper on explanation
>   b. criticisms
>   (1) omission of information
>   (2) lack of contextual sensitivity
>   2. experiments and observation
>   a. trade-offs
>   b. appropriate areas
>   B. Contextual Sensitivity
>   etc.

When you have completed your outline (and revised it) you will have done the bulk of the work for the paper. The ideas, arguments, and even references are contained in the outline. Once you invest the time to accomplish this, you will be surprised at how easy the actual writing process becomes. All that needs to be done now is to write out and enlarge upon each of your sections.

Fourth, the research for your paper should be reasonably thorough and documented according to one of the styles currently in use in the discipline that you are studying. Among other reasons for this choice, this style is likely to be preferred by your instructor. An early start to the paper assures you time to locate sources and even to request them on inter-library loans. In the case of research papers of significant scope, preliminary research will enable you to determine whether or not you can proceed with your chosen topic. The best of questions will languish if there are not sufficient sources to nourish them.

As you locate and examine research sources, make notes. We recommend the use of 3x5 cards for this purpose. A set of these can be devoted to the sources themselves and should contain full bibliographic references. Thereafter, as you make notes on points and select a few quotes for inclusion, these can be written on separate cards and tagged at the top with the author's name and page number. This is sufficient for most purposes and will allow you to interleave the note cards with your outline pages.

Fifth, the actual writing of the paper should be clear, in an active voice and without artifice. Students, whether due to an unfortunate, or even overweening, intellectual insecurity, or to a misplaced polyprothetic desire to impress the professor, or even to having encountered unfortunate examples, however erudite, in professional literature, sometimes feel that they must use constructions of a nearly labyrinthian complexity, recherché phrases, and voluminous verbiage to make their points. As you may have noted from the preceding sentence, such practices tend to obscure rather than to enhance one's message.

Computer Resources

Both for researching papers and developing the background for course assignments, web browsers and other computer applications have become important resources. There are also computer packages that format one's writing in certain styles, such as scientific (Friedman, 1987). We will provide some suggestions and discuss some of these resources shortly, but we wish to start with a caution. Those of you who have purchased this book presumably have done so because you wish to do well in college. Hopefully, that does not simply mean getting good grades. You need to develop a set of marketable skills, for it is for these, rather than for your resume, that people will pay you. Towards that end, while some of today's computer resources now save considerable time, they can also allow you, even encourage you, to bypass the development of useful skills. Thus, the ability to locate arcane facts on the web simply by typing a few key words into a search engine is a good resource, but it can inhibit your ability to develop library research skills and even to think sequentially and analytically – common accompaniments to the design of a research program. In short, we recommend that, at least for the time being, you access computer resources somewhat sparingly.

Computer programs. There are a variety of programs, mostly on CDs, that can be quite helpful as resources and which do not imperil the development of your skills (McArthur, 1987; Milone, 1996; Neuhoff, 2000; Niccaise, 1998). These include various data bases ranging from encyclopedias, to thesauri, to collections of specialized information such as quotes, science data, psychology experiments, the Human Relations Area Files, an anthropology data base of ethnographies, etc. There are also excellent dictionaries, such as American Heritage, that can be accessed either online or via CD-ROM. Finally, we have found bibliographic data bases, such as EndNote[a] to be extremely valuable, largely because they reduce the amount of repetitive and thoughtless effort involved in typing a bibliography. Of equal importance, such programs can serve as repositories of bibliographic information that can be reused when appropriate.

All of the preceding programs can be used as much as you might wish. Indeed, each can yield new insights into areas where you may have thought you were familiar with most ideas and materials. They are valuable means to augment your knowledge and your skills.

There are other programs such as interactive spell-checkers and grammar checkers that we hesitate to recommend, not because they lack utility, but precisely because they have great utility. If you come to rely upon these aids before you have developed the requisite abilities for yourself, you risk the good possibility that your spelling and grammar – two skills fundamental to written communication – will remain rudimentary and even wanting (Black & Bryant, 1995; Schwartz, 1996; Taylor & Taylor, 1990). Try to remember that there will be many occasions when you will need to write in the absence of a computer and computer aids. We appreciate that most will not heed this advice, but those who do will profit from it.

Business and other endeavors are making increasing use of computer-based expert systems. These are programs which access specialized databases and operate on them according to a set of parameters designed to mimic human decision making skills for that specialized domain (Storey, 1997; Utgoff, 1997). There are now expert systems that make judgments about traffic flow, that diagnose medical problems, that create architectural designs, and that even run investment strategies for major investment firms. These programs, while limited in scope, can accomplish more complex tasks than can humans, and they can do so at a much faster rate (Raybeck, 2000). The moral is simple. If you wish to be employable, you will need greater flexibility and better skills than these programs. These will not be acquired if you use computer abilities to replace, rather than to enhance your own.

The Web. The Web has grown exponentially until it now offers resources in virtually every field and for any purpose. On-line you can find riches ranging from translation programs, language databases, encyclopedias, dictionaries, to informational resources from such respected institutions as the Smithsonian, MOMA, The American Museum of Natural History, to the holdings of every major library in the world. These are enormously important and useful assets especially when researching a paper or presentation. Unfortunately, as with any tool it can be used well or misused.

Seeking out a specialized site such as the American Psychological Association web page or the Smithsonian allows you to utilize their resources in developing *your* project. When you have a sense of your project, but are unclear about what sites might be relevant, you can utilize search engines to narrow your quest. There are powerful search engines, such as MetaCrawler, that search other search engines and provide you with a list of potentially germane sites to visit. There are even search engines emerging that employ complex algorithms that enable context-sensitive searches. Such systems can determine whether the word "continent" is being referred to in the sense of abstinence or of a geographical area. These search engines are valuable starting places that can help you to discover obscure facts and to perceive unexpected relationships. However, to continue the theme above, they cannot substitute for your organization and intent. They are best consulted after you have a sense of what you wish to accomplish and what resources you will need.

Finally, we need to address one of the resources of the Web of which most students are aware. There are a variety of sites, such as Cheathouse.com, that offer undergraduate papers either for free or for a fee. The majority of papers collected by such sites are written by undergraduates and are listed along with the grade they received, as well as a summary of the papers contents. Thus, 'C+' students can acquire 'B' papers (but advisedly not 'A' papers) without arousing the undesired attention of the instructor.

We can give you several good pedagogical reasons why you shouldn't patronize such sites, but you are probably already familiar with these. In short, you know better, and you realize that not only is this cheating and dishonest, it is a short-term fix that will not advance your skills. (The people who lack this conviction are unlikely to have purchased this book.) Still, there are times when we all get caught short and the temptation to take a shortcut, such as purchasing a paper from the web, can be great. Let us give you additional practical reasons why this can result not only in a lack of learning, but also in severe penalties. At many institutions, the Dean of Student's Offices maintain subscriptions to these services and, at the request of faculty, can quickly review their contents. (A keyword or phrase search can quickly identify a paper.) In addition, students who visit such sites in search of an appropriate paper for an assignment have been known to submit *identical* papers to the same instructor. (This happened at one of the authors' institutions more than once.) Such "coincidences" can arouse the suspicion of even the most lethargic of instructors. The consequences of such coincidences can range from probation to expulsion, again depending on the institution.

In summary, our advice, as should be clear by now, is that the Web is an exceedingly valuable resource that should be selectively used, but not as a replacement for developing skills you will need later in life.

Some Additional Considerations

It may surprise you to learn that we actually do not expect most student readers to follow all of the advice in this chapter or throughout this book. Indeed, many of you will follow only a small minority of the suggestions we have made here. However, to return to where we started in this chapter, there are better and worse means to improve study skills, but there are no easy means (Apps, 1995; Longman & Atkinson, 1988; Luckie & Smethhurst, 1998; Reynolds & Werner, 1993/1994).

The profit you derive from this chapter relates directly to the amount of effort you are willing to expend on improving your academic performance. No one is apt to work all the time, nor do we expect that you should normally do so. The suggestions we have made in this chapter will enable you to do as well as you can or, if you prefer, as well as you wish to do. We especially recommend that you consult the Study Guides (Figures 18-21) when you are not sure on how to proceed with a particular study task. When these students describe how they studied for a test or prepared for a term paper, they often report having used only a few of the many appropriate techniques. Even students instructed in study skills often do not study any more effectively than students who have not been instructed. The instructed students explain that they did not use more techniques because – despite their training – they simply did not think of them. The Study Guides were developed to serve as external aids (Harris, 1984; Intons-Peterson, 1993; Intons-Peterson & Fournier, 1986; Intons-Peterson & Newsome, 1992) to remind students of the study techniques that may be applicable to particular study problems (e.g., planning a program of study; indepth reading procedures; extracting meaning from lecture notes and texts; preparing for exams; and taking exams). The motivated student, who wants to study properly, can merely glance at the Study Guides and be reminded of techniques that otherwise they might not have tried.

Irrespective of the amount of effort you decide to invest in your studies, we remain consistent in our general recommendations. Continually strive for an interrelated overview of the tasks before you, and continue to process information actively. You will improve both your understanding and your recall of the material you treat.

Tape recorders, cameras, and video camcorders can passively register enormous amounts of information far better than you can. However, unlike these machines, you can actively manipulate information to derive new insights and arguments. This, after all, is the real goal of education.

Summary

Doing better academically often involves changing your study habits. There are better and worse means to improve study skills, but there are no easy means to do so. The benefits you will derive from learning about study skills depend on how much effort and opportunity you have to expend on improving your academic performance.

One key to success is to discover and learn the particular techniques and strategies that apply to particular courses.

Another key to success is to learn and master some of the

more important general study skills, ones that are independent of any particular subject matter – yet are appropriate for any course. These general skills pertain to In-depth Reading Procedures, Meaning Extraction Techniques, Exam Preparation, and Exam Strategies.

Section IV.

Help from the World Around Us

10. The Physical Environment and External Aids

Our ability to learn and think is a result of adaptations we make with the environment (Anderson, 1990). We remember because cues elicit our memories. On exams, we remember because the words on the page connect with ideas in long-term memory. If we are not sufficiently prepared, we may not have our memory triggered by the words on the page. Similarly, if a professor uses wording on an exam that we do not recognize, we will not remember.

We also remember to do the tasks required of us because of cues around us. An alarm clock wakes us up in time to go to class. A notebook, planner, or an electronic device presents cues that help us keep track of all of our appointments, chores, assignments, and lectures. Failure to meet one of these obligations can cause us a lot of hassles.

If we are sensitive to the cues around us, life in college will go smoothly. In this chapter, we discuss how many kinds of cues affect your academic and especially your personal life. Obviously external cues, such as you have in your notes, are critical to academic success. However, a hassle-free personal life is also important to college success. If your life is hassle free, you will perform better on term papers and tests because you will have more energy to devote to your work.

The Power of Physical Stimuli

Physical stimuli have a powerful effect on memory because they capture attention more effectively than most ideas. Indeed, the external effect of physical stimuli on your memory is often greater than the internal effect of mental manipulations (Harris, 1984). Great detectives, such as Sherlock Holmes, often have witnesses return to the scene of the crime because the physical environment can be expected to awaken memories far better than mental efforts to remember the crime scene. Newscasters and performers on TV often have cue cards to prompt them in case they forget what to say.

Because physical stimuli may aid memory so well, many external aids have been developed both informally and commercially. You are using an informal external aid when you put an object near your front door to remind you to take it away the next time you leave. You are using an external aid when you set an alarm to remind you to make a call, go to a meeting, or put an ingredient into something you are cooking. The rest of this chapter focuses on the use of external aids to control the environment so that you will remember when necessary.

External aids. An image, a sound, a touch, or a movement often will register a more vivid trace – or will stimulate a memory to emerge more rapidly – than will a verbal description of the same sight, sound, touch, or movement. Consequently, external aids that can present an image, a sound, a touch, or a movement can facilitate learning and remembering better than ideas in memory.

External aids are used often by all of us. Several surveys have shown that both young adults and elderly people use external aids to cope with memory problems substantially more than they use mental manipulations (Cavanaugh, Grady, & Perlmutter, 1983). Even memory experts admit that they too use external aids much more than mental manipulations (Park et al., 1990).

Because external aids can assist your memory so powerfully, knowledge of them is essential to improving memory in everyday life. This chapter reviews how to take good advantage of external aids to facilitate your memory performance and, in some cases, to even relieve you of the burden of having to perform some memory tasks. Some of the aids can be applied to academic responsibilities, such as devices that may remind you when to study. Most of the aids serve to make your everyday life less stressful. If you can succeed in lowering the amount of stress in your life the better you will do academically, and you will enjoy your college years more.

Possible side effects from memory aid use. Although there are many reasons to be enthusiastic about external aids, you may want to consider an ancient question about their effects on memory ability. It has been argued that external aids reduce a person's reliance on memory per se, and that this reduced use may decrease a person's memory abilities. For example, a person might use external aids for each and every memory task and, thereby, never use his or her own memory.

It is true that the use of an external aid for certain kinds of memory tasks, especially over a prolonged period, can diminish one's memory ability for this task. However, ability for other tasks will not lessen. For example, suppose you purchase a telephone that stores the numbers of your friends and dials them at the push of a button. This may reduce your facility at memorizing phone numbers. If you cherish a certain kind of memory ability, then you may not want to use an external aid for the tasks served by that ability. But reliance on the phone will not affect your ability to remember the rules of games or past events of your life. Alternatively, external aids can relieve you of the mental burden of performing certain tasks. They also allow you to choose which tasks you want to relegate to an aid and which tasks you prefer to manage with your own memory system.

External aid use. Each section of the rest of this chapter discusses external aids as they apply to four broad categories of memory tasks in everyday life: physical memory for actions, studying, memory tasks at work, and personal memory tasks. Some external aids address registration, others retention, retrieval, or a combination of these memory phases. There are many memory tasks for which no external aid has been developed yet.

If you are satisfied with your memory performance in one or more of the broad task categories, skip ahead to a category that you find more challenging. For categories of interest, skim through until you find tasks on which you would like to improve. For many tasks, several external aids are discussed. Identify the external aids that you feel will be most useful to you, write them down as you read so that you will later remember which ones you want to obtain and use.

An effective use of these aids requires effort in planning, rather than in executing, the manipulations of external aids. So many memory tasks arise unexpectedly and end quickly (such as introductions). There is often no time to go in search of an external aid if one is not at hand. If you don't have an external aid (such as a notepad or an alarm) handy, you will have to make the effort to use a mental manipulation or not try at all.

Physical memory. Successful remembering of an action entails remembering the parts of the action and the precise sequence in which the parts are put together. Improved ability to remember actions has long been known to depend greatly on how much you practice them. Nevertheless, there are many actions that we perform infrequently, making it difficult to develop expertise at executing them. We may sometimes have to fix something, such as a toaster or a lawn mower, and then not have to repeat the actions involved for years. Such situations preclude becoming practiced at the task.

In lieu of practice, you can create external aids that you can later call upon when you have to attempt the action again. One manipulation is to take notes that break a task – such as a home repair – into steps. You might also create a checklist for the several parts of the action. If the action is a common one, you can obtain instruction manuals. They often include diagrams that illustrate actions you might otherwise forget. Most movements in sports occur in the context of a playing field. If you are attempting to acquire an athletic movement, make sketches of the movement on the playing field, court, alley, or rink showing the standard lines or markers. Later, when you are confronted by the real memory task, these lines and markers will externally aid your recall of the movement.

Academic Aids

Studying

Throughout life, you have to study information for work, responsibilities at home, and leisure activities. Studying is, of course, crucial in school or training situations (Flippo & Caverly, 1991). In work situations, where we generally have less time for studying, it can be especially important to learn information quickly in order to cope with a question or problem. At home we must learn many things, from using our appliances to filing our income tax. It is even necessary to learn just to have fun. When playing a new card or board game, you have to know the rules.

External aids help studying in two ways: by facilitating learning and by providing external sources should one fail to remember something learned previously.

Notes. Everyone uses notes sometimes when they study. Notes taken in class, meetings, or from a book serve to focus your attention and facilitate your registration of key material. Crib sheets facilitate last minute preparation for exams. Notes do not replace the need for mental manipulations. Rather they ensure that you mentally manipulate the right information and force you to better organize your mental records (Anderson & Ambruster, 1991; Intons-Peterson & Newsome, 1992).

"Teaching machines." Machines that teach have been around since at least the 1930s (Benjamin, 1988). Today, microcomputer stores stock shelf after shelf with instructional schemes and programs on a wide variety o

topics that facilitate learning (including learning how to use microcomputers). Many of these programs can accelerate your learning over your normal rate.

Memory art. An old learning device, not so well known today, is art. Paintings, drawings, and sketches have been designed by artists specifically to help people use the mental manipulation – the method of loci – discussed in the previous chapter. This method involves learning a list of items by mentally placing each item in different rooms of a familiar building. For example, if you have an interest in England, you might hang a map of it on the wall of the room where you study. When you have a small list of items to remember, mentally "place" each item in one distinct region of the map. Repeat the placements several times to yourself. When you need to "retrieve" the list, travel the map mentally from region to region, "picking up" the items as you go. In the 14th, 15th, and 16th centuries, artists drew or painted floor plans of houses, cathedrals, amphitheaters, and other buildings so people could similarly "locate" and memorize information in this way (Yates, 1966). The use of art to aid memory today is uncommon, but you might find it a personally intriguing and effective way to learn a list of items.

Superstitious memory aids. Sometimes people use an object to aid memory on the basis of an unfounded belief that the object has a power to influence memory. Usually, they justify this belief on the grounds that the object brought good luck to past memory tasks. Some students wear a special article of clothing, like a "thinking cap," to exams because they did especially well while wearing it in the past. Other students will use a "lucky" pen or bring their books even to closed-book exams. The use of lucky memory objects is particularly common among college students, but it is also not unusual among other professions, where a certain suit, briefcase, or pointer might be linked superstitiously to good performance. If you are inclined to use such an aid, go ahead. It won't hurt, and it may help by putting you in a mental state conducive to good memory performance.

Knowledge sources. For most subjects, we do not expect ourselves to remember every single detail. To back your memory up on topics you are likely to forget, you should use external knowledge sources. Some knowledge sources you develop on your own, such as notes from meetings, readings, and lectures. Other source materials are developed by others, such as work-related professional books and manuals. Many general sources (dictionaries, encyclopedias, thesauri, Guinness Book of Records, and Farmer's Almanac) are useful in any office. The more knowledge sources you have at your fingertips, the less time you spend going back and forth to the library.

Other books serve more personal needs, like skill improvement, travel, product supplies, or conference proceedings. All these sources keep facts readily on hand that might otherwise fail to come immediately or accurately to mind. Of course, they also provide you with information that you never knew in the first place. A knowledge source that is valuable to most people is a spelling aid. Either because we have forgotten a spelling or because we have forgotten the rules that govern its spelling, we are uncertain of how to spell certain words. There are now excellent devices that address spelling difficulties.

Instant speller. Computers commonly conduct a spell check of your writing. If you would like spelling assistance when you are away from your computer, you can purchase portable spellers.

Foreign language study. Learning the language of another country can be a formidable task. Nowadays, there are translation calculators that can help you in your studies, CD Rom courses (such as Linkword), as well as instructional programs on the Web.

Nitewriter. If you are the kind of person who awakes in the middle of the night with brilliant ideas, you might find a pen with a tip that lights up useful to record ideas. The light is bright enough to write down your thoughts while not so bright as to awaken someone else in the room.

The "memory-friendly" desk. When we work under high pressure, timing is essential. Often there is no time to be wasted in trying to remember the forgotten location of a misplaced folder, contract, or some other piece of information. Thus, it is important that your desk be arranged so that it is "memory friendly," allowing you to easily remember and find what you need. Keep the top of your desk in an order that facilitates finding what you need (Hertel, 1988; Malone, 1983). The order you impose need not be neat, but it should be predictable to you. Office supply stores sell a variety of products that help keep and find materials routinely in their place: e.g., desk organizers, pen holders, eyeglass holders. Similarly, you can use drawer organizers, which keep envelopes, letterhead sheets, etc., readily accessible. A good set of knowledge sources, such as technical manuals and other communications, should also be kept within arm's reach.

Meetings and classes. Often we take part in meetings, informal or formal, that we later remember less precisely than we wish. We forget critical statements, sometimes important decisions. You can avoid these memory failures by either writing down careful notes or by tape recording those meetings you expect to have to recall later.

Copying. Courses often require you to encounter documents that you may later need to know about. You can, of course, get copies made. If you can afford it, you might want to get a portable copier. However, it might justifiably be argued that the "Xerox Revolution" has created even more memory problems in giving us so much more information to file and retrieve. Thus, many have offered this sensible suggestion: copy only those documents you will genuinely need and use.

Work. Success at most occupations hinges critically on your ability to access information and communicate with others (Holland, 1994). These demands necessitate performing a stream of memory tasks each and every workday. You must remember the responsibilities of the moment, and also have pertinent information and the facts of past events at your fingertips.

Obligations

Work requires you to be – and appear to be – aware of many schedules and events. To be in touch, it is necessary to know your professional obligations, both day by day and well into the future. One common factor of your obligations is that they must be performed by a certain deadline. Another common factor is that obligations entail the remembering of details.

One valuable way to deal with memory burdens imposed by obligations is to use a record system that will manage those details for you. For many people, the primary record system is an appointment book or some form of notes, such as a chore list. The thought that we have an impending obligation often occurs to us at odd moments. If we forget to record this thought, we usually forget to meet the obligation. Some use the note itself as a reminder. Others copy the note onto a chore list or appointment book they consult regularly throughout the day. Keeping memo pads in key places of one's house facilitates getting a new obligation on the list before the intention to do the chore is forgotten. Some people carry this practice so far that they put a memo pad at their bedside in case chores occur to them in the middle of the night.

Since all obligations involve a deadline, they require you to be aware of the time. Some people can rely on memory alone to recall deadlines or dates, but many use aids such as notes or calendars. Accessibility is the key. Some people need a calendar in one or more rooms of the home or office.

Appointments. Research indicates that people forget appointments or project deadlines infrequently. Such a failure is to be avoided, if possible, because it is commonly taken as indicating a lack of interest in the person to be met or in the project to be done. Nevertheless, we do forget appointments or deadlines at times. Because appointment failures are so disturbing, people have developed a variety of external-aid manipulations to insure that such failures rarely occur.

The first thing to do to minimize your forgetting of appointments is to keep a daily record of your obligations – a to-do list. The act of keeping a daily record forces you to review the events of the day and fosters prompt realization of appointments. A daily schedule can be written on any scrap of paper, but you may wish to use any of a variety of appointment books that have been designed to organize your schedule and trigger the remembering of appointments. For example, you can use an appointment book, record book, address book, wallet, cardholder, and electronic systems for monitoring projects.

A second way to minimize your forgetting of appointments is to keep multiple records of your forthcoming obligations: in appointment books, lists of chores, diaries, and calendars. If you do this, you give yourself added mental rehearsal of the details of these obligations.

Remembrance file. A card file box with an opening in the front to allow the card to be read – which has spaces to record the date and what is to be done on that day.

Take-aways. Work routinely requires us to remember to take things away to another destination when we leave. In order to remember to do so, many people reserve a spot in their office or home for routinely putting things they intend to take away. To be maximally effective, the spot should be convenient and near a major exit, like a table or stairs near the front door. It should be checked habitually whenever one exits.

Similarly, a shirt pocket, a fold in your wallet, or section in your purse can be set aside as a portable spot for putting things you do not wish to forget. Tickets for a plane or play, check and personal letters are some of the "easy-to-lose" items that could be put in a special pocket. A portable memory spot will save you the time and worry of searching through all of your clothing to find important material.

When it is especially important that you remember to bring an object or papers somewhere at a certain time, you may need a more dramatic reminder. Rather than using your routine memory spot, you should put the "take-away" item in a conspicuous spot. The conspicuous placement manipulation is a common practice that experts regard as very effective (Winograd & Soloway, 1985). You can hardly ignore an object left against the front door or on the hood of your car. If the object to be taken is to large to be put in the doorway, then tape a reminder to the front door or on the steering wheel of your car.

Timing devices. You may be reminded of your obligations by more sophisticated devices. Instead of hoping that your obligations will spontaneously emerge and tell you what you are to do, you can use devices that take over most of the mental work. These devices can register the times of an appointment and the information about who is to be met, and later signal you with a light or sound at the time of your obligation.

Wireless remote control systems turn office or household machines on and off at preset times. Timer centers control from eight to 16 devices. Many computers come with calculator, tape recorder, phone terminal, and memo pad, as well as being capable of reminding you of appointments, errands, phone messages, birthdays, and holidays.

Pocket sized reminding devices. These devices are pocket-sized and can do calculations, hold data, as well as give you reminders. They have come to be called "palmtop computers" or "personal data assistants" by many stores and catalogs that sell them. They can be connected to a microcomputer to call up files concerning phone numbers, flight schedules, and other information (Herrmann et al., 1999a).

Simple timers. Sometimes called "kitchen timers," these devices buzz or ring, providing effective cues to short-term appointments or chores.

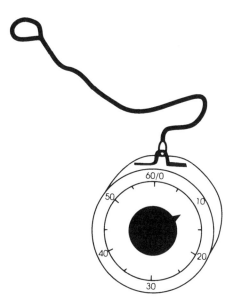

Figure 23. A Short-Term Practical. Attachable Timer (from 1 to 60 minutes)

Mechanical, wind up timers are often used when cooking. Radio alarm clocks often include a "snooze" button that lets your radio play up to an hour before automatically shutting off. The alarm or shut-off may be used as a cue. Also, pocket-size digital timers are useful (Herrmann et al., 1996, 1999a).

Symbolic Reminding

When you are in a hurry or do not have the time to make a note, you can create an external aid of your obligation by changing some aspect of your immediate physical environment. The unusual placement of an object increases the likelihood that a person will remember an appointment, because the sight of the object "out of place" provides an obvious symbol to remind you. For example, a person calls while you are hurrying out of the office and asks you to drop by later in the day. Because you don't have time to make a note, you turn your wristwatch over or switch it from one wrist to another. This manipulation, called "symbolic reminding," is often criticized as an inadequate method of remembering because the unusual change in the environment may not later suggest the precise obligation you intended to meet. Despite this shortcoming, symbolic reminding remains one of the most popular memory aids. You may also find symbolic reminding useful when you want to have a backup to an alarm watch or clock. Here are several examples of symbolic reminding that many people find beneficial for at least some tasks:

Examples of Symbolic Reminding

- Carry an object. (Pick up some small object and carry it until you have done whatever you did not want to forget to do.)
- Clothespin or paper clip in a buttonhole or pocket of a shirt or blouse.
- Connect a cord from your wrist to your belt. (Moderate or large gestures will simultaneously pull on your wrist and belt.)
- Knot in handkerchief.
- Position furniture oddly.
- Rubber band around a wrist.
- Scotch tape on a finger.
- String on the bridge of your glasses.
- String on your finger.

- Switch the pocket of your wallet.
- Switch the shoulder on which you normally carry something (such as a purse or golf bag).
- Switch your watch from the usual wrist to the other wrist.
- Switch your wedding ring to your other hand. (It is advisable to tell your spouse about this.)
- Turn your ring over.
- Turn your watch over (face down).
- Wear your belt two or three notches tighter.
- Wear your clothes in an unaccustomed manner. (If you normally wear a certain article of clothing, like a vest or a sweater, don't; or wear an article of clothing you normally would not, like an ascot or a scarf.)
- Wear "memory" jewelry. (For example, you can wear a "memory" bracelet, necklace, or tie that you reserve for reminding you to do important tasks. To be most effective, jewelry should be ostentatious in some way – unusually heavy, noisy, glittery, or cumbersome).
- Wear "memory" clothing. (To be most effective, it should be unusual in design, pattern, or color. If you are especially bold, it should be distasteful – a loud tie or a "shocking" scarf. Distasteful clothing has the advantage of attracting comments, and thereby eliciting additional reminders.)
- Similarly, you can position or "dress" notes and other papers symbolically with memo clips that call attention to them. Magnets are sold that keep grocery lists, recipes, phone numbers, and memos close at hand on the refrigerator. You can also buy a huge paper clip bearing the words "Don't Forget," which can be clipped to high priority paperwork in an obvious place.

Some people find appointment books difficult to keep or easy to neglect. Even if you have recorded an appointment, you may need to post further notices that are explicit reminders. One option is to stick your reminder where you will be sure to "run into" it. The convenient (and ubiquitous) Scotch "Post It" self-sticking notes work well for this manipulation. They can be placed on the front door, a frequently used mirror, the lid to the toilet, or any other spot you know you will pass regularly. Another option is to put up a message board, file, or cabinet that provides a constant reminder of things you have to do.

Phone Use

Whether you use phones heavily at work or casually at home, your use relies on several memory tasks that you could avoid. Perhaps because of the telephone's importance, the business world has produced aids of varying sophistication to assist with these memory tasks. From little black books to computers, you can find devices for every level of phone use.

Phone numbers. You can attempt to memorize frequently called numbers, or you can let one of several available indexes retain this information for you. You may also use these systems to record the names and numbers of business contacts generally.

If your phone use is heavy, and you can afford it, you may prefer an automatic dialing device. These dialers retain numbers that you key into the device, along with the name of the person corresponding to the number. When you are ready to call someone, you push the button on your dialer alongside the name of the person you want to call and the dialer dials the person's number. Some dialers are portable. These devices work the same as the non-portable ones except that a push of the button activates the tones corresponding to numbers. You simply hold the device against the telephone receiver and it dials the appropriate number.

What was said. It often becomes important to remember what someone said in a previous phone conversation, especially if you study with someone over the phone. Recall of prior conversations is typically inaccurate. If you anticipate needing to remember phone conversations precisely, you may want to install equipment that will record calls. However, if you decide to obtain a recorder, bear in mind the pitfalls of using one. Etiquette dictates that you inform the people you talk to that the call is being recorded. The goodwill of friends and acquaintances can be lost in an instant if it becomes known after the fact that a phone call, especially a sensitive one, has been "tapped." Legally, if you do not inform someone that a call is recorded, and this person discloses information that you would like to use in a legal action against them, your failure to inform them renders their disclosure inadmissible evidence.

Turn on your answering machine. Many people who use an answering machine frequently forget to turn the machine on. This memory failure can cause you to miss important calls. Some machines allow you to turn them from a remote location.

Personal Memory

College insulates you from a lot of this, but it does not insulate you from a variety of activities concerning finances and self care.

Personal finances. Keeping up with (and within) a budget involves several different memory tasks. For many people, successful budgeting demands more memory effort than they are willing to put out. Each kind of budget (household, gift, vacation, business travel) has its own pattern of expenditures and overall balance. Central to any budget is the paying of bills.

Paying bills. Probably the most important financial task we face is paying our monthly bills. If you are disciplined, you can combine all your bill-paying obligations by setting aside a day each week or month to handle this chore. The date itself may be chosen for its memorableness, such as the 1st, 15th, or 30th. You need not rely on your memory to record payment dates and schedules. Calendars are one place you can record the due-dates for recurring bills. Gathering or labeling the bills in a conspicuous fashion is another helpful manipulation. They can be marked or clipped as they arrive to show which bills remain unpaid.

Some people do not trust themselves to follow a routine or to notice a conspicuous reminder to pay bills. Others simply prefer to avoid the burden of remembering. For them, more active reminders are available. Many people find such a device too expensive and prefer disciplined use of a calendar to remind them of when bills must be paid.

A variety of businesses and institutions will now carry out financial transactions for you. These automatic financial services can reduce your financial memory load considerably. For example, you need not remember to deposit your paycheck. Banks now customarily provide "direct deposit" by arrangement with many employers. You also need not remember to pay many of your bills. Most banks will pay certain bills by deducting, with your permission, money from your checking account.

Your checkbook balance. People often put off balancing their checkbook. Since the advent of credit cards, knowing how much money you have in your account has become even more difficult to determine. No one who uses credit cards more than infrequently can expect to reliably remember all of their purchases and the amounts. Fortunately, new devices exist that make it easier to facilitate your recording of checks and credit card expenditures, enabling you to keep track of all your accounts. There are calculators that let you key in deposits and expenditures by check or credit card, give you a balance for the checking account, two credit card accounts, and overall.

Self Care

When we were children, our parents remembered what we were supposed to do to take care of our health. As adults, however, we must remember to take care of ourselves on our own. We must remember to eat right, get exercise, see doctors as needed, and to take medications when appropriate. Self-care requires that we perform a variety of memory tasks.

Cooking. A good cook is a bit like an orchestra conductor. To begin with, it is necessary to take frozen foods out so they can thaw. Since this is a task that many people forget, it is often useful to own a microwave that will allow you to thaw in minutes. You must either remember how to cook a dish or remember where the recipe for the dish is kept. Obviously, a recipe file is essential to the latter task. Prior to cooking, ingredients must be taken out of the refrigerator or cabinets. By dating foods, you can make sure to use older items before newer ones and avoid spoilage. As for the meal itself, there are a variety of products that can automatically start and stop one or more dishes on the stove that are not automatically timed.

Exercise. Exercise improves your cognitive functioning so you will be better off intellectually. If you are disciplined, you may find it easy to remember to exercise. But many people find that their schedule is so hectic that they simply forget to do so. If this applies to you, it is advisable to plan ahead and arrange times in your schedule to exercise. If you arrange to exercise with someone else, that person will serve as an added external memory aid – besides giving you extra incentive to follow through.

Taking medication. Some people make notes to remind them to take pills. Others lay out the full daily number of pills in a dish each morning, and then check the number left at each medication time. Others make use of devices that remind them to take their medication. Two kinds of devices are sold to assist remembering medications: passive devices (remind you when you happen to look at them) or active devices (signal you with a light or a buzzer). Passive reminders, a refinement of the dish manipulation just described, provide a systematic scheme for sorting out the pills to be taken, e.g., pocket-sized plastic boxes that organize daily doses in four separately-opened compartments. Active reminders are more useful for those who tend to forget or "skip" medication times.

Locations of possessions. The simplest way to keep track of your possessions is to be organized. Everyone misplaces or mislays things from time to time (Winograd & Soloway, 1985). Indeed, misplacing things is one of the most common and annoying memory failures. Placing of things is usually so mundane an act that we often pay too little attention at the time, and the lack of attention leads us to fail to register the experience properly.

One simple way to avoid this recurring annoyance is to organize the locations of your possessions using drawers, cabinet shelves, closets, shoe boxes, cardboard cartons, egg cartons, etc. "Organizing" does not necessarily mean becoming overly neat and tidy. The fundamental principle is to consistently place your various possessions in the same spot. By following a consistent pattern for placing objects, you avoid the problem of remembering where each object was last put: the organizational scheme does the remembering for you. Dime stores, department stores, and many other retailers sell devices that are intended to introduce order into your life: e.g., file boxes, parts cabinet, pattern-keeper notebook, sewing box, tackle box.

Location of possessions in drawers and cabinets. A sophisticated way to organize your possessions is to label containers, including drawers, cabinets, shelves, boxes, and filing cabinets. Labeling facilitates memory in two ways. First, labels on closed containers tell you at a glance what's inside. When boxes, files, or other containers are not labeled, the search for a particular object can be frustrating, if not fruitless. Second, labeling possessions can aid in their recovery if they are lost. Especially for items like clothing, which are often left in public places unintentionally, labels help others return your gloves, jackets, or hats to you. But labeling can be applied to other common tasks as well. By getting in the habit of labeling containers and other possessions, you can relieve your memory of many frustrations and conflicts over issues of location and ownership. Labeling requires only a pen or some paint, but you may prefer to purchase products that come pre-labeled with your initials or first name.

Locations of valuable or personally important possessions. Organization and labeling are not foolproof aids to remembering where your things are. In the case of valuables, it may not be sufficient to have a general idea of their whereabouts. For greater security, you will want to record the location of such possessions. Many people use either a plain notebook or a book sold explicitly for this purpose. Such a record is important when applying for home insurance and claims on home insurance. Unfortunately, when people are asked to recall what they own, they typically forget many items, because the sheer number of our possessions is beyond the capacity of our memory. And insurance companies will only cover what we "know" we own.

One possession you definitely do not want to lose track of is your personal papers (insurance, wills, and other records). Although you may keep such papers in a safety deposit box, you are likely to forget them when you need to consult them. Thus, you can find the papers you need faster if you have them stored in an organized fashion.

Locations of frequently used items. Certain objects seem to get misplaced more often than others. Keys, purses, wallets, and jackets are frequently misplaced. "Lost and found" notices often testify to such errors on public bulletin boards. When we accidentally leave something in a public place, our only hope is that we will remember doing so soon enough to retrieve it, or that a lost-and-found office will call us. But at home, a fancy homing device may be useful for chronic misplacers, such as an electronic search-and-find system (such as a sonic detector system that helps you locate frequently misplaced items).

Other objects are prone to being carried off absentmindedly. For example, people often walk off with borrowed keys, pens, or flashlights. By changing the appearance of objects in an obvious way, you can make them

Figure 24. An Example of a Memory Aid for Keeping Track of Possessions and Their Locations. The book sketched here was sold in the mid-19th century in England (one is on display at the Styal Mill museum, Styal, England), but similar books are easily purchased today. The title of the book straightforwardly indicates its purpose and, at the same time, the frustration that comes when a possession cannot be located.

easier to find or more difficult to forget to return. Painting them with iridescent colors, tying colorful yarn to them, or attaching them to large objects are among the many things that can be done to make possessions more noticeable.

Keeping your possessions. College life is a transient communal exist-ence. You share your room with people you never knew before, and visi-tors are not uncommon. To avoid having people inadvertently walking off with your possessions, mark them in a conspicuous manner. There are many ways to mark possessions for identification. Use luggage tags. At-tach a bright ribbon or yarn. Attach personalized straps to cameras, musi-cal instruments, and other objects you carry separately. Use a passport protector to keep your most important personal papers. Get a credit card case which has an alarm that goes off if you close the case without return-ing the card.

Inventory. From time to time you may want to take inventory of what you have. One way to deal with such a task is to have automatic recording devices in operation. However, many counting jobs are relatively inconse-quential and do not warrant a costly automatic system.

Addresses. Although you "know" where you live, remembering your address takes a little effort and a little time (more effort and time if you have moved often). Considering how often you must address letters, the accumulated time over a lifetime probably amounts to several months. A variety of charities and printing services offer for a few dollars pre-ad-dressed stickers that will serve this purpose error-free.

Where you put your keys. For many of us, the most common, recurring, vexing, annoying, and frustrating memory problem is to try to remember where we put our keys. The easiest way to minimize this problem is to have a special place for them. By routinely putting the keys in a certain shirt, pants, or purse pocket, you can eliminate frequent searches through all of your clothing. If you are more inclined to put your keys down, do so in a pre-established spot, such as your dresser top or a hook by the door. It is wise to keep a set of duplicate keys available somewhere in your home or car. If you are inclined to use these extra keys often, give another set to a trusted neighbor. If you start going to your neighbor often (because you've lost several sets of keys), you may need to re-examine your "memory condition" (as discussed in Chapter 3).

You may want to make your keys conspicuous by attaching them to something large and visible. Many hotels have caught on to this external aid. To keep guests from departing with their room keys, hotels attach unforgettable objects, such as a large heavy disk, a wooden pear, or a piece of leather about as long as one's forearm. At home, this manipulation can work well for special keys that you use infrequently.

A variety of products are sold to help you remember your keys. Many keychains can be attached directly to you by one of various means. Other keychains are designed with messages or iridescent paint to make you unlikely to forget them. If all else fails, you can purchase a small Hide-a-key metal box that attaches under your car or stays in an obscure spot near your front door.

Chores. An apartment or a house asks a lot of the tenant or owner. The costs of heat and electricity can skyrocket if memory fails to turn them off when they are not needed. Likewise, maintenance of houseplants and a yard can become a financial loss if one forgets to water them as necessary.

Similarly, every apartment or house contains many appliances. Misuse of these can increase the cost of utility charges and may pose a threat to safety. Many of the timing devices discussed earlier can also be hooked up to regulate the turning on and off of appliances. Additionally, there are many more appliances that "remember" to turn themselves on or off. If you are going to buy a major appliance, car, house, boat, or any other very expensive product, inquire into what memory functions the product possesses. After all, why not try to buy the product that does what you want it to do and also facilitates memory?

Shopping. Shopping combines several memory tasks: the items to be purchased, the comparative prices at different stores, and the "running tab" of groceries in a shopping cart. A pad of paper and a pencil is obviously helpful for all of these tasks, but here are more specific aids as well.

Your shopping list. When your college allows, you may avoid eating in the dining hall in order to cook in your room or apartment. While being free to prepare your own food is a perk (especially after eating the food at most college dining halls), it is also a chore. The standard grocery list is one of the simplest and most effective external memory aids (see Figure 25). Many people use photocopies for each week's shopping. A checklist cues you to items you might otherwise forget, is quicker to fill out than a written list, and spares you the effort of dredging up potential needs from memory. Posting a blank list in the kitchen will allow you to mark items as you run out. Grocery stores sometimes sell checklists in convenient pads. Finally, you can avoid having to constantly remember to buy staple items by buying in bulk. When you have the habit of buying certain products in large quantities a few times a year, the presence of the products at home tends to remind you not to worry about purchasing them. And you'll save money, too.

Baby Food		**Fresh Fruit**	
Cereal	❑	Apples	❑
Fruit	❑	Grapefruit	❑
Meat	❑	Lemons	❑
Vegetable	❑	Oranges	❑
Baked Food		**Fresh Vegetables**	
Bread	❑	Beans	❑
Cake	❑	Carrots	❑
Cookies	❑	Lettuce	❑
Pie	❑	Peas	❑
Baking Needs		Potatoes	❑
Baking Powder	❑	Tomatoes	❑
Flour	❑	**Frozen Food**	
Mixes	❑	Fruit	❑
Shortening	❑	Ice Cream	❑
Sugar	❑	Juices	❑
Yeast	❑	Meat	❑
Beverages		Vegetables	❑
Coffee	❑	**Household Goods**	
Fruit Juice	❑	Bleach	❑
Soft Drinks	❑	Paper Napkins	❑
Tea	❑	Paper Towels	❑
Canned Food		Pot Cleaner	❑
Evaporated Milk	❑	Soap	❑
Fruit	❑	Stationery	❑
Fruit Juice	❑	Toilet Tissue	❑
Soup	❑	Wax	❑
Vegetable	❑	Wax Paper	❑
Condiments		**Meats**	
Catsup	❑	Bacon	❑
Mayonnaise	❑	Beef	❑
Mustard	❑	Hamburger	❑
Relish	❑	Pork	❑
Salt	❑	Weiners	❑
Spices	❑	**Poultry, Sea Food**	
Dairy Food		Chicken	❑
Butter	❑	Turkey	❑
Cheese	❑	Fish	❑
Cream	❑	**Miscellaneous**	
Eggs	❑	Cereal	❑
Milk	❑	Gelatin	❑
Dried Foods		Macaroni	❑
Prunes	❑	Pet Food	❑
Raisins	❑	Rice	❑
Drugs & Sundries		_____	
Beauty Aids	❑	_____	
Cigarettes	❑	_____	
Drugs	❑	_____	
Toothpaste	❑		

Figure 25. A Checklist for Shopping

Prices. When planning a shopping trip, you may need to determine how much you are likely to spend. Depending on your budget or cash-on-hand, this estimate can be important to your buying decisions. In making such a determination, your memory for the prices of different brands or stores may be unreliable. Books concerning product price and quality, such as those put out by Consumer Reports, can serve as a worthwhile memory aid.

Your "running tab." Getting "caught short" at the checkout counter can be embarrassing. Many grocery stores sell a shopping counter that keeps track of the total cost of items in your cart. Hand calculators can do the same chore.

How much you've spent. Obviously, you can do this task by writing down what you spent or by keeping and totaling receipts. Nevertheless, some people find it faster and more efficient to record purchases using a device such as a checkbook calculator (a large, easy-to-use calculator with checkbook holder and pen).

To take coupons. Part of being a good shopper is taking advantage of bargains. To do so requires keeping track of the sales opportunities and being able to put your hands on coupons and sales information when they can be used. A device to organize sales information facilitates your remembering to make use of this information and save money, e.g., such as a budget planner (a divider used to organize coupons before and during shopping and to maintain accurate budget records).

Party supplies. A party, especially if it involves many people and elaborate plans, requires you to perform several memory tasks: remembering who should be invited; remembering to send the invitations; remembering to buy food, drink, and gifts. There are aids that will facilitate your remembering the things you have to do when planning a party.

Special Days and Dates

With different degrees of elaborateness, people traditionally give cards, notes, or calls to friends and relatives on special days. For some people, passive reminders are sufficient for recalling dates. Such devices tell you "whom and when" to honor only when you happen to look at them. The timing devices discussed in the Appointments section can also be used to actively remind you of special days. Long-term timing devices will signal when a special day has arrived.

Personal history – records of your past. Your college days are very important now and will remain so all of your life. If you keep records of your experiences, you will be grateful later in your life. But all records take some planning. We must either anticipate that an experience will be one we will later wish to remember, or take action immediately following it. For example, when we take a camera to an event, we are obviously anticipating the event is worth recording. If we don't bring a camera, we might jot down our reminiscences after the event is over.

Some people keep a daily record in the form of a diary or log. The act of keeping a daily record facilitates memory in three ways. It relieves memory of having to retain all of the details of an event. But it also fosters a better memory for the event, because the process of making a record provides a prompt additional review of what happened. Finally, at a later point in time, the personal notes will enhance retrieval processes better than any other form of questioning or material.

Mementos can also be useful. You may never have occasion to think of certain personal events again unless a cue reminds you of them. Souvenirs, programs, tickets, and other objects serve more than sentimental purposes. They provide the clues necessary for us to remain as close as possible to the positive aspects of our pasts (Graumann, 1985). Some people complain that mementos just create a lot of clutter, but what appears to be clutter to you now may bring back vivid memories years from today.

Reminiscing. Of course, photo albums, films, and mementos are helpful to this end. However, you may also want to look back on an important time or event for which you have no photos or mementos. On such occasions, try to find sensory cues from the relevant period. Appropriate sensory cues can often help the desired memory to emerge. Play music that you have associated with this period. A collection of old records or tapes is rich with memory cues. Aromas from perfumes, prepared foods, fruits, or other sources can also provide potent cues to moments otherwise lost to time. Some products are specifically intended to link experiences and past memories with fragrances, e.g., the Aromance 2100 (a "diffuser" generates environmental fragrances that awaken memories through the playing of a "fragrance" record).

Choosing and Using External Aids

Your choice of an external aid should depend on its purpose, its effectiveness, and whether the aid suits your tastes. The purpose of an external aid is paramount in your choice because external aids differ greatly in how they assist memory. They are designed to assist registration, retention, and/or retrieval for a certain memory task that arises in a particular situation of everyday life (Intons-Peterson, 1993; Intons-Peterson & Fournier, 1986; Intons-Peterson & Newsome, 1992; Petro & Herrmann, 1991; Petro, Herrmann, Burrows, & Moore, 1992). One aid will assist a memory task concerned with an activity at home (such as timing the baking of bread), another an activity at work (keeping appointments), another some form of recreation (remembering the rules of a game). Some aids have broader applications than others, but all apply best to a restricted range of memory tasks. Thus, you should not hope to find an external aid that will improve your memory in general. Instead, you should seek external aids that assist memory for the specific memory tasks you find important.

Your choice of an external aid should be based on a careful consideration of how well it might apply to the memory task of interest to you. Often an aid that seems like it would be effective on initial examination, turns out not to be. For example, a piece of string tied around one's finger is often touted as a way to remember to do things. Nevertheless, a piece of string on your finger is rarely effective because it does not tell you what you have to remember. Because of its ineffectiveness, the piece-of-string aid is hardly ever used despite it being a universal symbol of memory use. Another example of an ineffective aid is the current "findable" keychains, which help you locate them by beeping when you whistle or clap. Unfortunately, these keychains beep to any random noise, interrupting conversations and other activities. In the end, they are not very useful.

Your choice of an external aid should rest on a realistic appraisal of whether it suits your tastes. Some people will advise you to make reminders of appointments by writing on your hand. This might work for you, but not if you dislike being seen with hands covered with ink. Similarly, many state-of-the-art commercial aids, such as memory watches, are not very popular because they require too much time and effort to use properly. If you sense that you will not put in the effort to learn to use them, or if you are easily intimidated by gadgets, hi-tech memory aids might not be for you. If you are a "gadget freak," several mail order companies sell various kinds of memory aids. Contact: The Sharper Image (P.O. Box 26823, San Francisco, CA 94126-6823), Marklinc (14 Jewel Drive, Dept.W, Wilmington, MA 01887-9988), and the Sporting Edge (22121 Crystal Creek Blvd., Bothell, WA 98021).

Summary

A sight, sound, touch, or movement captures attention so well that the best way to improve memory is often through the use of an external memory aid. Consequently:
- A knowledge of a variety of external aids, and how to make the best use of them, is essential to improving memory,
- External aids exist to help task-categories concerned with

physical memory, studying, work memory, and personal memory.

Learning and remembering may be facilitated by: a checklist, manuals, diagrams, sketches, notes, "teaching machines," memory art, superstitious objects, knowledge sources, a "memory-friendly" desk, etc. There are hundreds of devices that assist you not only with schoolwork but also personal life. These include devices that assist with personal finances, cooking, maintaining one's health, keeping track of one's possessions, carrying out routine chores, having fun, staying in touch with your past, and aid other personal memory tasks.

11. Social Context

Our relationships with others are very important in life, in general, and in college. In order to obtain assistance from other students and from professors, we must interact successfully with them. It will do you no good to clash with your professors. Similarly, it won't help if you antagonize your classmates. This chapter explains how good relationships with others facilitate your academic performance.

Getting along with other people rests largely on courtesy and on empathy. Part of getting along with others is cognition. You must make and meet appointments, repay favors, do chores that others depend on you to do. Your performance of such tasks helps determine how others judge and treat you. Failure to perform these memory tasks can lead your family, friends, and acquaintances to make negative judgments about your caring, sensitivity, manners, or even intelligence. Alternatively, successful performance can lead others to make corresponding positive judgments about you. Because your relationships with others can be seriously affected by your performance of various memory tasks, successful memory performance becomes especially important in social contexts (Best, 1992; Wyer & Srull, 1989).

Ironically, your memory is more likely to fail when you are with others than when you are alone. For example, it is harder to remember what you have learned when you are in class than when in your dorm room or apartment. Your memory performance fails you in social contexts in one of three ways. You fail sometimes because you simply do not realize that a person expects you to remember something, or to remember it to a certain degree. You fail other times because social situations are too distracting to use your memory effectively. Finally, even if you have successfully performed the memory task expected of you, you may still fail to communicate adequately that you have learned or remembered something.

This chapter will explain how various aspects of social situations affect your academic performance (Baron & Byrne, 1994). You will examine the memory performance that others expect of you: which tasks you should perform and how well you should perform them. Your increased awareness of these expectations will demonstrate to your family members, friends, and acquaintances that you can remember the information important to your relationship with them. You will examine how interacting with others distracts you and reduces your ability to concentrate on memory tasks. You will learn how to control the flow of conversations so as to have more mental time to perform memory tasks. You will examine the communication factors that render a person's recall less than convincing despite possessing an underlying memory that is accurate and complete. Your greater appreciation of these factors will enable you to recall what you remember in a more plausible fashion.

Myosotis arvensis
Common
Forget-me-not

Cupid

Figure 26. Internationally Recognized Symbols that Direct a Person to "not Forget" Certain Information: to carry out actions, a string around the finger; to remember the past, an elephant; to remember a loved one, "forget-me-not" flowers and cupid.

Recognizing the Memory Performance Expected of You

Task Expectations

Level of performance of a memory task. Often, others feel you have failed at a memory task even though you believe you have succeeded. For example, you may feel that you correctly recalled what was addressed in class, only to have your professor say he or she regarded your answer as incorrect. This discrepancy occurs because other people often have different expectations for what constitutes good academic performance.

Your academic reputation. Perhaps of the greatest importance to the way others judge your academic performance is your academic reputation. In any circle of acquaintances or co-workers you have known for a while, you have a reputation for how you succeed or fail at your courses. Like reputations for other characteristics (such as loyalty, diligence, or discretion), academic reputations are based generally on our past behavior patterns.

Most people would regard a reputation for a good memory as desirable when in college. If your memory reputation is excellent and you forget some fact or something you were to do, others will say you were tired or that even the best will falter sometimes. However, a "good" reputation is also likely to bring extra responsibilities. If you are known for "always remembering details," people may ask you to remember more than your share of chores or projects. A bad memory reputation is usually regarded as an undesirable emblem of weakness or incompetence. When your reputation is terrible, others may hold it against you. If you succeed in remembering some obscure fact, or actually do as you promised, others will say it was a fluke. However, a bad-memory reputation can free one from excessive impositions. If you are known to be "absentminded," people will be reluctant to burden you with memory tasks, giving you extra free time.

Memory stereotypes. Many people recognize the dangers of stereotypes. However, people are often surprised to find that stereotypes can govern how others judge our memory performance. Some examples of some memory stereotypes are listed in Table 11-1. This table presents the average ratings made by a dozen college students at Hamilton College, Clinton, New York. They were asked to estimate four kinds of memory ability as a function of a person's age, occupation, and marital role. The table shows expectations in memory performance are a function of the specific kind of task and the person's role. Notice how the ratings are lowest for a child, highest for young and middle-aged adults, and lower again for the senior citizen. Among the occupations, pilots are judged to have the best memory overall, although lawyers and professors are judged higher than pilots regarding knowledge. However, the participants in this study were judging from their knowledge of stereotypes, because no study has been done that examined the memory of people in all of these occupations. Memory stereotypes have also been established for gender (Crawford, Herrmann, Randall, Holdsworth, & Robbins, 1989; Herrmann, Crawford, & Holdsworth, 1992; Loftus, Banaji, Schooler, & Foster, 1987) and age (Best, 1992; Best, Hamlett, & Davis, 1992).

If stereotypes can affect the way ratings are made regarding memory performance, then it is likely that stereotypes affect the way we are judged by others in college life. Thus, when someone's reaction to your academic performance is unrealistically high or low, consider whether it may be because of stereotypical beliefs associated with your age, occupation, gender, or other characteristics. In such a case, you cannot expect to change their stereotype, because it has been established with years of learning. You should know that there are committees and college officials on your campus who can help you if you feel that prejudicial attitudes about your memory ability (or any other characteristic) are interfering with your academic performance or a professor's evaluation of your performance.

Table 11-1. Memory Stereotypes

	Knowledge	Events (personal experiences)	Intentions (things to do)	Actions (skills)	Average
Family					
Young adult	4.4	4.8	4.5	4.5	4.6
Wife	4.6	5.1	4.7	4.0	4.6
Husband	4.8	4.8	4.0	4.4	4.5
Middle-aged person	5.1	4.7	4.1	4.2	4.5
Senior citizen	4.6	4.2	3.4	3.5	3.9
Child	2.5	3.4	3.5	3.5	3.2
Occupation					
Airline pilot	6.0	5.1	5.8	6.4	5.8
Lawyer	6.6	5.4	5.1	5.1	5.6
Professor	6.9	5.2	4.8	4.5	5.4
Mechanic	5.2	4.0	5.0	6.4	5.2
Reporter	5.4	5.8	4.9	4.7	5.2
Receptionist	4.9	4.9	5.3	5.0	5.0
Politician	5.9	5.3	4.8	4.1	5.0
Police officer	4.9	4.5	5.0	5.7	5.0
Plumber	4.7	3.8	5.0	5.8	4.8
Company spokesperson	5.5	4.5	4.7	4.1	4.7
Salesperson	5.3	4.4	4.4	4.3	4.6

Note: A rating of 7 corresponded to a very superior memory; a rating of 1 corresponded to a very inferior memory.

Feedback. Students get feedback continually about how well or how poorly they performed an academic task. However, this " feedback" cannot be taken at face value (Best, 1992). People often deliberately *contrive* to make memory performance appear better or worse than it really is. Some students who get poor grades are actually capable of high grades. They do so in order to achieve certain social goals (Gentry & Herrmann, 1990). Comments about your academic performance may be intended to flatter or insult you, or they may be intended to show you kindness or anger.

Regardless of the intention behind a contrivance, it is important to distinguish contrived feedback from accurate and deserved feedback. As discussed in Chapters 3 and 5, you are best off if your attitudes about your memory and study skills are accurate. If you believe a negative contrivance about your memory, it will lower your confidence and lead you to perform the memory task poorly. A classmate stands to gain if you lose confidence because you will be more likely to make them look good on an exam. Believing positive contrivances will only hamper your performance because they will give you an unrealistic sense of your memory ability. Again, classmates are likely to look better than you if you have an exaggerated sense of confidence and study less for an exam. Six kinds of contrivances are especially common:

Contrivances of Others About Your Memory

Memory insult. A person points out a memory failure of yours that otherwise might have been overlooked and claims that the failure is indicative of a "bad memory." You forget that Columbus' third ship was the Santa Maria and a companion lambastes you for your idiocy. Chances are that the person who says this is angry with you for something unrelated to their love of history.

Memory praise. A person praises your success at a memory task far beyond what it deserves and claims your success is indicative of a "good memory." You remember the Nina, Pinta, and Santa Maria and a colleague declares you are brilliant! Enjoy the praise but beware that the other person wants something.

Memory alibi. A person makes excuses for a memory failure you have. You forgot to pick up a quart of milk on the way home from work. Someone present forgives this mistake, noting that after a long day you have a right to be tired. Perhaps, but the comment may be based on a desire to get a favor from you later.

Memory responsibility charge. A person claims that performing a memory task was your responsibility and not someone else's (such as the person making the claim). You arrive home without the milk, thinking that someone else was to pick it up, only to be accused of being irresponsible.

Memory non-cooperation. A person fails to help you at a memory task, although he or she is capable of doing so. In response to a query, you say the "Nina, Pinta, and Santa" (but you just can't get it) and a friend, who surely knows Columbus' saga, volunteers nothing. Such an obvious decision not to help when help could be offered shows your friend has some concern about your friendship.

Memory fraud. A person claims your memory is in error on some point, although you both know that this claim is untrue. Such a refutation of you bodes ill for your relationship with this person. Of course, people will also contrive about their own memory performance as well as yours.

Be alert to the social motives behind another's contrivance about his or her own memory. Generally, you should be careful about using another person as the standard for judging your memory ability.

Using Others as Memory Aids

Sometimes we do not feel like making an effort to remember what we know about something that arises in conversation. Instead, we ask someone present to serve as a human memory aid. We may ask them to answer the question, even though we could have answered it if we really tried. Or we ask them to register information in their memory and to tell us about it later. Or we may ask them to remind us later when we are supposed to do something.

Unfortunately, there are definite disadvantages to using a friend, acquaintance, or classmate as a memory aid. First, the person you regard as having a good memory may actually provide you with inaccuracies (Goldsmith & Pillemer, 1988). Using others as a "reminder service" can get you into trouble if the person aiding you has a faulty memory. Even if the person has a good memory and can be counted on to remember or register memories for you, there is no such thing as a free lunch. People who are willing to remember for you will eventually expect to be paid back. They know you have imposed on them. The use of others as memory aids is a last-ditch manipulation.

Social Pressures

Influence of People Present on What we Remember

Sometimes people assert that our recall is inadequate. Because of their doubt, we are often inclined to doubt ourselves. Even if we are initially sure of our recollection, we may come to disbelieve our own eyes and accept the account of several other people. People find it especially difficult to hold a lone dissenting view among well-respected friends or authorities (Asch, 1956). For example, in a study group several people may claim that a certain fact is true, when in fact it is not. In such a case, you may well revise your memory according to their version. The effect of social pressure on your confidence in what you recall is summarized in Figure 27.

It is not possible to suggest an easy way to insulate your memory from the influence of all group pressures. But bear in mind that your memory and understanding of course material may be right when others say it is wrong. Because you could be right, you should guard against revising your memories simply to lessen the social pressures disagreement can trigger. If others attack your recall, check later for corroborating evidence. Don't alter your memory just because others challenge it.

Influence of Groups with Which We Identify

The accuracy of your recall for information can be affected by the influences of groups to which you belong – even when the members of a group are not present. We learn and retain more about matters that are consistent with our religious, political, and social beliefs.

Considerable evidence shows that we edit our memories so they record our actions or words in a socially more favorable light (Greenwald, 1980). We also tend to better retain ideas that are consistent with our socially relevant interests. For example, after reading a balanced passage that discusses the pros and cons of a political issue, most people retain more accurately the facts about the side they favor, and less accurately facts from the position they oppose (Levine & Murphy, 1943).

To avoid having biased memories, spend extra time studying the facts that stand contrary to your position. For example, when you overhear an argument, pay special attention to the points you disliked because they are the ones you are likely to forget. This extra care will lead your memory to be more accurate. A by-product of this balanced rehearsal is that people disinclined to your point of view will give you additional credit for being open-minded because you possess an unusually accurate memory for the other point of view.

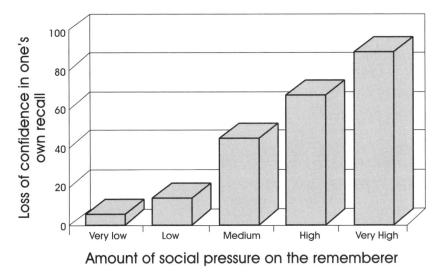

Figure 27. The Effect of Social Pressure on a Person's Confidence in what He or She Recalls (hypothetical data based on the research literature)

Communicating About Your Memory In a Convincing Manner

Assuming you have successfully recalled something in a social context, you may still have a problem convincing others that your recall is correct. There are three ways you can increase the likelihood that others will believe in what you recall. You can express your recall with an appropriate degree of confidence; you can strive to make the contents of your recall include the most essential details; and you can couch your recall in language that best describes your memory performance.

Expression. Overstatement or understatement of the confidence in your recall will likely hurt your credibility. Considerable research has demonstrated that witnesses in court will be regarded as remembering the truth if they sit up and speak confidently. John Dean, of Watergate fame, was regarded as having an excellent memory because he conveyed his recall of the events of Nixon's presidency in a convincing fashion (despite later investigation having shown Dean's recall was full of inaccuracies; Neisser, 1982).

Content. To be convincing, your memory claim should be internally consistent. Although inconsistencies appear in even highly accurate reports from memory, major contradictions between facts make a report appear illogical and indicate the memory underlying the report is distorted. The people you interact with will invariably discount what you recall if it contains obvious inconsistencies. Your recall will tend to be better accepted if you have a corroborating source, such as newspapers, books, or memos. Or your source can be someone whose memory is trusted, who can "back up" what you say.

Memory language. When you are called upon in class, your recall will be more credible if you couch it in appropriate memory vocabulary – the terms and catch phrases we use to describe our memory states. A range of commonly used verbs can express varying degrees of certainty. Thus, you may indicate that you suspect, believe, think, know, guarantee, or even swear that something you remember is true (Searle, 1969). Different memory terms have subtly different meanings. If you become more sensitive to memory terminology, you can express yourself better. For example, after having forgotten to do something for a friend, you may choose to excuse yourself by saying your memory was "overloaded." The success of this claim will depend on whether you can demonstrate why your memory was overloaded (Schvaneveldt, Reid, Gomez, & Rice, 1998; Tindall-Ford, Chandler, & Sweller, 1997). Or you may excuse yourself by saying you have a memory "like a sieve." The success of this claim will depend on whether your friend knows or can be convinced that your memory fails with unintentional and unusual frequency.

Besides appropriate use of memory language, you can improve your communication of memory performance even more by effective use of nonverbal signals. Many nonverbal signals concerning memory are virtually universal. When we recognize someone on the street, a smile or a widened gaze can be sufficient to signal our recognition. If you fail to remember something, you may groan or shake your head. If you want a moment longer to come up with something that you are sure you can remember, you may repeatedly mutter "oh" or shake your hand in the air. Combining appropriate nonverbal signals with verbal claims can make for an even more persuasive case that your memory is accurate.

The Current Status of Your Relationships with Other People

This obvious point cannot be left unsaid: people will be inclined to judge your memory and cognitive powers favorably or unfavorably depending on how you are getting along with them. The status of your relationships with others will depend on how you have treated them regarding many matters, including their performance of memory tasks. The sympathy or harshness with which others view your memory will in part be a function of how you have treated their memory performance. There is an unwritten social code of memory etiquette, and your adherence or rejection of it will usually come back to haunt you (see Table 11-2).

Table 11-2. Some Rules of Memory Etiquette

---

1. Do not comment on another's lack of memory ability. If someone in a discussion continually forgets items just mentioned, do not point this out or else you will appear rude.
2. If you must correct a memory error, do so politely. When a friend recalls some information incorrectly and you must correct lest someone else be set wrong, do so in a considerate manner ("you meant XXX, didn't you?)
3. Ignore unimportant memory errors (especially if the person is a loved one).
4. Do not point out unintentional repeated recalls (especially if the person is elderly). If grandpa is going to tell you the Battle of Bullrun for the two hundredth time, consider that you'll be doing the same before too long.
5. Remember what another person was talking about prior to an interruption in a conversation. Failure to remember what someone was just talking about may make you seem actually uninterested and insincere.
6. Remember another's successes, and forget their failures.

Also, the regard of other students and faculty for you will depend in part on one's courtesy. However, it is a difficult task for a number of reasons. First, names are usually meaningless. Second, we often don't attend to names when we are introduced, and make no effort to relate a name to a face, believing falsely that no effort is needed. Later when it is clear to a person that we failed to remember his or her name, this person will very likely be offended. Like people in all walks of life, students need the good will of their classmates and their teachers. Fortunately, there are procedures that can make it easier to learn another person's name and remember it later.

Visual imagery has been shown to relate a name to a face in a number of studies (e.g., Morris, Jones, & Hampson, 1978) to increase name-face association memory very considerably.

The method is very simple. It involves taking a major characteristic of the face you need to remember and linking it by means of imagery to the name. Suppose, for example that you need to remember Mr. Hill. What you do is imagine a hill growing out of the top of Mr. Hill's nose. If Mr. Hill's nose is not a prominent feature, you can always imagine it as a prominent feature – after all Mr. Hill won't know what you are thinking!

Where names are not easy to imagine, such as Mrs. Bruce, Mr. Sykes and so on, you have to make a word you can imagine, which is similar in sound. So Mrs. Bruce sounds like Mrs. Bruise – so imagine Mrs. Bruce with a bruise on her cheek. Mr. Sykes sounds like Mr. Socks, so imagine Mr. Sykes wearing socks on his head. While there is a slight danger of mis-remembering, it is only a slight danger, and will not be a problem if you meet the person regularly. Use this method with care. The effort involved in making an image severely interferes with a person's ability to hold a sensible conversation in a social situation. Only use the method if you are sure you will want to remember the person in the future, and then only create an association after the social interaction is finished. For example, you can excuse yourself to go to the toilet. Make the association between name and face and then go back. If you try to carry on a conversation and make an image, you risk being thought cognitively disadvantaged! In many social situations, you know you will be introduced to people you will never meet again. There is no point in trying to remember their names. Occasionally you will make a mistake, but so what! On the other hand, the method, when it is used, has been shown to be effective not only for young adults but for the elderly too, showing an advantage up to 6 months after the initial association was made (Yesavage et al., 1989).

Summary

Social situations require us to perform many memory tasks. This chapter has shown that there are several things you can do to make your memory perform better in social contexts.

Recognize what memory tasks others expect you to perform. Recognize factors that indicate what level of memory performance others expect of you (your reputation, stereotypes that apply to you).

Use conversational manipulations to keep from being distracted, to buy time, and to gather information that will enable you to perform memory tasks in class. Resist social pressures to recall facts and events as others might want you to. Recall plausibly by remembering logically consistent information and by expressing yourself with appropriate memory language and nonverbal signals.

Section V.

Integration of the Fundamentals with How you Feel, Store and Remember, and Get Help from the Environment

12. Study Savvy

The preceding chapters have given you hundreds of options on how to improve your memory and study skills. You have been thoroughly instructed in the multimodal approach. You have good knowledge now on how your academic performance is affected by physical states, emotive states, social interaction, the environment, and mental manipulations. In addition, you have learned how to design your own domain-specific repertoires (Williams, 1996) that take account of the specific situation in which knowledge will be used (Brent & Myers, 2000; Greeno, Smith, & Moore, 1993; Lave, 1988; Scribner, 1984). Repertoires enable you to deploy manipulations suitably, quickly, and efficiently.

The only knowledge remaining for a complete approach to improvement is to develop and practice your skills at applying this knowledge to your own memory performance. As a person practices manipulations they also increase in understanding, i.e., in savvy, about the right circumstances for memory skills to be used. A person with memory "savvy" knows how to recognize memory problems, link them with appropriate manipulations, and employ these manipulations in ways most suited to memory tasks (Bellezza & Buck, 1988; Ericsson, 1985; Herrmann, 1990a).

Improving the Appropriateness of Manipulation Use

In deciding whether a manipulation is appropriate for a given task, ask yourself two key questions. First, do you find the manipulation compatible with the context involved? For some people, the content to be studied for an exam should follow from class notes. They might register it more effectively by attending to the meaning of the items than by attending to their pronunciation. However, some students may want to study the notes by rote, with very little notion of the ideas, and might find the pronunciation manipulation more appropriate. Second, does the manipulation require more effort than you want to give to the task? Although a manipulation may be appropriate to registering or retrieving a certain kind of information, the effort required by the manipulation may not suit you. For a big exam, however, manipulations that form retrieval structures might well be an appropriately rigorous choice. To answer these two questions, you must blend knowledge about your own skills and inclinations with a clear understanding of both your targeted memory tasks and the manipulations you could apply to them.

Self-Observation of Memory Performance

The simplest way to improve the appropriateness of your use of manipulations is to critique your performance when you have actually applied manipulations to a given memory task (Herrmann & Searleman, 1990). As we discussed in Chapters 4 and 5, a key time to learn about appropriateness is when you have just failed at a study task. On such occasions, you should note possible adjustments to the technique or in your effort that might have enabled you to succeed at the task (Brennen et al., 1986; Herrmann, Grubs, Sigmundi & Grueneich, 1986). For example, we sometimes fail to learn a fact in class, despite having heard it clearly when it was said. If we make a note that we failed to do so, we are more likely to take steps to avoid making the same mistake in the future. Alternatively, there are certain memory tasks that we know we are good at. An awareness of the manipulations that make you skillful at these tasks may suggest ways to improve your performance on other tasks.

Self-observation can also be conducted in a more ongoing and systematic fashion. As described in Chapter 3, a study/memory diary can give you useful information about your current successes and failures at academic tasks. The results of a diary may make it easier to identify tasks that deserve more effort. Even if you don't keep formal records, you might routinely stop to mentally review your recent performance.

Interpreting Feedback about Your Memory Performance

Other people can be a useful and independent source of information about our memory performance (Best, 1992). Their praise or criticism, however, should not be accepted at face value. It must be interpreted and assessed. As we learned in Chapter 11, other people frequently offer distorted views of our performance (Gentry & Herrmann, 1990). Accepting inaccurate praise and criticism at face value can mislead you into approaching memory tasks inappropriately. Therefore, evaluate the feedback you get. If it does not square with your own impression of your abilities, but you suspect the person may be right, monitor your performance of the task for a few weeks. Your performance during a period of self-observation will indicate whether you need to prepare specifically for the task. If the feedback does not square with your own impression, and you have good reason to believe the person is wrong, then disregard the feedback.

Comparison of Your Memory Performance with Others

Watching others or listening to the comments they make about their own memory performance allows you to compare your performance to theirs. Perhaps they exploit specific techniques more effectively, or perhaps they "naturally" approach a task in a way that could be useful to you. If your performance compares favorably, you may confirm the appropriateness of your manipulations. Such comparisons are only effective, however, to the extent that people allow you to witness their memory successes and failures. Just as people distort the comments they make about our performance, they may also distort the comments they make about their own performance. Research indicates that people sometimes downplay, or even deny, their superiority at memory tasks, because they feel that to do otherwise would be immodest or might make others feel inferior. People may also feign poor memory performance in order to attain other goals (as discussed in Chapter 11).

Because of this, interpret others' memory performances judiciously. The surest sources of comparisons are people you know well enough to distinguish their actual performance from their motives and capacities for controlling apparent performance. If you are fortunate enough to have a friend who shares your interest in memory, frank discussion of how you approach certain memory tasks would provide the best possible form of comparison.

Continuing Education

Continued learning of memory and study skills will keep your knowledge about manipulations growing. New trade books and magazine articles on memory improvement, tapes developed as improvement guides, and occasional TV shows on specific scientific developments in memory research may opportunely inform and inspire your interest. Courses or training programs in memory improvement can challenge and inform you even more fully. Continued study of memory will deepen your theoretical understanding, enabling you to make better use of your memory manipulations.

Bad Habit Identification and Control

In addition to learning more about the appropriateness and use of manipulations, you should periodically attempt to identify and eliminate habits that hinder your memory performance. Some bad habits are fairly general and interfere with many kinds of tasks (Breme & Rosen, 1982; DiYanni, 1997). For example, going out with your friends night after night is going to hinder your academic performance. Other bad habits are very specific. For example, letting your mind wander when you start to read a textbook for a course you do not like results in poor learning and a waste of time. On the next two pages is a form which you can use to assess your bad memory habits.

This checklist resembles the ones presented in Chapters 4 and 5. It differs, however, because it focuses on bad habits, what not to do, rather than what to do. It assumes you have already put some thought and effort toward specific improvement, including an attitude assessment. In fact, its utility depends on your having sufficient experiences to recognize habitual memory patterns.

Your responses to this checklist can be evaluated in a few ways. An overall score can be accumulated by adding the values of all responses that you circle according to the following scale: "never" – 1, "sometimes" – 2, "half-the-time" – 3, "often" – 4, and "very often" – 5. The overall score will vary quite a bit depending on a person's age and background, but a typical answer for most items will be either "sometimes" or "half-the-time." A more important way to evaluate your responses involves comparing answers to different questions. Obviously, those habits you rated as most frequent may be ones that interfere with your performance. They most likely should and can be changed – with effort.

Checklist for bad memory habits. Directions: Indicate how often you act in the manner described.

Habits	Never	Some-times	Half the time	Often	Very Often
Memory Attitudes					
1. Holding a memory task in low regard.	x	x	x	x	x
2. Holding your memory ability in low regard.	x	x	x	x	x
Conditioning					
1. Assuming that poor physical condition won't hinder memory performance, or tolerating fatigue before an expected memory challenge.	x	x	x	x	x
2. Using adverse substances when performing or about to perform memory tasks.	x	x	x	x	x
3. Living an excessively busy lifestyle.	x	x	x	x	x
4. Living an excessively routinized lifestyle.	x	x	x	x	x
5. Not making or not referring to a daily schedule.	x	x	x	x	x
Environmental Use					
1. Keeping possessions in a disorganized state.	x	x	x	x	x
2. Memory arrogance — not using mental manipulations or environmental aids because you feel that it should be possible to perform the task without added effort or use of an aid.	x	x	x	x	x
Mental Manipulations					
Registration					
1. Half-hearted rehearsal learning while with others or while watching TV.	x	x	x	x	x
2. Learning indiscriminately, without selecting main points or ideas for greater concentration.	x	x	x	x	x
3. Daydreaming or letting your thoughts wander when you should be learning.	x	x	x	x	x

4. Intentional disattention — going through the motions of learning while aware your mind is elsewhere.	x	x	x	x	x
5. Cramming rather than using a series of study sessions.	x	x	x	x	x

Remembering

1. Failure to prepare — not studying prior to a known challenge to your ability to remember.	x	x	x	x	x
2. Tolerance of memory errors — accepting a memory error because correcting it seems too difficult or inconvenient.	x	x	x	x	x
3. Compulsive remembering checks — repeatedly checking whether you have done or remembered something, even when you remember just making such a check.	x	x	x	x	x

Development of Managerial Skills

Superior memory skill requires more than the learning of an array of memory manipulations. You must also be able to skillfully manage these manipulations according to the demands of different tasks and situations. Whether you are registering information during learning or retrieving it during remembering, you can take steps to organize and check your efforts. These managerial manipulations will help you use memory aids and practices as efficiently as possible.

Managerial Manipulations for Learning

1. Make sure that you are registering the correct information. Familiarize yourself with everything to be learned before you begin to register information (Gruneberg, 1973).
2. Consider whether your learning would be more efficient if you studied the material in parts or in its entirety. If you employ part learning, spend time subsequently studying the whole of the material.

3. Use more than one kind of manipulation when possible for the same material. For most tasks, you can find both an appropriate strength and attribute manipulation. For example, you might learn a list of items by first rehearsing the items, then by making attribute judgments on each item. Most experts believe that the use of different techniques leads to a more durable and accessible memory trace.

4. Distribute your studying over several occasions. Massed practice usually leads to slower learning than distributed practice. A study session of two hours is usually less effective in fostering registration than two one-hour study sessions separated in time. However, whether you mass or distribute your practice, it is a bitter truth that the amount learned is directly related to the amount of time spent in practice (Ebbinghaus, 1885).

5. Repeatedly test yourself as you learn. Before a study session, first estimate how much you will recall. Be prepared for plateaus in your learning, in which continued efforts at registration are not followed by increases in recall. Plateaus will eventually give way to additional increases in recall. Overlearn the material if it is especially important or detailed: after you have learned 100% of it, study and test yourself further.

6. As you test yourself, imagine the situation in which you will be called on to remember the information you have learned. Be sensitive to whether you will be required to recall information in a forwards direction or backwards. For example, if you are learning French, study vocabulary from English-to-French as well as from French-to-English.

7. Study on a schedule (Britton & Tesser, 1991), and review periodically after learning.

Managerial Manipulations for Remembering

1. During remembering, recall at a relaxed pace. Hurrying leads you to miss recalling parts of the information you remember. Hurrying is also more likely to elicit inaccuracies than a slow, deliberate recall. If possible, try to delay giving your recall when the desired information is not yet accessed.

2. Recall in an order that is optimal for the information and presentation conditions.
   a. Follow a chronological order when possible, such a when trying to recall a story or an event.

    b. When information has been presented briefly and recently, recall recent information first, then initial information, and finally the information in between.

    c. When a considerable amount of information is involved, and it is not chronologically organized, it will help to break the task down into parts. After you have done so, alternate between attempting to recall the parts and the entirety of the memory trace.

3. Question yourself in a balanced manner. Ask yourself related questions, which call for specific bits of information. Then ask yourself divergent questions, which relate indirectly to the information you want to remember. Alternate between convergent and divergent questions until recall succeeds, or until you feel that you are blocked.

4. Mentally edit what you have in mind before you recall it to others. You can check the correctness of your retrieval in several ways.

    a. Estimate the likely accuracy of your recall (Johnson & Raye, 1981; Schooler, Gerhard, & Loftus, 1986). People usually have a reasonably good idea of what they know. One way to form your estimate is to ask yourself how likely you would be to recognize the right answer. For subjects you know well, your estimate should be high. You should tend to have much lower estimates for unfamiliar subjects. You may, however, have further reasons to doubt or trust your recall for given facts, regardless of your general familiarity. Whether high or low, your estimate is likely to be right more times than not. Of course, a feeling of knowing is still not a guarantee that you remembered correctly (Koriat, 1993, 1994). When you need stronger assurances, take time to perform further checks.

    b. Check the content you have recalled. Is it internally consistent and plausible? If not, your retrieval may have been flawed. Try to remember again, using other manipulations if possible.

    c. Be sensitive to the fact that you may err in many ways. Initially, you might misinterpret the question or query posed for remembering. You can intentionally or unintentionally leave something out (omission). A memory trace can emerge that is either not called for (a false alarm intrusion) or is related to another trace just remembered (a repeat intrusion). Correct traces might be remembered out of sequence, at the wrong time (such as remembering an appointment after it occurred), or in the wrong place (such as recalling information that is socially inappropriate). With continued attempts to remember, erroneous retrievals can repeat their emergence (a double false alarm intrusion). Finally, after retrieving part of the desired information, you may think you have finished remembering, when you are not actually done (Reason & Mycielska, 1983). Double-checking these sources of error can be a way of cross-examining your recall process.

   d. Screen your recall to be sure that you don't "blurt out" something from memory that may be offensive.

   e. Give extra scrutiny to answers that come quickly and seem very familiar. Some errors are "strong habits" that intrude upon retrieval.

5. If your recall or recognition efforts fail despite conscientious attempts, avoid frantically repeating them.

   a. Give the task a rest. Chances are good that the desired item will eventually emerge into consciousness.

   b. Try the Yoga method of recall. Lay down in a quiet spot where you won't be disturbed. Systematically relax the muscles in your body. When you are extremely relaxed, put questions to yourself about the information you would like to recall.

6. Claim an honest level of confidence in the accuracy of your memory. Express your certitude or doubt prudently.

7. For recurring memory problems, establish a routine sequence of steps to guide your recall process. Include checks for errors (for instance, intrusion or omission) you have found yourself prone to commit.

Improving the Efficiency of Manipulation Use

Knowledge about how to improve memory and study skills will only go so far. Proficient academic performance requires gaining experience in the use of memory manipulations during memory tasks (James, 1890; Watson, 1925). As described in the preceding chapter, when people have acquired considerable experience at certain memory tasks, impressive memory abilities often result. For example, prolonged occupational experience may lead to excellent memory abilities for job-related memory tasks. Thus, if you desire a superior memory, you must be prepared to practice memory tasks over a considerable period of time (Wilding & Valentine, 1997). You can no more expect to improve memory skills by merely reading a book than you would your tennis or golf game by doing the same. Hard work and practice are unfortunately essential.

Practice

As mentioned earlier, a good way to excel at a learning task is to practice it directly (Anderson, 1982; Payne, 1992). Research has shown that the normal maximum memory for a series of numbers – around seven – can be increased by practice over several months, so a person will recall as many as 80 digits in a row. Remembering lists of digits probably is not a task at which you care to excel. But the dramatic improvement practice this task affords indicates how much you stand to gain by vigorously practicing an academic task of special interest to you. Acquisition practice is probably the best way to produce a dramatic and durable change in memory ability. However, it must be pointed out that practice requires a great deal of hard work (Chase & Ericsson, 1982).

Practice may also be used to develop retrieval skills for certain tasks. If you know that a particular retrieval task occurs on many occasions, a sure way to excel at this task is to engage in remembering practice (Herrmann, et al., 1987). For example, suppose you sell a line of products, and you want to be facile with the different types or models. After you have learned to identify each product type, practice recalling them – without restudying. Next, practice recalling the entire product line – all of it – again without restudying. Then practice recalling again, and again, until you are satisfied with your improvement. You will discover that the speed and number of words you recall will increase. Typically, a half-dozen repetitions or about 10 minutes per recall are necessary to produce substantial progress. Research has indicated that daily attempts over a few weeks may triple the number of items recalled.

Remembering practice is also very effective for enhancing retrieval of information you once knew well but now recall poorly. If you expect to be called upon at a meeting about some topic that is now hazy, practice retrieving the topic several times beforehand. Even without any relearning, you will recall more information and have faster access to it. By combining relearning with remembering practice, you can further improve your performance.

Contrived Practice

Daily life presents numerous opportunities to practice certain memory tasks. We frequently have occasion to remember names we may know but do not readily retrieve, such as those of old movie stars or distant relatives. If you are interested in improving your performance of common tasks, you will naturally get a lot of practice. Other tasks present far fewer opportunities. We seldom get "practice" at receiving and remembering directions to a new location. When this task does arise, it is usually important that we arrive on time, and most people rely on maps, written directions, or other memory aids. Few people trust their recall of verbal directions enough to engage in practice. If you are interested in improving your performance of uncommon tasks, you will need to devise ways to simulate the experience.

Computer Simulated Practice

Several software packages will now take a person through training exercises that teach the use of various memory manipulations. Most of the manipulations taught are the technical mnemonics (such as the ones taught by the "Einstein Memory Trainer" package). More diversified packages are likely to appear in the near future. The names of some of these software packages may be obtained from any computer store which stocks educational software.

Mental Practice

Even without direct or simulated practice, you can "run through" tasks in your mind. Imagine a memory situation you would like to conquer. Next, imagine yourself carrying out appropriate manipulations: you are taking good care of yourself ahead of time; adopting a positive view towards the task; making use of the environment when you perform the task; and using the mental manipulations most appropriate for the task. Athletes report that "mental practice" focuses their approach in actual competitions. It can do the same for your memory (Hardy & Ringland, 1984).

Role Playing

If there is a person you feel comfortable about asking, enlist that person to help you recreate the situation you want to improve. Suppose that you want to improve your ability to learn names at an introduction. (By the way, this is the most disliked memory task by young and old alike. The sequence of introductions is often unpredictable, and we are socially expected to engage in conversation while registering the name in memory.) In order to practice learning names at introductions, you must have similarly distracting and brief circumstances. Solitary practice is inadequate. Instead, ask your friend to assume any made-up names and introduce him- or herself to you in a natural way. If practiced thoroughly, simulated introductions will improve your use of manipulations during actual introductions. By reversing roles in the situations you create, you can also obtain a good comparison between your own memory performance and your partner's.

Summary

The preceding chapters presented ways on how to improve your memory and study skills. You have been thoroughly instructed in the multimodal approach. You know how repertoires enable you to deploy manipulations suitably, quickly, and efficiently.

A superior memory requires a response to memory tasks that is prompt, appropriate, and proficient. This chapter has explained how bad habits interfere with memory and study skills.

You can work towards a superior memory by developing a knowledge of a variety of manipulations; learning how to manage these manipulations so you use them to best effect; observing your performance; eliminating bad memory habits; and practicing using manipulations.

It is now clear that memory and studying are much more complex than envisioned in the past. Instead, academic performance is best improved by providing a person with many methods, and allowing a flexible response to diverse memory tasks. Our memory is good only in so far as we are prepared with those manipulations that enable us to respond effectively to the specific tasks that challenge us.

Epilogue

The College Success Formula

Success in college is a matter of simple arithmetic. Estimate how much time you spend in preparing for class (P), time you spend in class (C), time spent in self care (SC), and time spent in nonacademic activities unrelated to your schoolwork (N) across a day.

Time spent in preparing for class = P   _____

Time spent in class = C   _____

Time spent in self care (eating, sleep, rest, relaxation) = SC   _____

Time spent in nonacademic activities = N   _____

Total   _____

College Success = P + C + SC + N   _____

Then add these four numbers (P, C, SC, N) up. If your total exceeds 24 hours, go back and think through your estimates again. This is a sign that you may be trying to do too many things. If your total is less than 24 hours, you have obviously failed to take account of something you are doing.

If your total is exactly 24 hours, lets consider how your time is distributed. To some extent, grades depend on P and C. If either is close to zero, there is a problem. Generally, college professors expect two to three hours of preparation for each hour in class. Thus, if you have 3 hours a day in class, you should be spending at least 6 hours in preparation outside of class. Grades depend not on P per se, but also on a proper balance of P + C + SC. The relative size of P, C, and SC will vary from one person to another. There is no ideal combination for everyone but there is an ideal combination for you. Nevertheless, SC for many college students should be 12 (8 hours of sleep, 3 hours for meals, and 1 hour for bathing, dressing, etc.). This leaves 3 hours for nonacademic activities ($N = 24 - (9 + 12)$), such as sports, getting together with friends, watching TV.

If your grades are satisfactory, then you probably have your life in balance. However, if your grades are satisfactory but you are pushing yourself too hard, then you need to make adjustments. In this case you probably need to settle for a less active social life and devote more time to taking care of yourself. If you fear that slowing down your social life will lead to a loss of friends, recognize that genuine friends will be understanding. You might also consider accepting somewhat lower grades as satisfactory. The improved health and peace of mind may be worth it.

If you would like better grades, then you will want to increase your preparation time while reducing the time you spend on nonacademic activities. Sometimes students decide to reduce their time in self care in order to get more time to spend in preparation, or even to have more fun in nonacademic activities. However, the consequences of not taking care of yourself will likely lead to becoming physically or emotionally ill. Also, lack of sufficient self care can make people accident prone.

If your grades are not satisfactory, then your self diagnosis requires a fair amount of self examination. If you are spending a sufficient amount of time in preparation and class, then you are either neglecting your self care or devoting too much time to nonacademic activities, or both. As noted above, neglecting self care is unwise.

If your grades are not satisfactory but you have everything else in balance, you should seek assistance with your studying and/or test taking. Your campus is most likely to have some professionals who are there to advise you on studying and, when appropriate, to help you find a tutor. It may be that you are experiencing test anxiety, a common condition among college students and fortunately very easy to remedy. It may also be the case that you have yet to find the major or even college that is right for you. While in college, learn what really interests you. No one can learn information that is boring or creates anxiety. You are capable of doing many things in life that you would not imagine. A substantial number of students change their major every year or transfer to another institution. If that is on the cards for you, it is better to make such a change earlier than later.

It is easy in college to get in a "time crunch." When this happens, it is a sign that you need to evaluate your College Success Formula. Decide whether or not you are devoting too much time or too little time to P, C, SC, or N.

Make an concerted effort to learn what your college and your professors say would be beneficial for you to learn. If you have career objectives that require high grades, do your best to achieve them. But remember that your physical and emotional health should come first. You deserve to have your share of happiness in life. If your goals (not the goals that your friends, teachers, or parents want you to have) ask too much of you, consider changing your priorities or consider developing new goals. Use the knowledge conveyed in this book to strike the right balance among P, C, SC, and N and to achieve what you hope for.

Glossary

Absentmindedness	When a person intends to do one thing but unintentionally does another.
Absorption	A process by which the contents of working memory are recorded in long-term memory as a result of mentally processing these contents.
Accessibility of a trace	The potential of a trace to be found with sufficient cues, i.e., able to be retrieved.
Acetylcholine	A neurotransmitter that can improve or retard memory.
Acoustic encoding	Encoding of acoustic stimulation or of acoustic information inherent in verbal stimuli.
Acronym	A procedure to facilitate the learning of a list of words by arranging the words so that the first letters of the words themselves make a word (see first letter mnemonic).
Acrostic	A procedure to facilitate the learning of a target word by making a sentence in which each word of the sentence begins with one of the letters making up the target word.
Activation of a trace	The increase in the strength of a trace in long-term memory due to information represented in the trace, or related to the trace, being held in working memory.
Agnosia	An inability to recognize sensory stimuli.
Agreements to perform memory tasks	Tasks whose future performance is divided into parts and allocated between individuals.
Alzheimer's disease	A fatal disorder in which memory loss is a prominent initial feature.
Amnesia syndrome (sometimes called classic amnesia syndrome)	A person has linguistic abilities, intellectual abilities, and STM intact but no ability to form long-term memories.
Anterograde amnesia	The failure to form long-term memories.
Applicability of manipulations	The range of tasks for which mental manipulation will be effective: generally applicable manipulations facilitate most

	or all memory tasks, while specifically applicable manipulations facilitate just certain tasks.
Architecture of memory	The arrangement of information flow between components of the memory system.
Arousal	A general increase in energy to pay attention and to perform.
Articulatory control process	The process that permits rehearsal in the phonological store of the phonological loop.
Arts of memory	Paintings, posters, or maps that have been designed to aid memory either in registration of new information or in remembering of old information.
Assessment of memory and study abilities	Identification of strengths and weaknesses at memory tasks in general as revealed by self-observation or by formal testing by a psychologist.
Associationism	The view that memory is ultimately explained by forming associations between items (see connectionism).
Associations of a trace	One of the four aspects of a trace that may be affected by a mental manipulation. Associations join traces to one another in either a unidirectional or bidirectional manner.
Associative mental manipulations	Techniques that focus attention on two or more details of information at the same time in working memory, thereby leading traces of these details to be absorbed together in long-term memory.
Attention	The process of orienting to and observing the world around us and the contents of working memory.
Attitude manipulations	Manipulations of a person's attitude toward a memory task and toward one's ability to perform the task, so as to enhance memory performance.
Attribute mental manipulations	Techniques that foster deeper comprehension of aspects or qualities in the material to be learned.
Attributes of a trace	One of the four aspects of a trace that may be affected by mental manipulation. An attribute is one facet of the meaning of the information in a trace.
Autobiographical memory	A person's memory for the events of his or her life.
Availability heuristic	Judging the frequency of an event based on how quickly or easily instances of the event can be remembered.
Availability of a trace	Status of a trace as either in memory or not in memory (because it was never learned in the first place or because biological processes destroyed the trace over a retention inter-

	val); that information has been, and continues to be stored in memory.
Backward retrieval strategy	A search of memory beginning with the most recent memories to those that are most distant.
Bad memory and study habits	Automatic ways of responding to memory tasks that impair memory performance.
Benzodiazepines (BZ)	Tranquilizers (such as Librium and Valium) used to treat psychological symptoms (e.g., anxiety, depression, tension) that also impair memory.
Biological theoretical perspective	The view that memory is ultimately explained by biological processes.
Central executive (processor)	A component of the memory system that selects and implements manipulations of any type to facilitate memory performance.
Characteristic features	Features of concept that allow some but not all instances of a particular concept to be classified as such (see defining features).
Clustering	The tendency to organize items into groups in memory based on having a membership in the same category (see subjective organization).
Coding of information	The features of a stimulus or of associations of a stimulus that are stored in memory.
Cognitive maps	A mental map of a particular environment.
Commercial memory aid	A product that was specifically designed by the manufacturer to help a person with memory tasks, including: memory prosthetic, memory correctors, memory robots, and memory friendly products.
Compliance	The choice to perform or not perform a memory task because the person is or is not motivated to do so.
Components of memory	The parts of the memory system as viewed physiologically (parts of the brain) or conceptually (parts of memory processes).
Conceptually driven tasks	Those tasks that require active organization and elaborative processes (also called "top down").
Confabulation	When a person unintentionally makes up a story concerning a past event in his or her life (see false memory syndrome).
Connectionism	The theoretical view that memory is explained ultimately by the formation of connections between items and connections between sets of connections (currently used to describe computer models of memory based on connections).

Consolidation	The physiological process that progressively transforms temporary memories into durable memories held for the long term.
Constructive changes in memory	Changes in the content that occur during encoding, such as by misperception or by the storing in memory one's interpretation of an event as what actually happened (see reconstructive changes).
Content process modes	Manipulations of information in STM, the physical environment, and the social environment to enhance encoding, retention, and retrieval.
Context dependent memory	The superior recall of items which occurs when recall is attempted in the presence of a context that was also present during learning (see encoding specificity principle, state dependent memory, mood dependent memory, and transfer-appropriate processing).
Control processes	Flexible strategies a person uses to select, manipulate, and transform information in memory (see maintenance rehearsal and storage rehearsal).
Conversational flow manipulations	Verbal techniques that delay or redirect the flow of conversation so as to gain time for memory processing.
Credibility of memory performance	The surface validity of a person's remembering dependent on how the person expresses the remembering and on the content of that recalled.
Cryptomnesia	When a person produces something (such as writes a story or a song) believing it to be the product of her or his mind when objectively what produced was previous created by someone else (unintended plagiarism).
Cue-dependent forgetting	An inability to remember when retrieval cues are not present.
Cue gathering	Looking or listening for things that might facilitate your registration or remembering.
Cueing	The beneficial effect of physical cues on learning or remembering.
Cultural memory tasks	Traditions of social interaction that involve performance of certain memory tasks.
Cumulative rehearsal	Rehearsing a set of items over and over (see noncumulative rehearsal).
Data driven tasks	Those tasks that require passive and elementary processes (also called "bottom-up").
Decay of a trace (law of disuse)	The physiological erosion or fading of a memory trace.

Decay theory	The explanation of forgetting as being due to memories growing weaker and weaker with the passage of time.
Declarative memory	A kind of knowledge or memory of facts that is directly accessible to conscious recollection.
Defining features	The essential features of concept that allow an object to be considered an instance of a particular concept (see characteristic features).
Deja vu	The feeling that a person has already experienced a situation while objectively the person knows that she or he has never encountered the situation before.
Dementia	Disorders which result in a deterioration of all intellectual abilities and produce drastic changes in personality, including the progressive dementias (primary undifferentiated dementia, primary differentiated dementia), and secondary dementia.
Depression	The well known emotional state of being down, which can occur naturally or can be induced; depression often leads to lessened memory ability (see anterograde amnesia).
Diary studies	Research in which people keep a diary of memory failures in general or of a particular kind of memory failure.
Digit span	A test in which the subject is presented with a series of digits and then required to recite them in the order of presentation, called forward digit span, or in the reverse order of presentation, called backward digit span; both procedures being an instance of serial learning.
Directed forgetting (suppression)	The conscious forgetting of a memory by deliberately trying not to think about it.
Discrepancy detection principle	The increased likelihood that a person will change recall of an event to include information about the event presented after it when the person does not detect the discrepancy between the post-event information and their memory for the original event.
Displacement of memory	The hypothesis that new information can displace old information similar in kind, such that the old information is gone forever.
Dissociations	When one variable affects performance differently than another variable.
Distinctiveness hypothesis	This hypothesis holds that deeper levels of processing result in better learning than shallower levels of processing, because the deeper processing makes material more distinctive from other memory traces (see elaboration hypothesis).

Distortion of a trace	An alteration of a memory trace in which inaccuracies are usually undetected.
Distribution of practice	When a person spaces or distributes his or her studying over time.
Dynamics of social interaction	Aspects of communicating with others, e.g., its pace and content, that affect encoding and retrieval of information.
Efficiency of manipulation use	The speed with which one is able to execute a manipulation.
Eidetic imagery (photographic memory)	The ability to maintain an image of a visual stimulus after the stimulus has been removed from view.
Elaboration hypothesis	Deeper levels of processing result in better learning than shallower levels of processing because the deeper processing makes the memory for the material richer than other memory traces (see distinctiveness hypothesis).
Elaborative rehearsal (Type II rehearsal)	Repetition of information in order to analyze it more deeply and form a long-term memory of the information.
Emergence	A process in which traces in long-term memory become sufficiently active and re-enter your working memory.
Emotional state manipulations	Manipulations of a person's mood and emotionality so as to enhance memory performance.
Encoding	The registration of an experience in memory incidentally or intentionally.
Encoding congruency	The selective effect of mood on the encoding of information (see recall congruency).
Encoding specificity principle	The superior recall of items which occurs when recall is attempted in the presence of cues that were also present during learning (see context dependent memory, state dependent memory, mood dependent memory, and transfer-appropriate processing).
Engram	The physical material (neuronal or chemical) in which a memory trace resides.
Environmental manipulation	A behavior that focuses on, and takes control of, objects or events around you to stimulate, or even substitute for, memory.
Exceptional memory	A person who can learn and/or remember in ways that are clearly superior to most people; includes experts, memorists, mnemonists, and idiot-savants.
Exhaustive serial search	A search of item by item in memory, regardless of whether the correct item has been found before all items have been examined (see exhaustive serial search).

Experimental approach to the study of memory	Identifies and documents the existence and nature or memory phenomena with observations that are systematically collected.
Expert knowledge	The knowledge of experts that allows them to perform impressive memory feats in their area of expertise.
Explicit encoding (intentional)	Willful trying to register information in memory.
Explicit memory tasks	Tasks that do require conscious recollection of prior learning (see implicit memory tasks).
Explicit remembering	Conscious recall that occurs intentionally or unintentionally.
External knowledge sources	Sources of information that one may have known at one time but which one cannot access in memory.
External memory aids	The use of objects and devices to remember to perform prospective memory tasks or retrospective information (see internal memory aids and commercial memory aids, reminding services, and external knowledge sources).
Face-name imagery technique	A technical mnemonic for learning a person's name by imagining an object suggested by the name superimposed on the person's face, resulting in rapid and effective learning of the name in response to seeing the person's face.
False memory syndrome	The recall of fictitious events, usually traumatic, with the belief that the events are genuine.
Feedback about memory performance	Praise or criticism from others about a person's performance (see memory contrivance).
First letter mnemonic	A procedure to facilitate the learning of a list of words by arranging the words so that the first letters of the words themselves make a word (see acronym).
Flashbulb memories	Recollections of highly emotional and stressful events, suggested by some to be especially well registered in memory and immune from forgetting.
Forgetting	The decrease in remembering over time.
Forgetting function	The shape of the decrease in remembering over time.
Formal assessment of memory abilities	Determination of specific memory abilities from performance of a variety of tests, administered and interpreted by a psychologist.
Forward retrieval strategy	A search of memory from the most early memories on up to the present.
Free recall learning	When a person attempts to recall a list of items, and does so in any order.

General mental manipulations	Manipulations that supposedly apply to many memory tasks.
Generation effect	The superior recall for items that were generated by oneself.
Gestalt psychology	The theoretical perspective that memory is ultimately explained by the patterns of items which are acquired.
Gist	The essential idea inherent in a message of information that is encoded and held in memory.
Group pressures on memory performance	The influence of others' (people you are with, normative groups to which you belong) expectations or memory performance, which may lead one to doubt or disavow one's recollection.
Habitual prospective memory tasks	Those prospective memory tasks that we engage in on a regular basis, e.g., brushing one's teeth (see episodic prospective tasks).
Hierarchical knowledge	Knowledge structures that help people organize what they know into various domains, allowing for quick learning and retrieval when in new situations.
Hierarchical network	A propositional network in which different concepts are represented by nodes that correspond to a certain level of abstraction and whose features, which are pertinent to the level, are stored alongside of the concept.
Iconic memory	A term used to refer to sensory memory (or the sensory register) which provides a brief but highly accurate record for stimuli impinging on sensory receptors.
Immediate memory	The retention of information for about 30 seconds or less (see STM or primary memory).
Implicit memory tasks	Tasks that do not require conscious recollection of prior learning, but whose performance shows evidence that such learning occurred, because performance can be shown to have been affected by the learning (see explicit memory tasks).
Incidental learning	Learning that does not occur consciously.
Incidental manipulations	Behaviors of any type that raise attention level, without focusing on details, for a period after the manipulation is carried out.
Incremental learning	Learning which proceeds bit by bit, feature by feature, rather than all at once ("all or none learning.")
Information-processing approach	The theoretical view that memory is best explained as a computer which learns and remembers mental programs, or routines, that direct the learned behavior.

Instructional variables	Aspects of the directions given to subjects regarding how to perform a memory task.
Intentional forgetting	Willful forgetting due to deliberate inattention to the memory trace.
Intentional manipulations	Behaviors of any type that raise attention to a particular memory task and, in addition, consciously focus on certain details of the information encountered in the task.
Interference between traces	A source of forgetting in which the primary memory trace to be remembered is confused with one or more other memories.
Interference hypothesis of repression	The explanation of repression as due to the anxiety associated with repressed memories interfering with the person's ability to recall the memories.
Interference theory of forgetting	A theory that assumes forgetting occurs because the primary memory trace to be remembered is confused with, and hence inhibits the recall of, one or more other memories.
Internal memory aids	The use of mental strategies to remember to perform prospective memory tasks or retrospective information (see external memory aids).
Intrusion	An item recalled incorrectly as having been learned.
Jamais vu	The feeling that a person has never experienced a situation while objectively the person knows that she or he has encountered the situation before.
Kinesthetic cues	Information about where body parts are positioned with respect to each other when something is learned.
Knowledge base	The information that someone knows about a topic.
Language of memory	Common words or colloquial expressions that describe memory performance.
Law of contiguity	The law that two events or experiences occurring closely in time will, with some probability, become associated with each other.
Law of disuse (decay theory)	The explanation of forgetting as due to the decrease in habits over time.
Leading questions	Questions whose content suggest the answer to be given.
Learning practice	Development of skill at learning in a particular kind of memory task through repeated attempts at the task.
Levels of processing	The perspective that stresses how memory is processed over where, or by what component, it may be processed.

Lexical decision task	The task of deciding whether a string of letters is a word or not.
Link mnemonic	A technical mnemonic in which an image is formed of the object represented by each word on a list to be memorized and then visualizing each successive pair of objects interacting, forming a link from one word to another.
Linkword mnemonic	A technical mnemonic in which foreign language vocabulary is learned by forming an image of an object suggested by the foreign word interacting with an image suggested by the English word.
Localizationist position	The hypothesis that memory functions are performed in a certain portion of the brain.
Long-term memory	A component of the memory system that holds information indefinitely (see secondary memory).
Long-term recency effect	The superior recall of the final items in a list where the list was presented on a previous occasion.
Maintenance rehearsal (Type I rehearsal)	Repetition of information with shallow processing in order to just keep it in consciousness, and not to learn the information (see elaborative rehearsal).
Managerial memory manipulations	Techniques that enhance memory skill through organizing one's use of manipulations.
Manipulation (to improve memory)	A behavior that acts on the world around one or on one's mental processes to facilitate memory performance.
Mediation deficits	When an individual cannot make use of any appropriate memory strategy, either spontaneously or when the strategy is provided.
Memorist	A person who has developed superior memory skills without the use of traditional image-based mnemonics.
Memory aids	An object or device that facilitates memory performance.
Memory aids, commercial	A product that facilitates memory performance or even does the memory task for one.
Memory anomalies	Experiences of remembering or lack of remembering where the individual knows that his or her remembering experience is incorrect (see deja vu, jamais vu, time-gap experience, cryptomnesia).
Memory attitude manipulation	A behavior that corrects misimpressions of a person's memory performance; fosters a positive, realistic, and adaptive approach to memory tasks.
Memory attitudes that	Attitudes that are negative or unrealistic toward a task,

affect memory performance	motivation to perform a particular task, a person's self concept about their abilities to perform the task, negative feelings about information to be registered or remembered.
Memory before birth	Memories for sounds while a baby was in utero.
Memory blocks	When a person tries repeatedly to recall something but is unable to succeed.
Memory communication	Ways of making claims, verbally or nonverbally, about memory performance that affect another's acceptance of the claims.
Memory contrivance	A deliberate distortion that portrays someone else's memory performance as better or worse than it actually was in order to achieve certain social goals.
Memory corrector	A commercial memory aid that corrects memory errors.
Memory disorder	A psychological and/or physiological condition that renders a person's memory performance less than normal, and often renders the person unable to function adequately in daily life.
Memory etiquette	Rules of behavior concerning how one should react when someone else fails at a memory task.
Memory friendly product	A product whose use involves a memory task and which has a memory aid built in to perform or assist in performing the memory task.
Memory improvement	A program of imparting better memory processes to those with memory functioning in the normal range (see memory rehabilitation).
Memory language	Vocabulary and idioms that convey memory states (e.g., remember vs. believe).
Memory organization packet (MOP)	A collection of scenes or scripts that are highly related, e.g., the scripts for having a party: calling people ahead of time, preparing food and drinks, meeting people as they arrive (see thematic organizational points).
Memory pacts	Agreements between individuals wherein one person assumes responsibility for performing certain memory tasks in exchange for the other person performing other memory tasks.
Memory prosthetic	A commercial memory aid that facilitates memory performance. A product that was specifically designed by the manufacturer to help a person with memory tasks, including memory prosthetic, memory correctors, memory robots, and memory friendly products.
Memory questionnaires	Tests of knowledge in questionnaire format that indicate the amount of information in long-term memory on a certain topic.

Memory reactivation procedure	A test of memory for something that an infant has apparently forgotten by presentation of reminders of part of an original situation before testing retention of memory for the full situation (see refreshing).
Memory rehabilitation	A program of restoring lost memory functions due to disease, disorder, or accident (see memory improvement).
Memory reputation	The beliefs that others commonly hold regarding the likelihood one will succeed or fail at different memory tasks.
Memory rituals	Memory tasks customarily expected of individuals in certain cultural situations.
Memory robot	A commercial memory aid that performs memory tasks for the owner.
Memory role expectations	Memory tasks customarily expected of individuals in certain relationships (e.g., formal and information knowledge which people of a certain occupation are expected to know).
Memory savvy	Knowledge about how to recognize memory problems, link them with appropriate manipulations, and adjust performance to fit the memory tasks that arise.
Memory slips	When a person accidentally recalls something other than what was intended.
Memory span	The number of items recalled in correct order from a list presented serially.
Memory stereotypes	Beliefs people hold about the memory performance of others based on group characteristics (gender, race, physical appearance, or occupation).
Memory strategies	The mental activities used to enhance encoding and retrieval.
Memory tasks imposed by others	Situations in which you are expected to perform certain memory tasks, as dictated by social norms and events, or by personal relationships. College is a special case in which faculty impose many memory tasks on students.
Memory test battery	A collection of standardized memory tasks that are administered in order to develop a comprehensive account of an individual's memory functioning (see assessment).
Mental conditions that impair memory performance	Lack of concentration, excessive emotions, anxiety, mood difficulties.
Mental manipulation	A behavior that orders and organizes thoughts to assist registration, retention, and remembering.

Mental status exam	A series of tests presented as an interview in which the examiner assess the individual's ability to attend, communicate, remember, and think.
Metamemory	Knowledge about how to perform memory tasks, based on knowledge of memory strategies and awareness of one's own memory processes, abilities, and interests.
Metamemory questionnaires	Tests of self knowledge of memory performance and memory strategy use (see memory questionnaires).
Method of loci	A technical mnemonic in which a person first memorizes or calls to mind a set of familiar locations (such as the rooms in one's house) and then mentally places each item on a list in the different rooms, resulting in rapid learning of the list.
Minerva	The Roman god of memory (circa 1000 B.C.).
Misinformation effect	The tendency for people to recall information about an event presented after the event's occurrence as what was originally encoded.
Mnemonics	Often used to refer to the ways of learning or remembering something more effectively by relating it to something one already knows; more technically, mnemonics refers to image-based technical strategies for memory improvement, such as the method of loci.
Mnemonists	Often used generally to refer to someone with a superior memory; more technically, a mnemonist is someone who possesses a superior memory because of using the traditional image-based mnemonics.
Mnemosyne	The Greek goddess of memory (circa 1000 B.C.).
Mood-dependent memory	The hypothesis that memories may be retrieved best when a person's mood at the time retrieval is attempted is the same as when the memory was formed (see encoding specificity and state-dependent memory).
Mood induction	The process of presenting stimuli that will elicit, or facilitate entering into, a particular mood state.
Motivated forgetting	Forgetting which occurs because the person consciously suppresses or unconsciously represses a memory.
Motivation	The psychological processes that lead people to attempt to perform memory tasks because of incentives or drives.
Multi-modal theoretical perspective	The view that memory is best explained by taking account of all psychological processes, including memory and non-memory processes (such as perceptual, motivational, physiological, emotional, social processes).

Multiple personality disorder	An extreme form of a dissociative disorder in which a person's personality structure divides into two or more distinct identities (see psychogenic amnesia and psychogenic fugue).
Naive mnemonics	Mnemonic techniques that people naturally use without formal training or instruction.
Network models	Models of semantic memory that link concept nodes together in a broad network of interconnections.
Neural nets	Groups of interconnected neurons hypothesized to retain memories (see cell assemblies and macrocolumn). A term descriptive of the neural organization of the cerebral cortex; a term also used to refer to connectionist models.
Neuron	The smallest anatomical unit of the nervous system, consisting of a cell body, dendrites and an axon, and separated from other neurons by a gap called a synapse.
Neurotransmitter	Substance released by a neuron into synapses and stimulates other neurons.
New approach to improving memory and study skills	The improvement of memory ability with scientifically-validated manipulations that affect memory directly or indirectly through other psychological functions (physical and mental condition, memory attitudes, perception and use of the physical environment, social interaction).
Next-in-line effect	The phenomenon where a person who is about to speak in a group remembers poorly what was said by others who spoke before or after this person.
Noncommercial memory aid	Objects in the environment that have other purposes but which people adapt to help perform a memory task.
Noncumulative rehearsal	Rehearsing a single item at a time (see cumulative rehearsal).
Non-declarative memory	A synonym for procedural memory and for heterogeneous learning abilities capable of many amnesic patients.
Nonsense syllable	Three letter combinations of a consonant, a vowel, and a consonant that are supposedly devoid of meaning.
Nonverbal memory language	Gestures, facial expressions, and nonverbal sounds that convey memory states of efforts to remember and successfully remember.
Number-letter mnemonic	A technical mnemonic in which number-letter pairs, that map the digits 0 to 9 with particular consonants, are memorized; then the letters of words to be learned are converted into numbers or numbers to be learned are converted into letters, resulting in rapid learning of the word or numbers.

Olfactory cues	The smells present during learning and remembering.
Organismic variables	A type of independent variable; permanent or relatively permanent characteristics of a person (e.g., intelligence, physical condition, or health) that influence memory performance.
Organization (organizational strategies)	The process by which individual items are grouped together because of some shared characteristic.
Overlearning	Increasing the likelihood that material will be remembered by continuing to study the material after complete recall has been demonstrated.
Paired associate learning	The learning of pairs of items so that one can recall the second item when the first is presented.
Parallel distributed processing (PDP)	The kind of processing that occurs in the brain as different functions of sight, hearing, thought, and others occur simultaneously; the kind of processing which occurs in connectionist models.
Parallel search	The simultaneous access and retrieval of multiple items in memory.
Pattern recognition	The recognition of an arrangement of stimuli (such as pieces on a chess board).
Peg system	A technical mnemonic in which a person first memorizes a series of mental hooks on which to "hang" items to be learned.
Peg word system	A technical mnemonic in which a person first memorizes a series of number-object pairs, usually in a rhyme ("one is a bun, two is a shoe, three is a tree, etc."), and then mentally places each item on a list to be learned on an object, resulting in rapid learning of the list.
Permastore	A theoretical memory storage system in which material is not lost from memory over a long interval.
Person schema	A mental model or representation, built up through experience, about a person (their traits and typical behaviors).
Phonological loop	The part of working memory responsible for manipulating speech-based information with an articulatory control process in a phonological store.
Photographic memory (eidetic imagery)	The ability to maintain an image of a visual stimulus after the stimulus has been removed from view.
Physiological state memory manipulations	Manipulations to improve memory performance by correcting sensory deficiencies, treating major and minor health problems, providing good nutrition, avoiding use of adverse substances, reducing fatigue, and ensuring adequate sleep.

Physiological state modes	Manipulations of one's own physical condition, emotional state, and attitude in order to enhance encoding, retention, and retrieval.
Physiological states that impair memory performance	Sensory deficiencies, major and minor health problems, poor nutrition, use of adverse substances, stimulants, fatigue, lack of sleep.
Picture elicitation method	A test for eidetic imagery in which a picture stimulus is presented briefly, and then removed while the subject continues to look where the stimulus had been, and attempts to "see" and recall certain details of the picture.
Placement manipulations	Placing objects in conspicuous locations to facilitate the remembering of an intention.
Pollyanna principle	The fact that information and events are more likely to be freely recalled if they are pleasant rather than if they are unpleasant.
Pragmatic approach to the study of memory	An approach that seeks to develop new or better ways to improve a person's ability to learn and remember.
Pragmatic implications	A statement that leads a person to believe something that is neither explicitly asserted nor necessarily implied.
Preparation manipulations	Learning and retrieval manipulations that are used prior to registration and remembering tasks to facilitate the effectiveness of manipulations used at that time.
Presentational variables	The aspects of the visual, auditory, or temporal manner in which stimulus materials are presented in memory tasks.
Primacy effect	The superior recall of the initial items presented relative to items in the middle of a list; the initial portion of the serial position curve.
Primary memory	The contents of consciousness (sometimes regarded as short-term memory).
Primary memory measure	The amount of information indicated as held in memory.
Priming	The increase in trace strength that results from familiarizing oneself with the material to be learned or retrieved.
Proactive interference (PI)	When prior learning acts forward in time to interfere with the recall of something learned more recently.
Procedural memory	A kind of knowledge or memory of actions or sequences which is demonstrated by performance and not accessible to conscious recollection.

Production deficits	When an individual fails to spontaneously generate an appropriate memory strategy to handle a memory task.
Proposition	A unit of knowledge that can be asserted as being either true or false.
Proprioceptive cues	Information about what body parts are doing when something is learned.
Prospective memory	The ability to remember to carry out intended actions, tasks, and plans (see retrospective memory and Type A personality).
Prototypes	A pattern that is common to other patterns.
Psychogenic amnesia	An amnesia brought on by an extremely stressful or anxiety provoking event in the individual's life (see psychogenic fugue and multiple personality disorder).
Psychogenic fugue	An amnesia brought on by an extremely stressful or anxiety provoking event in the individual's life in which the individual will move away from home and assume a new identity (see psychogenic amnesia and multiple personality disorder).
Qualitative assessment procedures	Tests that assess nonquantitative aspects of performance, such as affect expressed during recall (see secondary memory measure).
Reality monitoring	The detection of memories as representing events that have, or have not, actually occurred.
Realization	The incidental form of remembering.
Recall	The task of saying or writing what was presented or what occurred.
Recall congruency	The selective effect of mood on the recall of information during recall (see encoding congruency).
Recency effect	The superior recall of the final items presented over that for items in the middle of a list; the final portion of the serial position curve.
Recent memory	Memory for events that happened longer than that characteristic of STM (i.e., 30 seconds), to as much as several hours or a few days.
Recognition	The task of indicating whether or not a stimulus is what was presented or descriptive of what occurred.
Reconstructive changes (reconstruction)	Changes in the content of recall that occur during retrieval and which subsequently become part of the memory, such as by the storing in memory one's interpretation of the event after remembering it (see constructive changes).
Refreshing	The revival of a memory for an event by presenting some or all of a record of the event.

Registration of a memory	The encoding of information into STM or LTM.
Reminding	When a physical stimulus leads information in memory to come to consciousness.
Reminding service	A business whose purpose is to remind people about special occasions in their personal lives and to carry out personal memory tasks such as sending gifts and cards.
Reminiscence	Prolonged attempts at autobiographical recall, often for personal purposes (such as for pleasure or for coping with an unpleasant period). In memory theory, "reminiscence" also has a technical meaning: an increase in recall after a retention interval, rather than the usual decrease.
Remote memory	Memory for events that happened in a person's distant past.
Repertoire (of manipulations)	A set of task-specific manipulations tailored to particular memory tasks.
Repertoire, natural	A set of task-specific manipulations that one instinctively applies to a particular memory task.
Repisodic memory	The formation of a memory that blends together the memories of similar episodes (see schematization, gist).
Repression (motivated forgetting)	The unconscious lessening of the accessibility or forgetting of extremely unpleasant memories or experiences.
Resource-allocation hypothesis	The detrimental effect on cognitive processing that occurs when the number of cognitive tasks required by a situation exceeds a person's processing limit. This hypothesis is sometimes used to explain the poorer memory performance of depressed people who presumably have a lower limit on cognitive resources.
Response bias	The tendency of people to recall information in a way that will be acceptable to their audience.
Retention	The holding of a mental representation of stimuli for a limited or unlimited interval.
Retrieval	Remembering of information, often regarded as deliberate (see implicit and explicit memory).
Retrieval practice	Development of skill at retrieval in a particular kind of task through repeated attempts at the task.
Retrieval structure	A set of secondary information that may direct retrieval to the information that one wants to remember.
Retrieval structure manipulations	Developed by creating trace information that suggests the information in another trace.

Retrieval structure of a trace	One of the four aspects of a trace that may be formed by a mental manipulation.
Retroactive interference (RI)	When recently learned information acts backward in time to interfere with the recall of something learned previously.
Retrograde amnesia	A loss of memory for events prior to the onset of brain damage.
Retrospective memory	The ability to remember past events or information (see prospective memory).
Savant	Literally, a person of great learning; in recent times, the term has been used to refer to people with unusual knowledge of a certain type or a certain mental skill.
Savings score	A quantitative measure of the effort "saved" in relearning the list due to what was retained from original learning.
Schema	A mental model or representation, built up through experience, about a person, object, situation, or event.
Schema activated encoding	The hypothesis that schemas influence encoding through affecting four stages: selection of relevant cues, abstraction of relevant meaning, interpretation based on prior knowledge, and integration into a single memory.
Schematization	The merging of memories for individual episodes into scripts, of personal and cultural importance, that guide subsequent learning and remembering.
Script	A particular type of schema that describes the kind of knowledge that people can abstract from common, frequently occurring events.
Secondary dementias	Dementias that derive from illnesses that do not attack the brain.
Secondary measures	Measures that are concerned with aspects of memory other than the primary measure of amount in memory.
Secondary memory	Information in memory which is not in immediate consciousness (see long-term memory).
Selective recall	The superior recall for information consistent with a person's attitudes in comparison to recall of information inconsistent with his or her attitudes.
Self-awareness explanation of mood congruency	The hypothesis that mood congruency effects are most likely to be evident when a person is aware of being in a certain mood state.
Self-observation of memory performance	Taking stock of one's performance in a variety of memory tasks by completing questionnaires and keeping a memory diary.

Self-reference effect	The superior recall that occurs when people decide how well the material applies to themselves.
Self-schema	A mental model or representation, built up through experience, about oneself (one's traits and typical behaviors).
Self-terminating serial search	A search of item by item in memory until the correct item is found (see exhaustive serial search).
Semantic encoding	Encoding of meaning inherent in, or associated with, verbal stimuli.
Sensitization	The increase in responding to a repetitive stimulus (see sensitization).
Sensory memory	The fleeting memory for a stimulus wherein the memory has the sensory properties of the stimulus (e.g., a visual icon for something just seen).
Sensory modality specific cortical areas	The initial sites of short and long-term declarative memories.
Sensory register	The component of the memory system responsible for sensory memories.
Serial learning	Learning to recall an entire sequence of items in order.
Serial position curve	A plot of the probability of recall as a function of the serial order in which items were studied.
Serial search	The access and retrieval of several items in the order they were stored in memory.
Short-term memory (STM) phenomena	The retention of information for about 30 seconds or less (see immediate memory or primary memory).
Short-term memory (STM) system	A component of the memory system hypothesized to retain small amounts of information for about 30 seconds (see primary memory).
Skilled memory theory	A theory that individual differences in memory performance do not derive from differences in innate ability but in differences in practice at memory tasks.
Social context manipulation	A technique that identifies social factors harmful to performance or that alters social behaviors to maximize memory performance.
Social contexts that affect memory performance	Social tasks that make extra demands on memory (such as cocktail parties or receiving lines) and aspects of common interactions that influence performance (such as the pace of conversation).
Social information	Information about the attitudes, roles, and means for impressing others that affect one's own memory performance and that of others.

Social manipulation	A technique that identifies social factors harmful to performance or that alters social behaviors to maximize memory performance.
Spacing effect	The superior recall that occurs when students space out their study sessions relative to when study sessions are not spaced.
Stages of manipulation execution	A manipulation is elicited, modified to the particular task, applied to the task, and assessed for its effectiveness.
State dependent memory	The hypothesis that memories may be retrieved best when the "state" of a person at the time retrieval is attempted (such as when drunk) is the same as when the memory was formed (see encoding specificity and mood-dependent memory).
Stimulus variables (materials)	The physical stimuli for learning or remembering, including letters, words, sentences, and pictures.
Story mnemonic	A naive mnemonic in which a person creates a story which makes use of all of the words on a list to be memorized, resulting in rapid learning of the list.
Strength mental manipulations	Techniques that increase attention, usually through rehearsal, and thereby increase the strength of the traces absorbed.
Strength of a trace	One of the four aspects of a trace that may be affected by a mental manipulation. The stronger its trace, the more familiar we are with an item.
Stress	A process of adjusting to or dealing with situations that produce mental or emotional upheaval, disposing people to be absentminded.
Structural features of memory	Aspects of the memory trace or memory components containing the memory trace.
Study formulas	Sets of key words that are intended to orient a person properly for studying.
Study test procedure	A laboratory test which presents only half of the items presented earlier to be learned, allowing a person to correctly identify an old item (a hit), correctly reject a new item, incorrectly fail to identify an old item as old (a miss), and incorrectly reject a new item (a false alarm; see intrusion).
Subjective organization	The tendency to organize words into groups in memory seemingly based on no commonality but actually on features of meaning common to the words.
Superimposition method	A test for eidetic imagery in which a subject scans an array of dots that are meaningless in themselves and then mentally attempts to superimpose the image of this array on another dot pattern, which in combination with the first array produces an overall pattern (see picture elicitation method).

Superstitious environ-mental manipulations	Objects or actions that people believe will provide good luck to their memory performance.
Suppression (directed forgetting)	The conscious forgetting of a memory by deliberately trying not to think about it.
Symbolic memory tasks	Tasks whose performance, successful or unsuccessful, conveys respect or affection (or lack of it) and affects the state of a personal relationship between people.
Symbolic reminders	Drawings or sketches of culturally established symbols which conventionally convey that a memory task is to be performed.
Synapse	The space between neurons, sometimes called the synaptic cleft; secretion of neurotransmitters into *excitatory* synapses make the firing of an action potential more likely and the *inhibitory* synapse makes firing less likely.
Synesthesia	The phenomenon of sensation in one modality (e.g., hearing) simultaneously evoking sensory experience in other modalities (e.g., vision, touch).
Tagging	The theoretical assumption that information in memory is marked in some fashion.
Task menu	A term used in this book to refer to the set of manipulations that may be especially suitable for a particular task.
Task situations	Broad categories of daily life in which memory tasks occur: homelife, work, obligations, recreation.
Task-specific manipulation	A behavior that is especially effective for a particular kind of memory task.
Task variables	A type of independent variable which pertains to the characteristics of a particular memory task or situation in which the task is performed.
Technical mnemonics	Mnemonic techniques that people come to use only with formal training or instruction (see naive mnemonics).
Test anxiety	Fear and nervousness that inhibits memory performance, especially for a topic of particular importance to the individual.
Test wise	A knowledge of and ability for taking tests.
Theoretical approach to the study of memory	The approach that seeks explanations of the mechanisms of memory either with theories, models, or metaphors that capture part of a phenomena.
Theory of disuse	The explanation that forgetting from disuse is due to people having a limited capacity to retrieve information from memory, even well-learned information becoming inaccessible when not periodically retrieved, and to learning or retrieval of information that is similar to the material sought after in memory.

Thoth	The Egyptian God of learning, memory, and wisdom (circa 3000-4000 B.C.).
Time-gap experience	The feeling that little or no time has elapsed when objectively a considerable lapse has occurred.
Timeliness of manipulation use	The speed with which a manipulation is elicited when needed.
Tip-of-the-tongue phenomenon	When a person fails to recall a word or name, feels confident that he or she knows the correct answer, but cannot recall it at the moment.
Top-down processing	Those tasks that require active organization and elaborative processes (also called "conceptually driven").
Trace	A record in working memory or long-term memory of details of a percept or an idea.
Transfer-appropriate processing	The superior recall to cues which elicit the kind of processing in recall that was used when items were learned.
Two-stage model of memory formation	A model of memory formation in which memories are first represented in short term by reverberating circuits, and then by anatomical changes in these circuits by long periods of reverberation.
Type A personality	People who are highly competitive with a perfectionist attitude and who are more likely to remember prospective memory tasks than less competitive people (said to have a Type B personality).
Visuo-spatial sketch pad	The component of working memory that is responsible for manipulating visuo-spatial images and useful for planning spatial tasks.
Von Restorff effect	The superior recall of items that are perceptually and/or conceptually distinctive from other material studied.
Warm up	The increase in speed and proficiency at performing a memory task that results from initial attempts at the task.
Wechsler Memory Scale (WMS)	The oldest and possibly best known memory battery which assesses an individual's "personal and current information, orientation, mental control, logical memory, digit span, visual reproductive memory, and associative learning."
Whole report procedure	A test in which the recall of an entire stimulus array is attempted.
Word fragments	Test in which one attempts to recall the word that corresponds to segments and parts of the letters making up the word.
Word-stem completion	Test in which one attempts to recall the word that corresponds to some of the letters making up the word.

Working memory	The components of the memory system (phonological loop, visuo-spatial sketch pad, central executive) that holds information for approximately one minute.
Yerkes-Dodson Law	The relationship between arousal and performance, i.e., that performance increases from low to intermediate levels of arousal, but decreases at high levels of arousal.

References

Adams, L. T. (1985). Improving memory: Can retrieval strategies help? *Human Learning, 4,* 281-297.

Alzheimer, A. (1907). Über eine eigenartige Erkrankung der Hirnrinde. *Allgemeine Zeitschrift für Psychiatrie und Gerichtliche Medizin, 64,* 146-148.

Anderson, J. R. (Ed.). (1981). *Cognitive skills and their acquisition.* Hillsdale, NJ: Erlbaum.

Anderson, J. R. (1982). Acquisition of a cognitive skill. *Psychological Review, 89,* 396-406.

Anderson, J. R. (1983). *The architecture of cognition.* Cambridge, MA: Harvard University Press.

Anderson, J. R. (1990). *The adaptive character of thought.* Hillsdale, NJ: Erlbaum.

Anderson, R. C. (1985). Role of the reader's schema in comprehension, learning, and memory. In H. Singer & R. B. Ruddel (Eds.), *Theoretical models and processes of reading* (3rd ed.). Newark, DE: International Reading Association.

Anderson, T. H. (1980). Study strategies and learning strategies. In R. J. Spiro, B. C. Bruce, & W. F. Brewer (Eds.), *Theoretical issues in reading comprehension.* Hillsdale, NJ: Erlbaum.

Anderson, T. H., & Armbruster, B. B. (1991). The value of taking notes during lectures. In R. F. Flippo & D. C. Caverly (Eds.), *Teaching reading & study strategies: at the college level.* Newark, DE: International Reading Association.

Andrzejewski, S. J., Moore, C. M., Corvette, M., & Herrmann, D. (1991). Prospective memory skills. *Bulletin of the Psychonomic Society, 29,* 304-306.

Annis, L. F. (1983). *Study techniques.* Dubuque, IA: William C. Brown.

Apps, J. (1995). *Study skills for today's college student.* New York: McGraw-Hill.

Arkes, H. R., & Hammond, K. R. (Eds.) (1999). *Judgment and decision making: An interdisciplinary reader.* New York: Cambridge University Press.

Aronson, M. K. (Ed.) (1988). *Understanding Alzheimer's disease.* New York: Scribner's.

Asch, S. E. (1956). Studies of independence and conformity: I. A minority of one against a unanimous majority. *Psychological Monographs, 70,* 9 (Whole No. 416).

Atkinson, R. C., & Shiffrin, R. M. (1968). Human memory: A proposed system and its control processes. In K. W. Spence & J. T. Spence (Eds.), *The psychology of learning and motivation: Vol. 2.* New York: Academic Press.

Baddeley, A. D. (1982). Domains of recollection. *Psychological Review, 89,* 708-729.

Baddeley, A. D. (1986). *Working memory.* New York: Basic Books.

Baddeley, A. D. (1990). *Human memory: Theory and practice.* New York: Allyn and Bacon.

Bahrick, H. R. (1984). Semantic memory content in permastore: Fifty years of memory for Spanish learned in school. *Journal of Experimental Psychology: General, 113,* 1-29.

Baltes, P. B., & Kliegel, R. (1986). On the dynamics between growth and decline in the aging of intelligence and memory. In K. Poeck (Ed.), *Proceedings of the Thirteenth World Conference of Neurology*. Heidelberg, Germany: Springer Verlag.

Barnard, P. J., & Teasdale, J. D. (1991). Interacting cognitive subsystems: A systemic approach to cognitive-affective interaction and change. *Cognition and Emotion, 5,* 1-39.

Baron, R. A., & Byrne, D. (1994). *Social psychology: Understanding human interaction.* Boston: Allyn and Bacon.

Bauer, M. I., & Johnson-Laird, P. N. (1993). How diagrams can improve reasoning. *Psychological Science, 4,* 372-378.

Beach, K. (1988). The role of external mnemonic symbols in acquiring an occupation. In M. M. Gruneberg, P. E. Morris, & R. N. Sykes (Eds.), *Practical aspects of memory: Current research and issues:* Vol. 1. (pp. 342-346). Chichester, UK: John Wiley & Sons.

Beal, C. R. (1988). The development of prospective memory skills. In M. M. Gruneberg, P. E. Morris, & R. N. Sykes, *Practical aspects of memory: Current research and issues: Vol. 1.* New York: Wiley.

Beatty, P., Herrmann, D., Puskar, C., & Kerwin, J. (1998). When people say they do not know, do they know? *Memory, 4,* 407-426.

Bell, P., & Winn, W. (2000). Distributed cognitions, by nature and by design. In D. H. Jonassen & S. M. Land (Eds.), *Theoretical foundations of learning environments.* Mahwah, NJ: Erlbaum.

Bellezza, F. S. (1981). Mnemonic devices: Classification, characteristics, and criteria. *Review of Educational Research, 51,* 247-275.

Bellezza, F. S. (1982). *Improve Your Memory Skills.* Englewood Cliffs, NJ: Prentice-Hall.

Bellezza, F. S. (1983). Menemonic-device instruction with adults. In M. Pressley & J. R. Levin (Eds.), *Cognitive strategy research.* New York: SpringerVerlag.

Bellezza, F. S., & Buck, D. K. (1988). Expert knowledge as mnemonic cues. *Applied Cognitive Psychology, 2,* 147-162.

Bendiksen, M., & Bendiksen, I. (1992). A multidimensional intervention program for a solvent injured population. *Cognitive Rehabilitation, 10,* 20-27.

Bendiksen, M., & Bendiksen, I. (1996). Multi-modal memory rehabilitation for the toxic solvent injured population. In D. Herrmann, M. Johnson, C. McEvoy, C. Hertzog, & P. Hertel (Eds.), *Basic and applied memory research: New findings.* Hillsdale, NJ: Erlbaum.

Benjamin, L. T., Jr. (1988). The history of teaching machines. *American Psychologist, 43,* 713-720.

Benton, D. (1993). Blood glucose and human memory. *Psychopharmacology, 113,* 83-88.

Best, D. L. (1992). The role of social interaction in memory improvement. In D. Herrmann, H. Weingartner, A. Searleman, & C. McEvoy (Eds.), *Memory improvement: Implications for memory theory.* New York: SpringerVerlag.

Best, D. L., Hamlett, K. W., & Davis, S. W. (1992). Modification of memory complaint and memory performance in elderly adults. *Applied Cognitive Psychology, 6,* 405-416.

Biederman, I. (1987). Recognition-by-components: A theory of human image understanding. *Psychological Review, 94,* 115-147.

Birnbaum, I., & Parker, E. (Eds.) (1977). *Alcohol and human memory.* Hillsdale, NJ: Erlbaum.

Black, J., & Bryant, J. (1995). *Introduction to communication* (4th ed.). Chicago: Brown & Benchmark.

Block, R. I., & Wittenborn, J. R. (1984). Marijuana effects on semantic memory: Verification of common and uncommon category members. *Psychological Reports, 55,* 503-512.

Blumenthal, J. A., & Madden, D. J. (1988). Effects of aerobic exercise training, age, and physical fitness on memory-search performance. *Psychology and Aging, 3,* 280-285.

Bowen, J. D., & Larson, E. B. (1993). Drug-induced cognitive impairment: Defining the problem and finding solutions. *Drugs & Aging, 3,* 349-357.

Bower, G. H. (1981). Mood and memory. *American Psychologist, 36,* 129-148.

Bracy, O. L. (1986). Cognitive rehabilitation: A process approach. *Cognitive Rehabilitation, 4,* 10-17.

Brandimonte, M., Einstein, G., & McDaniel, M. (Eds.) (1996). *Prospective memory: Theory and applications.* Hillsdale, NJ: Erlbaum.

Bransford, J. D., & Stein, B. (1984). *The ideal problem solver.* New York: W. H. Freeman.

Breme, F. J., & Rosen, D. A. (1982). How to flunk out: A paradoxical approach to study skills. *ERIC Reports,* ED 240 478.

Brennan, S., Winograd, P. N., Bridge, C. A., & Hiebert, E. H. (1986). A comparison of observer reports and self-reports of study practices used by college students. In J. A. Niles & R. V. Lalik (Eds.), *Solving problems in literacy: Learners, teachers, and researchers.* Rochester, NY: National Reading Conference.

Brent, W., & Myers, K. M. (2000). Situated cognition in theoretical and practical context. In D. H. Jonassen and S. M. Land (Eds.), *Theoretical foundations of learning environments.* Mahwah, NJ: Erlbaum.

Britton, B. K., & Tesser, A. (1991). Effects of time-management practices on college grades. *Journal of Educational Psychology, 83,* 405-410.

Broadbent, D. E. (1958). *Perception and communication.* Oxford: Pergamon.

Broadbent, D. E., Cooper, P. F., Fitzgerald, P., & Parkes, K. R. (1982). The Cognitive Failures Questionnaire (CFQ) and its correlates. *British Journal of Psychology, 21,* 1-16.

Brown, A. L. (1978). Knowing when, where and how to remember: A problem of metacognition. In R. Glaser (Ed.), *Advances in instructional psychology: Vol. 1.* Hillsdale, NJ: Erlbaum.

Bruner, J. S., Goodnow, J. J., & Austin, G. A. (1956). *A study of thinking.* New York: Wiley.

Brunning, R. H., Schraw, G. J., & Ronning, R. R. (1999). *Cognitive psychology and instruction* (3rd ed.). Upper Saddle River, NJ: Prentice Hall.

Bugelski, B. R. (1968). Images as a mediator in one trial paired associate learning. *Journal of Experimental Psychology, 77,* 328-334.

Burt, C. D. B., & Forsyth, D. K. (1999). Designing materials for efficient time management: segmentation and planning space. *Cognitive Technology, 4,* 11-18.

Cacioppo, J., & Petty, R. (1982). The need for cognition. *Journal of Personality and Social Psychology, 42,* 120-121.

Cacioppo, J. T., Petty, R. E., & Morris, K. J. (1985). Semantic, evaluative, and self-referent processing: Memory, cognitive effort, and somatovisceral activity. *Psychophysiology, 22,* 371-384.

Carlson, R. A. (1997). *Experienced cognition*. Mahwah, NJ: Erlbaum.

Cavanaugh, J. C., & Baskind, D. (1996). Relations among basic processes, beliefs, and performance: A lifespan perspective. In D. Herrmann, C. McEvoy, C. Hertzog, P. Hertel, & M. Johnson. *Basic and applied memory: Practical Aspects*. Hillsdale, NJ: Erlbaum.

Cavanaugh, J. C., Feldman, J. M., & Herzog, C. (1998). Memory beliefs as social cognition: A reconceptualization of what memory questionnaires assess. *Review of General Psychology, 2,* 48-65.

Cavanaugh, J., Grady, J. C., & Perlmutter, M. (1983). Forgetting and the use of memory aids in 20 to 70 year olds' everyday life. *International Journal of Aging and Human Development, 17,* 113-122.

Cavanaugh, J. C., Kramer, D. A., Sinnott, J. D., Camp, C. J., & Markley, R. P. (1985). On missing links and such: Interfaces between cognitive research and everyday problem solving. *Human Development, 28,* 146-168.

Caverly, D. C., & Orlando, V. P. (1991). Textbook study strategies. In R. F. Flippo & D. C. Caverly (Eds.), *Teaching reading & study strategies: At the college level*. Newark, DE: International Reading Association.

Chase, W. G., & Ericsson, K.A. (1982). Skill and working memory. In G.H. Bower (Ed.), *The psychology of learning and motivation: Vol. 16*. New York: Academic Press.

Cohen, G. (1989). *Memory in the real world*. Hillsdale, NJ: Erlbaum.

Craik, F. I. M., & Lockhart, R. S. (1972). Levels of processing: A framework for memory research. *Journal of Verbal Learning and Verbal Behavior, 11,* 671-684.

Crawford, M., Herrmann, D., Randal, E., Holdsworth, M., & Robbins, D. (1989). Self perception of memory performance as a function of gender. *British Journal of Psychology, 80,* 391-401.

Dansereau, D. F. (1985). Learning strategy research. In J. W. Segal, S. F. Chipman, & R. Glaser (Eds.), *Thinking and learning skills* (Vol. 1). Hillsdale, NJ: Erlbaum.

Darley, C. F., Tinklenberg, J. R., Hollister, T. E., & Atkinson, R. C. (1973). Marihuana and retrieval from short-term memory. *Psychopharmacologia, 29,* 231-238.

Davies, G. M., & Thomson, D. M. (1988). *Memory in context. Context in memory*. Chichester, UK: Wiley.

DeBeni, R. (1988). The aid given by the 'Loci' memory technique in the memorization of passages. In M. M. Gruneberg, P. E. Morris, & R. N. Sykes (Eds), *Practical aspects of memory: Vol. 2*. (pp. 421-424). Chichester, UK: Wiley.

Dixon, R. A., Hertzog, C., & Hultsch, D. F. (1986). The multiple relationships among metamemory in adulthood (MIA) scales and cognitive abilities in adulthood. *Human Learning, 5,* 165-178.

DiYanni, R. (1997). *How to succeed in college*. Boston: Allyn and Bacon.

Druckman, D., & Björk, R. A. (1994). *Learning, remembering, believing: Enhancing human performance*. Washington, DC: National Academy Press.

Druckman, D., & Swets, J. A. (1988). *Enhancing human performance*. Washington, DC: National Academy Press.

Ebbinghaus, H. (1885). *Ueber das Gedaechtnis: Untersuchungen zur Experimentellen Psychologie*. Leipzig: Dunker & Humboldt. Translated by H. A. Ruger & C. E. Byssenine as *Memory: A contribution to experimental psychology*. New York: Dover, 1913.

Elias, M. F., Elias, J. W., & Elias, P. K. (1990). Biological and health influences on behavior. In J. E. Birren & K. W. Schaie (Eds.), *Handbook of the psychology of aging* (3rd ed.). San Diego, CA: Academic Press.

Ellis, J. (1996). Prospective memory or the realization of delayed intentions. In M. Brandimonte, G. Einstein, & M. McDaniel (Eds.), *Prospective memory: Theory and applications*. Hillsdale, NJ: Erlbaum.

Erdelyi, M. H., & Goldberg, B. (1979). Let's not sweep repression under the rug: Toward a cognitive psychology of repression. In J. F. Kihlstrom & F. J. Evans (Eds.), *Functional disorders of memory*. Hillsdale, NJ: Erlbaum.

Ericsson, K.A. (1985). Memory skill. *Canadian Journal of Psychology, 39,* 188-231.

Falkenberg, P. R. (1994). *15 days to study power*. Winston-Salem, SC: Greencrest Press.

Flippo, R. F. (1988). *TestWise: Strategies for success in taking tests*. Carthage, IL: Fearon Teacher Aids/Simon & Schuster.

Flippo, R. F., & Caverly D. C. (Eds.) (1991). *Teaching reading & study strategies: At the college level*. Newark, DE: International Reading Association.

Fodor, J. A. (1983). *The modularity of mind*. Cambridge, MA: MIT Press.

Folkard, S., & Monk, R. (1978.) Time of day effects in immediate and delayed memory. In M. Gruneberg, P. E. Morris, & R. N. Sykes (Eds.), *Practical aspects of memory*. London: Academic Press.

Folkard, S., & Monk, T. H. (1980). Circadian rhythms in human memory. *British Journal of Psychology, 71,* 295-307.

Forrest-Pressley, D. L.; MacKinnon, G. E., & Waller, T. G. (1985). *Metacognition, cognition, and human performance: Vols. 1 & 2*. New York: Academic Press.

Foster, J. K., Lidder, P. G., & Sunram, S. I. (1998). Glucose and memory: Fractionation of enhancement effects? *Psychopharmacology, 137,* 259-270.

Friedman, M. P. (1987). WANDAH - A computerized writers aid. In D. D. Berger, K. Pezdek, & W. P. Banks (Eds.), *Applications of cognitive psychology: Problem solving, education, and computing*. Hillsdale, NJ: Erlbaum.

Gagne, R. M., & Paradise, N. E. (1961). Abilities and learning sets in knowledge acquisition. *Psychological Monographs, 75,* No. 14 (Whole no. 518), 308.

Gardner, H. (1993). *Frames of mind: The theory of multiple intelligences*. New York: Basic Books.

Garry, M., & Polaschek, D. L. L. (2000). Imagination and memory. *Current Directions in Psychological Science, 9,* 6-9.

Geiselman, R. E., Fisher, R. P., MacKinnon, D. P., & Holland, H. L. (1986). Enhancement of eyewitness memory with the cognitive interview. *American Journal of Psychology, 99,* 385-401.

Gentner, D., & Stevens, A. (1983). *Mental models*. Hillsdale, NJ: Erlbaum.

Gentry, M., & Herrmann, D. J. (1990). Memory contrivances in everyday life. *Personality and Social Psychology Bulletin, 18,* 241-253.

Gibson, J. J. (1979). *The ecological approach to visual perception*. Boston: Houghton Mifflin.

Ginter, E. J., & Dwinell, P. L. (1994). The importance of perceived duration: Loneliness and its relationship to self esteem and academic performance. *Journal of College Student Development, 35,* 456-460.

Glaser, R. (1984). Education and thinking: The role of knowledge. *American Psychologist, 39,* 93-104.

Goethals, G. R., & Solomon, P. R. (1989). Interdisciplinary perspectives on the study of memory. In P. R. Solomon, G. R. Groethals, C. McKellyn, & B. R. Stephens (Eds.), *Memory: Interdisciplinary approaches.* New York: Springer Verlag.

Gold, P. E. (1987). Sweet memories. *American Scientist, 75,* 151-155.

Goldsmith, L. R., & Pillemer, D. B. (1988). Memories of statements spoken in everyday context. *Applied Cognitive Psychology, 2,* 273-286.

Grafman, J. (1984). Memory assessment and remediation in brain-injured patients: From theory to practice. In B. A. Edelstein & E. T Couture (Eds.), *Behavioral assessment and rehabilitation of the traumatically brain-damaged.* New York: Plenum.

Graumann, C. F. (1985). Memorabilia, mementos, memoranda: Towards an ecology of memory. In F. Klix & H. Hagendorf (Eds.), *Human memory and cognitive capabilities: Part A.* Amsterdam: North Holland.

Greeno, J. G., Smith, D. R., & Moore, J. L. (1993). Transfer of situated learning. In D.K. Detterman & R. J. Sternberg (Eds.), *Transfer on trial: Intelligence, cognition, and instruction.* Norwood, NJ: Ablex.

Greenwald, A. G. (1980). The totalitarian ego. *American Psychologist, 35,* 603-618.

Gruneberg, M. M. (1973). The role of memorisation techniques in finals examination preparation - a study of psychology students. *Educational Research, 15,* 134-139.

Gruneberg, M. M. (1985). *Computer Linkword: French, German, Spanish, Italian, Greek, Russian, Dutch, Portuguese, Hebrew.* Mount Pleasant, SC: Unforgettable-language.com.

Gruneberg, M. M. (1987). *Linkword: French, German, Spanish, Italian, Greek, Portuguese.* Chicago: McGraw Hill.

Gruneberg, M. M. (1992). The practical application of memory aids: Knowing how, knowing when, and knowing when not. In M. M. Gruneberg & P. Morris (Eds.), *Aspects of memory.* London: Routledge.

Gruneberg, M. M., & Jacobs, G. C. (1991). In defence of linkword. *The Language Learning Journal, 3,* 25-29.

Gruneberg, M. M., & Mathieson, S. (1997). The perceived value of mind maps (spider diagrams) as learning and memory aids. *Cognitive Technology, 2,* 21-24.

Gruneberg, M. M., & Monks, J. (1974). Feeling of knowing and cued recall. *Acta Psychologica, 38,* 257-265.

Gruneberg, M. M., Monks, J., & Sykes, R. N. (1976). The first letter search strategy. *IRCS Medical Science: Psychology and Psychiatry, 4,* 307.

Gruneberg, M. M., & Morris, P. E. (1979). *Applied problems in memory.* New York: Academic Press.

Gruneberg, M. M., Morris, P. E., & Sykes, R. N. (1978). *Practical aspects of memory.* London: Academic Press.

Gruneberg, M. M., Morris, P. E., & Sykes, R. N. (1988). *Practical aspects of memory.* Chichester, UK: Wiley.

Gruneberg, M. M., & Pascoe, K. (1996). The effectiveness of the keyword method for receptive and productive vocabularly learning in the elderly. *Contemporary Educational Psychology, 21,* 102-109.

Gruneberg, M. M., Smith, R., & Winfrow, P. (1973). An investigation into response blocking. *Acta Psychologica, 37,* 187-196.

Gruneberg, M. M., & Sykes, R. N. (1993). The generalizability of confidence-accuracy studies in eyewitnessing. *Memory, 1,* 185-190.

Halpern, D. F. (1997). *Critical thinking across the curriculum: A brief edition of thought and knowledge.* Mahwah, NJ: Erlbaum.

Hammand, K. R. (2000). *Judgements under stress*. New York: Oxford University Press.

Hardy, L., & Ringland, A. (1984). Mental training and the inner game. *Human Learning, 3,* 143-226.

Harlow, H. F. (1949). The formation of learning sets. *Psychological Review, 56,* 51-65.

Harma, M. I., Illmarinen, J., Knauth, P., Rutenfranz, J., et al. (1988). Physical training intervention in female shift workers: II. The effects of intervention on the circadian rhythms of alertness, short-term memory, and body temperature. *Ergonomics, 31,* 51-63.

Harris, J. E. (1984). Methods of improving memory. In B. A. Wilson & N. Moffatt (Eds.), *Clinical management of memory problems*. Beckenham: Croon Helm.

Harris, J. E., & Morris, P. E. (1984). *Everyday memory: Actions and absent-mindedness.* New York: Academic Press.

Harris, J. E., & Wilkins, A. J. (1982). Remembering to do things: A theoretical framework and an illustrative experiment. *Human Learning, 1,* 123-136.

Hasher, L., & Zacks, R. T. (1979). Automatic and effortful processes in memory. *Journal of Experimental Psychology: General, 108,* 356-388.

Hastie, R., Ostrom, T. M., Ebbesen, E. B., Wyer, R. S. Jr., Hamilton, D. L., & Carlston, D. E. (1980). *Person Memory.* Hillsdale, NJ: Erlbaum.

Hattie, J., Biggs, J., & Purdie, N. (1996). Effects of learning skills interventions on student learning: A meta-analysis. *Review of Educational Research, 66,* 99-136.

Herrmann, D. J. (1982). Know thy memory: The use of questionnaires to assess and study memory. *Psychological Bulletin, 92,* 434-452.

Herrmann, D. J. (1984). Questionnaires about memory. In J. Harris & P. E. Morris (Eds.), *Everyday memory: Actions and absent-mindedness.* New York: Academic Press.

Herrmann, D. J. (1987). Task appropriateness of mnemonic techniques. *Perceptual and Motor Skills, 64,* 171-178.

Herrmann, D. J. (1990a). Self perceptions of memory performance. In W. K. Schaie, J. Rodin, & C. Schooler (Eds.), *Self-directedness and efficacy: Causes and effects throughout the life course*. Hillsdale, NJ: Erlbaum.

Herrmann, D. J. (1990b). The representational bias of acquired memory processes. *Zeitschrift fur Psychologie (Centennial edition), 198,* 265-281.

Herrmann, D. J. (1990c). *SuperMemory.* Emmaus, PA: Rodale.

Herrmann, D. (1994). The validity of retrospective reports as a function of the directness of retrieval processes. In N. Schwarz & S. Sudman (Eds.), *Autobiographical memory and the validity of retrospective reports*. New York: Springer Verlag.

Herrmann, D. (1996). Improving prospective memory. In M. Brandimonte, G. Einstein, & M. McDaniel (Eds.), *Prospective memory: Theory and applications*. Hillsdale, NJ: Erlbaum.

Herrmann, D., Brubaker, B., Yoder, C., Sheets, V., & Tio, A. (1999a). Devices that remind. In F. Durso (Ed.), *Handbook of applied cognitive psychology*. Mahwah, NJ: Erlbaum.

Herrmann, D. J., Buschke, H., & Gall, M. (1987). Improving retrieval. *Applied Cognitive Psychology, 9,* 27-33.

Herrmann, D. J., & Chaffin, R. (1988). *Memory in historical perspective*. New York: Springer Verlag.

Herrmann, D. J., Crawford, M., & Holdsworth, M. (1992). Gender linked differences in everyday memory performance. *British Journal of Psychology, 83,* 221-231.

Herrmann, D. J., Grubs, L., Sigmundi, R., & Grueneich, R. (1986). Awareness of memory ability before and after relevant memory experience. *Human Learning, 5,* 91-108.

Herrmann, D. J., & Palmisano, M. (1992). The facilitation of memory. In M. Gruneberg & P. Morris (Eds.), *Aspects of memory: Vol. 1* (2nd ed.). London: Routledge.

Herrmann, D., & Parente, R. (1994). The multi-modal approach to cognitive rehabilitation. *Journal of Head Trauma Rehabilitation, 4,* 133-142.

Herrmann, D. J., & Petro, S. (1990). Commercial memory aids. *Applied Cognitive Psychology, 4,* 439-450.

Herrmann, D., & Plude, D. (1996). Museum memory. In J. Falk & L. Dierking (Eds.), *Public institutions for personal learning: The long-term impact of museums.* Washington, DC: American Museum Society.

Herrmann, D., Plude, D., Yoder, C., & Mullin, P. (1999). Cognitive processing and extrinsic psychological systems: A holistic model of cognition. *Zeitschrift für Psychologie, 207,* 123-147.

Herrmann, D., Raybeck, D., & Gutman, D. (1993). *Improving student memory.* Toronto, Canada: Hogrefe & Huber.

Herrmann, D., Rea, A., & Andrzejewski, S. (1988). The need for a new approach to memory training. In M. M. Gruneberg, P. E. Morris, & R. N. Sykes (Eds.), *Practical aspects of memory.* Chichester, UK: Wiley.

Herrmann, D., Schooler, C., Caplan, L. J., Darby-Lipman, P., Grafman, J., Schoenbach, C., Schwab, K., & Johnson, M. L. (2001). The latent structure of memory: A confirmatory factor-analytic study of memory distinctions. *Multivariate Behavioral Research, 36,* 29-51.

Herrmann, D. J., & Searleman, A. (1990). A multi-modal approach to memory improvement. In G. H. Bower (Ed.), *Advances in learning and motivation.* New York: Academic Press.

Herrmann, D., & Searleman, A. (1992). Memory improvement and memory theory in historical perspective. In D. Herrmann, H. Weingartner, A. Searleman, & C. McEvoy (Eds.), *Memory improvement: Implications for memory theory.* New York: Springer Verlag.

Herrmann, D., Weingartner, H., Searleman, A., & McEvoy, C. (Eds.) (1992). *Memory improvement: Implications for theory.* New York: Springer Verlag.

Herrmann, D. J., Yoder, C., Wells, J., & Raybeck, D. (1996). Cognitive technology: portable electronic scheduling/reminding devices. *Cognitive Technology, 1,* 36-44.

Hertel, P. (1988). External memory. In M. Gruneberg, P. Morris, & R. Sykes (Eds.), *Practical aspects of memory.* Chichester, UK: Wiley.

Hertel, P. (1992). Mood and improving memory. In D. Herrmann, H. Weingartner, A. Searleman, & C. McEvoy (Eds.), *Memory improvement: Implications for memory theory.* New York: Springer Verlag.

Hertzog, C. (1992). Improving memory: The possible roles of metamemory. In D. Herrmann, H. Weingartner, A. Searleman, & C. McEvoy (Eds.), *Memory improvement: Implications for memory theory.* New York: Springer Verlag.

Hertzog, C., Park, D. C., Morrell, R. W., & Martin, M. (2000). Ask and ye shall receive: Behavioral specificity in the accuracy of subjective memory complaints. *Applied Cognitive Psychology, 14,* 257-275.

Higbee, K. L. (1981). *What do college students get from a memory improvement course?* New York: Eastern Psychological Association.

Higbee, K. L. (1988). *Your memory* (2nd ed.). Englewood Cliffs, NJ: Prentice-Hall.

Higbee, K. L. (1999). 25 years of memory improvement: The evolution of a memory-skills course. *Cognitive Technology, 4,* 38-42.

Holland, J. (1994). *The occupations finder.* Odessa, FL:PAR Inc.

Howe, M. (Ed.). (1977). *Adult learning: Psychological research and applications.* London: Wiley & Sons.

Humphreys, M. S., & Revelle, W. (1984). Personality, motivation, and performance: A theory of the relationship between individual differences and information processing. *Psychological Review, 91,* 153-184.

Idzikowski, C. (1984). Sleep and memory. *British Journal of Psychology, 75,* 439-449.

Idzikowski, C. (1988). The effects of drugs on human memory. In M. M. Gruneberg, P. E. Morris, & R. N. Sykes (Eds.), *Practical aspects of memory.* Chichester, UK: Wiley.

Intons-Peterson, M. J. (1993). External and internal memory aids: When and how often do we use them? In C. Izawa (Ed.), *Applied cognitive psychology.* Hillsdale, NJ: Erlbaum.

Intons-Peterson, M. J., & Fournier, J. (1986). External and internal memory aids: When and how often do we use them? *Journal of Experimental Psychology: General, 115,* 267-280.

Intons-Peterson, M. J., & Newsome, G. L. III (1992). External memory aids: Effects and effectiveness. In D. Herrmann, H. Weingartner, & C. McEvoy (Eds.), *Memory improvement: Implications for memory theory.* New York: Springer Verlag.

James, W. (1890). *The principles of psychology.* New York: Holt.

Johnson, M. K., & Raye, C. L. (1981). Reality monitoring. *Psychological Review, 88,* 67-85.

Johnson-Laird, P. N. (1983). *Mental models.* Cambridge, MA: Harvard University Press.

Kahneman, D., & Tversky, A. (1973). On the psychology of prediction. *Psychological Review, 80(4),* 237-251.

Kahneman, D., & Tversky, A. (1982). The psychology of preferences. *Scientific American, 246(1),* 160-173.

Kasper, L. (1993). The keyword method and foreign language vocabulary learning: A rationale for its use. *Foreign Language Annals, 26,* 244-251.

Keogh, T. (1999). Remember, remember: The peg method. *Chemistry Review, 9,* 15.

Kernaghan, K., & Woloshyn, V. E. (1995). Providing grade one students with multiple spelling strategies. Comparisons between strategy instruction, strategy instruction with metacognitive information, and traditional language arts. *Applied Cognitive Psychology, 9,* 157-166.

Khan, A. U. (1986). *Clinical disorders of memory.* New York: Plenum.

Kiewra, K. A. (1985). Investigation notetaking and review. A depth of processing alternative. *Educational Psychologist, 20,* 23-32.

Kihlstrom, J. F., & Evans, F. J. (1979). *Functional disorders of memory.* Hillsdale, NJ: Erlbaum.

Klatzky, R. L. (1984). *Memory and awareness.* New York: W. H. Freeman.

Kolakowsky, S. A. (1997). Improving cognition through the use of nutrients, drugs, and other cognitive-enhancing substances. *Cognitive Technology, 2,* 44-54.

Kolodner, J. L. (1984). *Retrieval and organizational strategies in conceptual memory: A computer model.* Hillsdale, NJ: Erlbaum.

Koriat, A. (1993). How do we know that we know? The accessibility account of the feeling of knowing. *Psychological Review, 100,* 609-639.

Koriat, A. (1994). Memory's knowledge of its own knowledge: The accessibility account of the feeling of knowing. In J. Metcalfe & A. P. Shimamura (Eds.), *Metacognition.* Cambridge, MA: M.I.T. Press.

Lachman, M. E., Steinberg, E. S., & Trotter, S. D. (1987). Effects of control beliefs and attributions on memory self-assessments and performance. *Psychology and Aging, 2,* 266-271.

Landauer, T. K. (1986). How much do people remember? Some estimates of the quantity of learned information in long-term memory. *Cognitive Science, 10,* 477-494.

Landauer, T. K., & Ross, B. H. (1977). Can simple instructions to used space improve ability to remember a fact?: An experimental test using telephone numbers. *Bulletin of the Psychonomic Society, 10,* 215-218.

Lapp, D. (1983). Commitment: Essential ingredient in memory training. *Clinical Gerontologist, 2,* 58-60.

Larkin, J. H., & Simon, H. A. (1987). Why a diagram is (sometimes) worth ten thousand words. *Cognitive Science, 11,* 65-99.

Lave, J. (1988). *Cognition in practice.* Cambridge, UK: Cambridge University Press.

LeBlanc, J. (1998). *Thinking clearly: A guide to critical reasoning.* New York: W.W. Norton.

Levine, J. M., & Murphy, G. (1943). The learning and forgetting of controversial material. *Journal of Abnormal and Social Psychology, 38,* 507-517.

Lewis, M., & Sullivan, M. (1994). Developmental interventions in the lives of infants and parents. In C. Fisher & R. Lerner (Eds.), *Applied developmental psychology.* New York: McGraw Hill.

Loftus, E. (1980). *Memory: Surprising new insights into how we remember and why we forget.* Reading, MA: Wesley.

Loftus, E. F., Banaji, M. R., Schooler, J. W., & Foster, R. A. (1987). Who shall remember?: Gender differences in memory. *Michigan Quarterly Review, 26,* 64-85.

Loisette, A. (1896). *Assimilative memory: Or how to attend and never forget.* New York: Funk & Wagnalls.

Longman, D. G., & Atkinson, R. H. (1988). *College learning and study skills.* St. Paul, MN: West.

Luckie, W. R., & Smethhurst, W. (1998). *Study power: Study skills to improve your learning and your grades.* Cambridge, MA: Brookline Books.

Macan, T. M. (1994). Time management: Test of a process model. *Journal of Applied Psychology, 79,* 381-391.

Malone, T. W. (1983). How do people organize their desks? Implications for the design of office information systems. *ACM Transactions on Office Information Systems, 1,* 99-112.

Mandl, H., & Trabasso, T. (Eds.) (1992). *Learning and comprehension of text.* Hillsdale, NJ: Erlbaum.

Manning, C. A., Stone, W. S., Korol, D. L., & Gold, P. E. (1998). Glucose enhancement of 24-h memory retrieval in healthy elderly humans. *Behavioural Brain Research, 93(1-2),* 71-76.

Martinez, J. L., & Kesner, R. P. (Eds.) (1986). *Learning and memory: A biological view* (2nd ed.). San Diego, CA: Academic Press.

Mathews, G., Davies, R. D., Westerman, S. J., & Stammers, R. B. (2000). Human performance: Cognition, stress, and individual differences. Philadelphia: Psychology Press.

Matlin, M., & Stang, D. (1978). *The pollyanna principle.* Cambridge, MA: Schenkman.

Mayer, R. E. (1998). *The promise of educational psychology: Learning in the content areas.* Upper Saddle River, NJ: Prentice Hall.

Mayes, A. R. (1988). *Human organic memory disorders.* New York: Cambridge University Press.

McArthur, D. (1987). Developing computer tools to support performing and learning complex cognitive skills. In D. D. Berger, K. Pezdek, & W. P. Banks (Eds.), *Applications of cognitive psychology: Problem solving, education, and computing.* Hillsdale, NJ: Erlbaum.

McEvoy, C. L. (1992). Memory improvement in context: Implications for the development of memory improvement theory. In D. Herrmann, H. Weingartner, A. Searleman, & C. McEvoy (Eds.), *Memory improvement: Implications for memory theory* (pp. 210-231). New York: Springer Verlag.

McEvoy, C. L., & Moon, J. R., (1988). Assessment and treatment of everyday memory problems in the elderly. In M. M. Gruneberg, P. E. Morris, & R. N. Sykes (Eds.), *Practical aspects of memory: Current research and issues: Vol. 2.* Chichester, UK: Wiley.

McGaugh, J. L. (1989). Modulation of memory processes. In P. R. Solomon, G. R. Goethals, C. M. Kelley, & B. R. Stephens (Eds.), *Memory: Interdisciplinary approaches* (pp. 33-64). New York: Springer Verlag.

McWhorter, K. T. (1986). *College reading and study skills* (3rd ed.). Boston, MA: Little Brown.

Meacham, J. A., & Leiman, B. (1982). Remembering to perform future actions. In U. Neisser (Ed.), *Memory observed: Remembering in natural contexts* (pp. 327-336). San Francisco: Freeman.

Merry, R. (1980). The keyword method and children's vocabulary learning in the classroom. *British Journal of Educational Psychology, 50,* 123-136.

Meyer, B. J. F., Young, C. J., & Bartlett, B. J. (1989). *Memory improved: Reading and memory enhancement across the life span through strategic text structures.* Hillsdale, NJ: Erlbaum.

Middleton, A. E. (1888). *Memory systems: New and old.* New York: G. S. Fellows.

Miller, G. A. (1954). The magical number seven, plus or minus two: Some limits on our capacity for processing information. *Psychological Review, 101,* 343-352.

Miller, G. A., Galanter, E., & Pribram, K. H. (1960). *Plans and the structure of behavior.* New York: Holt.

Milone, M. (1996). *Beyond bells and whistles: How to use technology to improve student learning.* Washington, DC: American Association of School Administrators.

Milton, J., & Meara, P. (1998). Are the British really that bad at language learning? *Language Learning Journal, 18,* 68-76.

Morris, P. E. (1977). Practical strategies for human learning and remembering. In M. Howe (Ed.), *Adult learning: Psychological research and applications.* London: Wiley & Sons.

Morris, P. E. (1984). The cognitive psychology of self-reports. In J. Harris & P. Morris (Eds.), *Everyday memory, actions and absentmindedness.* London: Academic Press.

Morris, P. E. (1992). Prospective memory: Remembering to do things. In M. M.

Gruneberg & P. E. Morris (Eds.), *Aspects of memory: The practical aspects*. London: Routledge.

Morris, C. D., Bransford, J. D., & Franks, J. J. (1977). Levels of processing versus transfer appropriate processing. *Journal of Verbal Learning and Verbal Behavior, 16,* 519-534.

Morris, P. E., & Greer, P. J. (1984). The effectiveness of the phonetic memory system. *Human Learning, 3,* 137-142.

Morris, P. E., Jones, S., & Hampson, P. J. (1978). An imagery mnemonic for the learning of peoples names. *British Journal of Psychology, 69,* 335-336.

Mullin, P., Herrmann, D. J., & Searleman, A. (1993). Forgotten variables in memory research. *Memory, 15,* 43.

Neisser, U. (1978). Memory: What are the important questions? In M. M. Gruneberg, P. E. Morris, & R. N. Sykes (Eds.), *Practical aspects of memory*. London: Academic Press.

Neisser, U. (1982). *Memory observed: Remembering in natural contexts.* San Francisco: Freeman.

Neisser, U., & Winograd, E. (1988). *Remembering reconsidered.* New York: Cambridge University Press.

Neuhoff, J. (2000). Classroom demonstrations in perception and cognition using presentation software. *Teaching of Psychology, 27,* 142-144.

Niccaise, M. (1998). Cognitive research, learning theory & software design: The virtual library. *Journal of Educational Computing Research, 18,* 105-121.

Nist, S. L., & Diehl, W. (1985). *Developing textbook thinking.* Lexington, MA: Heath.

Nist, S. L., & Mealey, D. L. (1991). Teacher-directed comprehension strategies. In R. F. Flippo & D. C. Caverly (Eds.), *Teaching reading & study strategies: At the college level.* Newark, DE: International Reading Association.

Norman, D. A. (1981). Categorization of action slips. *Psychological Review, 88(1),* 1-15.

Norman, D. A. (1982). *Learning and memory.* New York: W. H. Freeman.

Nummedal, S. G. (1987). Developing reasoning skills in college students. In D. D. Berger, K. Pezdek, & W. P. Banks (Eds.), *Applications of cognitive psychology: Problem solving, education, and computing.* Hillsdale, NJ: Erlbaum.

Paivio, A. (1969). Mental imagery in associative learning and memory. *Psychological Review, 76,* 241-263.

Parente, R., & Herrmann, D. (1996). *Retraining memory strategies.* Gaithersburg, MD: Aspen.

Park, D. C., Smith, A. D., & Cavanaugh, J. C. (1990). Metamemories of memory researchers. *Memory & Cognition, 18,* 321-327.

Parker, E. S., & Weingartner, H. (1985). Retrograde facilitation of human memory by drugs. In H. Weingartner & E. S. Parker (Eds.), *Memory consolidation: Psychology of cognition.* Hillsdale, NJ: Erlbaum.

Pauk, W. (1984). *How to study in college* (3rd ed.). Boston, MA: Houghton Mifflin.

Payne, D. (1992). Memory improvement and practice. In D. Herrmann, H. Weingartner, A. Searleman, & C. McEvoy (Eds.), *Memory improvement: Implications for memory theory.* New York: Springer Verlag.

Pearson, P. D. (Ed.) (1984). *Handbook of reading research.* New York: Longman.

Peeke, S. C., & Peeke, H. V. (1984). Attention, memory and cigarette smoking. *Psychopharmacology, 84,* 205-216.

Perlmutter, M. (1988). Research on memory and its development: Past, present, and future. In F. E. Weinert & M. Perlmutter (Eds.), *Memory development: Universal changes and individual differences.* Hillsdale, NJ: Erlbaum.

Petro, S., Herrmann, D., Burrows, D., & Moore, C. (1992). Usefulness of commercial memory aids as a function of age. *International Journal of Aging and Human Development, 33,* 295-309.

Pfeiffer, K., Feinberg, G., & Gelber, S. (1987). Teaching productive problem solving attitudes. In D. D. Berger, K. Pezdek, & W. P. Banks (Eds.), *Applications of cognitive psychology: Problem solving, education, and computing.* Hillsdale, NJ: Erlbaum.

Plude, D. (1992). Memory improvement and attention training. In D. Herrmann, H. Weingartner, A. Searleman, & C. McEvoy (Eds.), *Memory improvement: Implications for memory theory.* New York: Springer Verlag.

Pollens, R., McBratnie, B., & Burton, P. (1988). Beyond cognition: Executive functions in closed head injury. *Cognitive Rehabilitation, 6,* 26-33.

Poon, L.W. (1980). A systems approach for the assessment and treatment of memory problems. In J. M. Ferguson & C. B. Taylor (Eds.), *The comprehensive handbook of behavior medicine, Vol. 1* (pp. 191-212). New York: Spectrum.

Poon, L. W., Gurland, B. J., Eisdorfer, C., Crook, T., Thompson, L. W., Kaszniak, A. W., & Davis, K. L. (1986). Integration of experimental and clinical precepts in memory assessment: A tribute to George Talland. In L. W. Poon (Ed.), *Handbook for clinical memory assessment of older adults.* Washington, DC: American Psychological Association.

Poon, L. W., Rubin, D. C., & Wilson, B. A. (Eds.) (1989). *Everyday cognition in adult and late life* (The Fifth Talland Conference). New York: Cambridge University Press.

Postman, R. D., Keckler, B., & Schneckner, P. (1985). *College reading and study skills.* New York: Macmillan.

Powell, E. (1974). Psychological effects of exercise therapy upon institutionalized geriatric mental patients. *Journal of Gerontology, 29,* 157-161.

Pressley, M., & Levin, J. R. (1983). *Cognitive strategy research.* New York: Springer Verlag.

Pugh, E. (1970). *A dictionary of acronyms and abbreviations.* London: Anchor Books.

Rankin, J. L., Bruning, R. H., & Timme, V. L. (1994). The development of beliefs about spelling and their relationship to spelling performance. *Applied Cognitive Psychology, 8,* 213-232.

Raugh, M. R., & Atkinson, R. C. (1975). A mnemonic method for learning a second language vocabulary. *Journal of Educational Psychology, 67,* 1-16.

Raybeck, D. (2000). *Looking down the road: A systems approach to future studies.* Prospect Heights, IL: Waveland Press.

Read, J. D., Lindsay, D. S., & Nicholls, T. (1998). The relationship between confidence and accuracy in eyewitness identification studies: Is the conclusion changing? In C. P. Thompson, D. J. Herrmann, J. D. Read, D. Bruce, D.G. Payne, & M.P. Toglia (Eds.), *Eyewitness memory.* Mahwah, NJ: Erlbaum.

Reason, J. T. (1988). Stress and cognitive failure. In S. Fisher & J. T. Reason (Eds.), *Handbook of life stress, cognition and health.* New York: Wiley.

Reason, J. T. (1990). *Human error.* Cambridge, UK: Cambridge University Press.

Reason, J. T., & Lucas, D. (1984b). Absentmindedness in shops: Its incidence, correlates and consequences. *British Journal of Clinical Psychology, 23,* 121–131.

Reason, J., & Mycielska, M. (1983). *Absentmindedness.* Hillsdale, NJ: Prentice-Hall.

Reder, L. M. (1987). Strategy-selection in question answering. *Cognitive Psychology, 19,* 90-134.

Rego, A., & Sousa, L. (1999). Performance in higher education: Toward an understanding. *Educational Research, 41,* 91-94.

Revelle, W., Humphreys, M. S., Simon, L., & Gilliland, K. (1980). The interactive effect of personality, time of day, and caffeine: A test of the arousal model. *Journal of Experimental Psychology: General, 109,* 1-31.

Reynolds, J., & Werner, S. C. (1993/1994). An alternative paradigm for college reading and study skills courses. *Journal of Reading, 37,* 272-278.

Richardson, J. T. E. (1991). Imagery mnemonics and memory remediation. *Neurology, 42,* 283-286.

Risko, V. J., Alvarez, M. C., & Fairbanks, M. M. (1991). External factors that influence study. In R. F. Flippo & D. C. Caverly (Eds.), *Teaching reading & study strategies: At the college level*. Newark, DE: International Reading Association.

Robinson, J. A. (1986). Temporal reference systems and autobiographical memory. In D. C. Rubin (Ed.), *Autobiographical memory*. Cambridge, UK: Cambridge University Press.

Rosenzweig, M. R. (1998). Introduction to the symposium on drug improvement of memory. *International Journal of Psychology, 33,* 81-85.

Ross, J., & Lawrence, K. A. (1968). Some observations on a memory artifice. *Psychonomic Society, 9,* 107-108.

Rupert, M. P., Eisendorfer, C., & Loewenstein, D. A. (1996). Normal aging: Changes in sensory/perceptual and cognitive abilities. In J. Sadavoy & L. W. Lazarus et al. (Eds.), *Comprehensive review of geriatric psychiatry* (pp. 113-134). Washington, DC: American Psychiatric Press.

Sameroff, A., & Feise, B. (1990). Transactional regulation and early intervention. In S. Meisels & J. Shonkoff (Eds.), *Handbook of early childhood intervention*. Cambridge, UK: Cambridge University Press.

Schacter, D. L. (1984). Toward the multidisciplinary study of memory: Ontogeny, phylogeny, and pathology of memory systems. In L. R. Squire & N. Butters (Eds.), *Neuropsychology of Memory*. New York: Guilford.

Schacter, D. L., & Glisky, E. L. (1986). Memory remediation: Restoration alleviation, and the acquisition of domain-specific knowledge. In *Clinical Neuropsychology of Intervention*. New York: Martibus Nijolf Publishing.

Schank, R. C. (1982). *Dynamic memory*. Cambridge: Cambridge University Press.

Schoenfeld, A. H., & Herrmann, D. J. (1982). Problem perception and knowledge structure in expert and novice mathematical problem solvers. *Journal of Experimental Psychology: Human Learning, Memory, and Cognition, 8,* 484-494.

Schooler, J. W., Gerhard, D., & Loftus, E. (1986). Qualities of the unreal. *Journal of Experimental Psychology: Learning, Memory, and Cognition, 12,* 171-181.

Schvaneveldt, R. W., Reid, G. B., Gomez, R. L., & Rice, S. (1998). Modeling mental workload. *Cognitive Technology, 3,* 19-31.

Schwartz, N. (1996). *Cognition and communication: Judgmental biases, research methods and the logic of conversation*. Hillsdale, NJ: Erlbaum.

Scribner, S. (1984). Studying working intelligence. In B. Rogoff & J. Lave (Eds.), *Everyday cognition: Its development in social sciences*. Cambridge, MA: Harvard University Press.

Searle, J. R. (1969). *Speech acts.* Cambridge, UK: Cambridge University Press.

Searleman, A., & Gaydusek, K. A. (1996). Relationship between prospective memory ability and selective personality variables. In D. Herrmann, C. McEvoy, C. Herzog, P. Hertel, & M. Johnson (Eds.), *Basic and applied memory: Vol. 2.* Mahwah, NJ: Erlbaum.

Searleman, A., & Herrmann, D. (1994). *Memory from a broader perspective.* New York: McGraw Hill.

Segal, J. W., Chipman, S. F., & Glaser, R. (Eds.) (1985). *Thinking and learning skills: Volumes 1 & 2.* Hillsdale, NJ: Erlbaum.

Shepherd, J. F. (1987). *College study skills* (3rd ed.). Boston, MA: Houghton Mifflin.

Shiffrin, R. M., & Schneider, W. (1977). Controlled and automatic human information processing: II, Perceptual learning, automatic attending and a general theory. *Psychological Review, 84,* 127-190.

Simon, H. A., & Gilmarten, K. (1973). A simulation of memory for chess positions. *Cognitive Psychology, 5,* 29-46.

Smith, A. (1988). Effects of meals on memory and attention. In M. M. Gruneberg, P. E. Morris, & R. N. Sykes (Eds.), *Practical aspects of memory.* Chichester, UK: Wiley.

Snel, J., & Lorist, M. M. (Eds.) (1998). *Nicotine, caffeine and social drinking: Behavior and brain function.* Amsterdam: Harwood Academic Publishers.

Spielberger, C. D., Gonzales, H. P., & Fletcher, T. (1979). Test anxiety reduction, learning strategies, and academic performance. In H. F. O'Neill & C. D. Spielberger (Eds.), *Cognitive and affective learning.* New York: Academic Press.

Spielberger, C. D., & Vagg, P. R. (Ed.) (1995). *Test anxiety: Theory, assessment, and treatment.* Washington, DC: Taylor & Francis.

Spilich, G. (1986, August). Cigarette smoking and memory: Good news and bad news. In G. J. Spilich (Chair), *Symposium on "Cognitive and environmental agents: Theoretical and pragmatic implications."* New York: American Psychological Association.

Stamford, B. A., Hambacher, W., & Fallica, A. (1974). Effects of daily exercise on the psychiatric state of institutionalized geriatric mental patients. *Research Quarterly, 45,* 35-41.

Sternberg, R. J. (1985). *Human abilities.* New York: W. H. Freeman.

Sternberg, R. J. (1986). *Intelligence applied: Understanding and increasing your intellectual skills.* San Diego: Harcourt Brace Jovanovich.

Stigsdotter-Neely, A., & Bachman, L. (1993). Long-term maintenance of gains from memory training in older adults. Two 3 year followup studies. *Journal of Gerontology, 48,* 233-237.

Storey, P. (1997). *Expert system.* Danbury, CT: Grolier Interactive Inc.

Squire, L. (1987). *Memory and brain.* New York: Oxford University Press.

Squire, L. R., & Butters, N. (1984). *Neuropsychology of memory.* New York: Guilford.

Swanson, J. M., & Kinsbourne, M. (1979). State-dependent learning and retrieval: Methodological cautions and theoretical consideration. In J. F. Kihlstrom & F. J. Evans (Eds.), *Functional disorders of memory.* Hillsdale, NJ: Erlbaum.

Sweller, J. (1989). Cognitive psychology: Some procedures for facilitating learning and problem solving in mathematics and science. *Journal of Educational Psychology, 81,* 457-466.

Talland, G. (1968). *Disorders of memory.* Harmonsworth, UK: Penguin.

Taylor, I. A., & Taylor, M. M. (1990). *Psycholinguistics: Learning and using language.* Englewood Cliffs, NJ: Prentice Hall.

Thomas, M. H., & Wang, A. Y. (1996). Learning by the keyword mnemonic: Looking for long term benefits. *Journal of Experimental Psychology: Applied, 2,* 330-342.

Thorndike, E. L. (1924). Mental discipline in high school studies. *Journal of Educational Psychology, 15,* 1-22; 83-98.

Tindall-Ford, S., Chandler, P., & Sweller, J. (1997). Cognitive load theory and instructional design. *Cognitive Technology, 2,* 48-59.

Tulving, E. (1983). *Elements of episodic memory.* Oxford: Oxford University Press.

Tulving, E. (1984). How many memory systems are there? *American Psychologist, 40,* 385-398.

Tulving, E., & Craik, F. M. (2000). *The Oxford handbook of memory.* Oxford: Oxford University Press.

Utgoff, P. E. (1997). *Artificial intelligence.* Danbury, CT: Grolier Interactive Inc.

Van Locke, P. (Ed.) (1999). *The nature of concepts: Evolution, structure and representation.* New York: Routledge.

Wark, D. M., & Flippo, R. F. (1991). Preparing for and taking tests. In R. F. Flippo & D. C. Caverly (Eds.), *Teaching reading and study strategies: At the college level.* Newark, DE: International Reading Association.

Watson, J. B. (1925). *Behaviorism.* London: Kegan Paul, Trench, Trubner.

Watts, F. N. (1988). Memory deficit in depression. In M. M. Gruneberg, P. E. Morris, & R. N. Sykes (Eds.), *Practical aspects of memory.* Chichester, UK: Wiley.

Wechsler, D. (1945). A standardized memory scale for clinical use. *Journal of Psychology, 19,* 87-95.

Weinstein, C. E., Goetz, E. T., & Alexander, P. A. (1989). *Learning and study strategies: Issues in assessment, instruction, and evaluation.* New York: Academic Press.

Weinstein, C. E., & Mayer, R. E. (1986). The teaching of learning strategies. In M. C. Wittrock (Ed.), *Handbook of research on teaching* (3rd ed.). New York: Macmillan.

West, R. (1985). *Memory fitness over forty.* Gainesville, FL: Triad Publishing.

Wheeler, R. J., & Magaletta, P. R. (1997). General well being and academic performance. *Psychological Reports, 80,* 581-582.

Whimbey, A., & Lochead, J. (1999). *Problem solving and comprehension.* Mahwah, NJ: Erlbaum.

White, D. R. (1971). *A glossary of acronyms, abbreviations and symbols.* Germantown, MD: Don White Consultants.

Wilding, J., & Valentine, E. (1988). Searching for superior memories. In M. Gruneberg, P. E. Morris & R. N. Sykes (Eds.), *Practical aspects of memory.* Chichester, UK: Wiley.

Wilding, J., & Valentine, E. (1997). *Superior memory.* Hove, UK: Psychology Press.

Williams, J. E. (1996). The relation between efficacy for self-regulated learning and domain-specific academic performance, controlling for test anxiety. *Journal of Research and Development in Education, 29,* 77-80.

Wilson, B. A. (1987). *The rehabilitation of memory.* New York: Guilford.

Wilson, B., & Moffat, N. (1984). *Clinical management of memory problems.* Rockville, MD: Aspen Systems.

Winograd, E. (1978). Encoding operations which facilitate memory for faces across the lifespan. In M. M. Gruneberg, P. E. Morris, & R. N. Sykes (Eds), *Practical aspects of Memory* (pp. 255-262). London: Academic Press.

Winograd, E., & Soloway, R. M. (1985). Hiding things from ourselves: Objects and special places. *Journal of Experimental Psychology: General, 115,* 366-372.

Wittenborn, J. R. (1988). Assessment of the effects of drugs on memory. *Psychopharmacology, 6,* 67-78.

Wolkowitz, O. M., & Weingartner, H. (1988). Defining cognitive changes in depression and anxiety: A psychobiological analysis. *Psychiatry & Psychobiology, 3,* 1-8.

Woodhead, M. M., Baddeley, A. D., & Simmonds, D. C. V. (1979). On training people to recognize faces. *Ergonomics, 22(3),* 333-343.

Wyer, R. S., & Srull, T. K. (1986). Human cognition in its social context. *Psychological Review, 93,* 322-359.

Wyer, R. S., & Srull, T. K. (1989). *Memory and cognition: In its social context.* Hillsdale, NJ: Erlbaum.

Wyon, D. P., Andersen, B., & Lundqvist, G. R. (1979). The effects of moderate heat stress on mental performance. *Scandinavian Journal of Work Environment and Health, 5,* 352-361.

Yantis, S. (2001). *Visual perception: Essential readings.* Philadelphia: Psychology Press.

Yates, F. (1966). *The art of memory.* Chicago: Chicago University Press.

Yesavage, J. A., Rose, T. L., & Spiegel, D. (1982). Relaxation training and memory improvement in elderly normals: Correlations of anxiety ratings and recall improvement. *Experimental Aging Research, 8,* 198.

Yesavage, J. A., Sheikh, J. I., & Lapp, D. (1989). Mnemonics as modified for use by the elderly. In L. Poon, D. Rubin, & B. Wilson (Eds.), *Everyday cognition in adult and late life.* New York: Cambridge University Press.

Yoder, C., & Elias, J. (1991). The role of affect in memory. In R. L. West & J. Sinnott (Eds.), *Everyday memory and aging: Current research and methodologies.* New York: Springer Verlag.

Zachs, R. T., & Hasher, L. (1992). Memory in life, lab, and clinic: Implications for memory theory. In D. Herrmann, H. Weingartner, A. Searleman, & C. McEvoy (Eds.), *Memory improvement: Implications for memory theory* (pp. 232-248). New York: Springer Verlag.

Zarit, S. H., Gallagher, D., & Kramer, N. (1981). Memory training in the community aged: Effects on depression, memory complaint, and memory performance. *Educational Gerontology, 6,* 11-27.

Author Index

Subject Index